C000084675

March by Moonlight

MARCH BY MOONLIGHT

A BOMBER COMMAND STORY OF OPS AND EVASION, CAPTIVITY AND FRIENDSHIP

JACK LOVE · BARRY LOVE

Published in 2016 by Fighting High Ltd,
www.fightinghigh.com

Copyright © Fighting High Ltd, 2016
Copyright text © Barry Love, 2016
Copyright text © Jack Love, 2016

The rights of Barry and Jack Love to be identified as the
authors of this book are asserted in accordance with the
Copyright, Patents and Designs Act 1988.

The print publication is protected by copyright. Prior
to any prohibited reproduction, storage in a retrieval
system, distribution or transmission in any form or by
any means, electronic, mechanical, recording or otherwise,
permission should be obtained from the publisher.

The ePublication is protected by copyright and must
not be copied, reproduced, transferred, distributed, leased,
licensed or publicly performed or used in any way except
as specifically permitted in writing by the publisher, as
allowed under the terms and conditions under which it
was purchased, or as strictly permitted by applicable
copyright law. Any unauthorised distribution or use of this
text may be a direct infringement of the author's and the
publisher's rights and those responsible may be liable in
law accordingly.

British Library Cataloguing-in-Publication data.
A CIP record for this title is available from the
British Library.

ISBN – 13: 978-09934152-1-0

Designed and typeset in Adobe Minion 11/15pt
by Michael Lindley. www.truthstudio.co.uk.

Printed and bound in China by Toppan Leefung.
Front cover design by www.truthstudio.co.uk.

Contents

Foreword *by Barry Love*

As a boy, I grew up with Grandad's RAF Bomber Command operational tales ringing in my ears, raising him up on to a pedestal as my very own hero with every new piece of his flying adventures puzzle. But not once did he talk (or even hint) about his other experiences of crash landing in occupied France, or of his eventual capture and time spent in prison camps; he would always drop the subject and discuss something else or find an errand or task to do, rather than drift into that extension of his story by natural continuation. Not surprisingly, I knew nothing of this episode of his life in the Second World War until I was into my early teens, and only discovered the partial truth when Dad let slip about his own childhood at that time, without his father around for a few years.

The revelation certainly came as a surprise – although I soon realised that I simply hadn't picked up on the clues with each imparted tale – but once that truth had emerged, I implored Grandad to tell me what he'd been up to as a POW, suddenly imagining my 'hero' as a crazy escaper or work-party saboteur, or something similar. For many years, however, I gained very little ground with that latter aim, as – like most of his ex-POW comrades – Jack Love, my grandfather, had been largely made to feel partly 'ashamed' that he had spent three hard years in captivity (in some ignorant eyes, a 'coward's way out of the war'). Some people felt that he ought to have taken every opportunity to escape and to return home, then get back up into 'the blue yonder', to carry on the scrap with the Jerries and continue to bomb important targets for the war effort – but of course, we now know that it simply wasn't anywhere near as easy as that, otherwise every prisoner of war would have 'strolled' home unobstructed to carry on the good fight.

Equally, once home and the damage reports filtering back from Germany, some people tried to make him feel guilty, too, for his role in the aerial bombing campaign, even though he could truthfully deny involvement in the horrific fire-bombing raids, as those particular attacks took place while he was a POW. He always upheld that he was simply doing his trained duty, targeting German industry in the hope of shortening and winning the war; his answer to detractors was usually something like, 'They started it [the bombing], so our instructions were to give it back to them, with interest and great precision.'

Every critic, of course, was an armchair warrior – most of whom would undoubtedly quiver in his (or her) boots at the prospect of even setting foot inside the linen-covered 'basket-weave' airframe that was the Vickers Wellington bomber, let alone flying in one on an operational jaunt – and as for being incarcerated for three long years in prisoner of war camps, in conditions that make today's criminal prisons look like luxurious holiday camps … well, perish the thought! Those critics simply wouldn't have survived.

Eventually, during a long, quiet holiday with Grandad in the late 1980s, I finally managed to extract his whole story and I became utterly enthralled as the details gradually unfolded – to the point where I felt that his story just had to be told, if only to help fill in a relatively small gap in the service history of the renowned 101 Squadron in which he was justifiably proud to have served; his time in operational service with the squadron was relatively brief, but it proved to be somewhat exciting.

I persuaded him to write out a draft for me, and promised that I would fill in any technical gaps in his memory by researching as time passed. He agreed, and set to work, but to my eternal chagrin – principally through interminable research delays and the challenges of life – it has taken me far too many years to fulfil my promise; sadly, Jack passed away long before his story could be told.

Here, finally, is his greatest 'adventure' – with a happier ending than might otherwise be imagined.

Barry Love
March 2016

Prologue

O, Lord! We Pray, Watch O'er Us,
Beneath Thy Heavenly Dome;
O, Pegasus! Spread Out Thy Wings,
And Fly Us Safely Home!

BL

High over France, abruptly, we were bracketed by a cluster of popping smoke puffs – not too close, but near enough to scare us – and we heard the rattle of shrapnel clattering off various parts of D-Donald as we took evasive action. It was a very nasty moment that brought our hearts into our mouths, but the barrage was over as quickly as it had begun – just a token flurry, apparently – and we settled back down to our individual tasks, checking for damage and reporting back to our pilot, Beecroft.

After a while, the steady, throbbing drone of the twin Hercules engines was like a comforting, reassuring background 'music' to my ears as we flew through the night, ever onwards to our target. As I raised my head into the observation dome it seemed as if the engines' roar sounded a little louder – even with my flight-hat's earpieces damping the din – but I knew that it was a figment of my imagination as there was little difference between the acoustic properties of the Perspex dome and that of the fuselage skin. As always, though, I was captivated by the sight that met my eyes.

Ahead and slightly to starboard of our nose – once my eyes had adjusted – I could just discern the glint of the tail turret cupola of our lead aircraft, and as I turned my head left and right, I saw another couple of Wellingtons in a loose but reassuring formation around us. I couldn't help but feel a surge of pride (and a little comfort in numbers) as our aircraft rumbled onward to Germany.

We were about to graze the top of another long cloudbank that was brightly lit by the moon, and with that came the heightened danger of being spotted by any night fighters that might be prowling above us. Given that it was such a clear night, we were all somewhat fearful of the likelihood of their presence – if we could see so well, then so could they, obviously – and given that our ground-schemed camouflage meant nothing against a glaringly blue-white blanket beneath us, every aircraft would stand out like flies skimming a rice pudding, presenting an easy sighting for an enemy.

Beecroft's voice crackled in our earpieces once more. 'Going over cloud … now! Keep your eyes peeled, lads – we don't want to be "bounced" now, do we?'

Almost on cue, as I thought about that very danger, a Glaswegian brogue crackled in my headphones. 'Aye, 'tis a braw, bricht, moonlicht nicht, t'nicht, laddies!' It was little Alec romanticising from the rear turret almost as though he had read my thoughts, and we all managed a few chuckles at his fine attempt to break the tension.

Right at that moment, the port-side engine spluttered, ran on again, then cut out altogether, although the propeller carried on windmilling.

Beecroft – uncharacteristically – let forth a string of profanities, and my heart lurched; we were well over foreign, occupied territory now – a long way from home – and we could most certainly do without frights like this.

It seemed to me that we were already beginning to lose height and drop out of the formation as our remaining engine roared louder than ever as it struggled to keep us flying. We were sitting ducks, and I felt the hairs rising on the back of my neck. …

Chapter 1

Always the conductor

As history now records, the 1920s and 1930s were dominated by a terrible recession; industry was dying on its feet, and as a consequence the basic standards of life were wilting, resulting in many thousands of people being plunged into abject poverty, and in many instances, starvation.

My home, the Northumbrian mining village of Ashington, was just one of several in the north-east to feel the pinch – yet somehow, I managed to lead a fairly ordinary life, despite the hardships of the time. I had won a scholarship at a grammar school, did quite well, and at the end of four years of hard study I had nine 'School Certificate' passes (equivalent to nine O-levels today), but I had no specific ambitions. Although my scholarship was renewed, circumstances at home determined that I could go no further with my education.

My father was a miner, but following a serious accident in 1922 he could only manage light work and earned very little as a result, so what modest money I could earn by finding a job was essential just to keep us from real poverty. I had no choice but to accept this responsibility, although the task of actually finding an occupation to match my qualifications proved extremely difficult, which was only to be expected of the time.

The only worthwhile jobs that turned up were two that required from me a premium of £80, which was a fortune to us in those days and quite impossible to raise, as a normal miner's wage was just 6s 9d per shift. Eventually, I took employment at the sawmill attached to North Seaton pit, where my father worked, and after two years there I obtained a job as a bus conductor, simply because the wages were better. That change in career was in 1930, and as the slump continued throughout the decade, there seemed little hope of getting out of the rut.

The bus company had a scheme whereby conductors could apply for driver training, so when my turn came along early in 1939, there looked to be the chance of at least an increased wage. We all had to pass a medical before being accepted for driver training, however, and to my surprise and great chagrin, I failed it; I had had a few weeks off with cystitis about a year before, and that was the reason given for my failure – which seemed grossly unfair to me, as it was the only illness I'd suffered in my life up until then! The GP said that it had left me with a heart murmur, and thus I found myself at the age of twenty-eight, now married with a seven-year-old son, and in a dead-end, humdrum job – a most uninviting prospect!

The war came, and as it dragged on – apparently pointlessly – little seemed to change. Conscription was in force, of course, and rather than run the risk of leaving my wife and child in possibly poorer circumstances by volunteering for duty, I decided to wait for my call-up papers to arrive.

Dunkirk and the ensuing Battle of Britain pulled us out of the 'phoney war', and in September 1940 I finally received my conscription notice. I opted for service in the RAF and went for an interview at the local drill hall, which turned out to be a lengthy affair, to say the least. I wasn't sure whether it was because I'd impressed the squadron leader to whom I talked, or perhaps it was my nine school certificates that did the trick, but I soon learned that I'd been accepted and I went home to await my 'orders'. When my papers arrived, I was very pleasantly surprised to discover that I'd been classified as 'Pilot U/T' (under training).

That did it! For the first time in my life, I saw myself (perhaps a little naively) as someone of importance; here was the chance of great adventure, the opportunity to break away from the rut in which I'd been confined for so long! I would really be somebody, doing something to help fight against the threat of German invasion and dominance!

Well, perhaps my thoughts were not quite so clear-cut as those words would seem to imply, but at any rate, I knew I would finally get to make a vital contribution to my country, instead of handing out three-penny bus tickets!

Firstly, though, I had to go to London for three days of preliminary testing – which was an exciting prospect for me, as I'd never been to the capital before – and not long after receiving my orders, I found myself lodging at the Union Jack Club, along with a few others due to take the same course.

The first two days were taken up with intelligence assessments of various kinds, and the third day was a series of medical checks. I managed to get through the intelligence tasks without difficulty, but I was dreading the medicals due to my experience with the bus company's tests. Would I fail and be pushed out of service for the entire war? What if …? But I needn't have worried; I was passed 'A-1 fit'! I wondered what the bus company's GP would have said if he'd known – unfit to drive buses, but fit enough to fly aeroplanes!

I didn't have much of a chance to wander around the city on sightseeing trips because we were there at a critical time. London was getting a pasting on Hitler's orders, and each night the air-raid sirens would go off at eight o'clock, with the roar of aero-engines and the crash of bombs going on right through the night until dawn. I was frankly appalled at the devastation I saw, and it made me appreciate the terrors that the Londoners had to withstand. What I saw made me all the more determined to get into the front line against the vile enemy.

Back home, and in a few days my movement orders arrived. I had to go to Blackpool for kitting-out, the usual inoculations and so on, and I had to undergo indoctrination into the ways of the Royal Air Force. In all, I was there for about a week, and then we were posted to Wilmslow, in Cheshire, for our 'basic training' – and basic, it certainly was! Foot drill, rifle drill and guard duty, fatigues (usually potato-peeling!), and yet more square-bashing in typical RAF fashion, with a few hours per day spent doing PT to get us fighting fit.

Not all of it was straightforward, however. The foot drill and the PT were all right – I actually enjoyed them – but the rifle drill was somewhat different from the RAF norm. With the German capture of huge quantities of British armaments at Dunkirk, there just weren't enough rifles to go around, so we ended up doing rifle drill only every other day, taking turns with the other training squads. And as for firing practice during my stay at Wilmslow, I fired precisely ten shots! The biggest laugh of all was guard duty; we had just brawn and pickaxe handles with which to guard the camp perimeter! If Hitler had only known what a perilous state our defences were in.

The chaps in our hut were very fortunate, because instead of the usual stridently bellowing drill sergeant, we were in the charge of a soft-voiced Jewish NCO, Corporal Sherman. His first advice to us was that the bawling, barking shouts heard regularly on the parade ground were quite unnecessary.

'Just get used to the sound of my voice,' he told us, 'and you'll pick it out quite easily' – and he was absolutely right. In no time at all, we were following his commands quite easily, in spite of the noise of other roaring sergeants and the tramping and stomping of booted feet. This went on almost incessantly throughout the day, but following our Corporal Sherman's advice, we got through the course quite comfortably.

The PT, with a little football and one or two cross-country runs thrown in to give some variety was – for me – the best part, and as we were being fed like fighting cocks, I found that in my six weeks there, my weight increased from ten to eleven stones. What was even better was that I was much fitter and stronger than ever before.

Corporal Sherman continued to be a great help, for he was always willing to sit and talk with us in the evenings, and from him we learned a great deal about life in the RAF. He was an informal but informative man.

At length, our time at Wilmslow came to an end, and we were sent on to our next stations. Those of us who were to become aircrew were given white flashes to sew on to the front of our forage caps, and it was a distinction that quickly brought us good-natured jibes from the others. 'What-ho! The Brylcreem Boys' and 'Only fools and birds fly!' were the commonest of all, but it was all just part of the fun, and we survived it all.

I was among a party sent to Newquay ITW (Initial Training Wing) in Cornwall, and a long, tedious journey it turned out to be. It wasn't all bad, however, for I made friends with two fellow north-easterners – Len Jackson from Newcastle and Bill Sykens from Middlesbrough – and when we reached our destination we were pleasantly surprised to discover that we'd been posted to what was then quite a seaside resort, with marvellous wide beaches. It was, we soon learned, one of the few places in Britain where surfing was possible, and when we arrived in early October we were not a little amazed to see swimmers enjoying this exhilarating pastime.

Our billets were a welcome surprise, too. No damp and dismal huts for us; we were lodged in various seaside hotels in the town, and my own 'squad' – which included 'Geordie' Jackson and Bill Sykens – was placed in one of the best! This was the Cliffside Hotel, right on the seafront, with comfortable rooms, and – as we found by probing among our fellow 'sprogs' – possessing the best cook in town. He was Swiss, a chef by profession, and although I'm sure he was supplied with the same rations as other cooks, he somehow always made them taste just that little better. What was more, there was always plenty of it, so we really had fallen on our feet!

My room-mates were Jackson, Sykens and Bill McCulloch. The latter was a real cosmopolitan; his father was Italian, his mother Scottish, he lived in Wales and worked in Shrewsbury! We all got on well together, and we remained a friendly foursome for all of our five months in Newquay.

As soon as we had settled in, we began our initiation into the first few steps on the ladder to becoming aircrew. The course was a strenuous one, taking in English, mathematics (particularly as used in navigation), meteorology, the rudiments of navigation itself, air force law and tradition, and, of course, PT and drill. The PT was done on the wide hard stretches of sand and, again, we were fortunate in having two excellent PT sergeants. One was a good-natured Lancashire lad in the same mould as Corporal Sherman, and the other was Billy Butler, the then lightweight boxing champion of the RAF. And to help us really enjoy our stay at Newquay, there were two extra bonuses.

Firstly, my new-found extra strength and fitness had greatly improved my footballing skills, and Bill Sykens and I quickly became regular members of the squadron football team. Wednesday was our usual games day, so Sykens and I were on 'football duty' every Wednesday and Saturday afternoons. Our star player was a young Scotsman named George Hendry, only nineteen, and the best player I'd ever seen outside professional football. Tragically, we learned later, he was killed during flying training.

The second bonus was rather more unusual. There was a girls' college in town, and they often played lacrosse on the beach right in front of our hotel – what a treat! Several of our boys became quite friendly with the girls, and they were always welcome visitors to our dances.

All this sounds as if Newquay was just a giant holiday camp, but in fact we were kept very busy indeed, for it was a very full and demanding course – especially as there was a great demand for fresh aircrew at that time.

We had a short break for Christmas, and then it was back to the grindstone once more. Our exams were in the middle of January 1941, and my room-mates and I found no great difficulty in getting through them. Came the results and we were all delighted to learn that we had passed – and even happier still that we had gained promotion to the rank of leading aircraftmen, with a pay rise and a fortnight's leave thrown in. Great stuff!

That leave was memorable, aside from the fact that other than the few days we'd had at Christmas it was our first real break. We'd been at Newquay for four months and the climate had been very mild all the time – we'd never even had to wear overcoats – but the weather in other parts of the country had been pretty bad. When I finally reached Newcastle after the long train journey from Cornwall, I was shocked to discover a heavy blanket of snow over everything. But I didn't realise just how severe it was until, walking from the railway station to catch a bus to Ashington, I saw two double-decker buses completely snowed-up in huge drifts in the middle of Northumberland Street, the main shopping centre. I reached home at last, however, to a joyful reunion with my wife Evelyn and son John, and I thoroughly enjoyed the time off.

As with all leaves it passed much too quickly, and back we all went to Newquay to await our next posting. It didn't come immediately, though, and in fact, we were at Newquay for a further four weeks. We spent the time doing some drill, and to keep us in touch with all that we had learned before, there was constant revision. A large part of the time was spent keeping fit, and we played lots of football, took part in athletics contests and indulged in long walks, so that my stay at Newquay remains in my memory as a pleasant, happy time.

At last, in early March, we received our postings and the squadron was scattered far and wide to begin our basic flying training. I was sent to Hatfield House, Hertfordshire, where the flying training was done in 'string-bag' de Havilland Tiger Moth biplanes, and I was placed under the expert care of a Flight Lieutenant Williams, a regular RAF officer who was a pilot of wide experience.

I was a little apprehensive, as was to be expected, but he soon put me at ease, and my first trip in a Tiger Moth became both an educational and pleasurable experience. Giving me a running commentary on his every move, he took us off the deck, then for the next twenty minutes or so he indulged in a series of aerobatics, designed, I believe, to see if I could take it without being sick. Fortunately I was too busy enjoying the flight to think of that and when we landed – again accompanied by a full running commentary – he seemed quite satisfied with me. In the days that followed, however, things became much more difficult as I began to operate the controls myself, and I didn't pick up the piloting skills quite as quickly as I'd hoped I would.

Flight Lieutenant Williams was very patient, though, and I gradually became more confident. I mentally excused myself with the knowledge that in most new things that I'd taken up, I'd often been a slow learner, but once I'd got the basic technique in my head, I generally picked up things fast. That had been the rule for most things in my life up until then, both at school and at work, but after four weeks of practising 'circuits and bumps', interspersed with practice sessions in a Link trainer, Flight Lieutenant Williams sat me down in an office and said, 'You're not doing quite as well as I'd hoped you would. I think you'd better have a session with Squadron Leader Holmes.'

Squadron Leader Holmes was the chief flying instructor at Hatfield House, and so the next day I met him and we went up for what I realised was to be my test. I took off well enough, and then I just had to follow whatever instructions he gave me. After about twenty minutes, during which I thought I had flown reasonably well, he told me to land. I got us down quite smoothly, and as we climbed out of the Moth, he said, 'Come into my office after you've changed'.

Once there, he told me, 'You didn't do too badly, but you're not so advanced as I think you really ought to be, by now.' Then he went through all the mistakes I'd made on my test flight, many of which I must admit I just hadn't realised I was making. 'This means, I'm afraid,' he concluded, 'that I must take you off the course.' Upon those words my heart sank into my boots, and I sat there, feeling totally dismayed and dejected. I really didn't think I'd done that badly. 'However,' he added with a smile, 'all is not lost. Your results from the ITW – particularly in navigation – mean that you can now go on to become a navigator. You've done enough preliminary work to give you a very good start. You'll get your new orders at the end of the week – and good luck!'

So, my dream of becoming a pilot was at an end. I was very disappointed, but I consoled myself that at least I would still be flying as a navigator, still doing a very useful job. 'Always the conductor, never the driver,' I thought, ruefully. I'm a fairly philosophical person, though, so I didn't let the disappointment get me down too much.

I was duly posted to Babbacombe, in Devon, where I began an observer's course (the observer being a combination of navigator and bomb aimer), and I was soon cheered by the fact that many of the chaps that I had met on the course had had the same experience as myself – ITW success, but failure at flying practice. What was more consoling to me was that most of them had received similar comments from their flying instructors, and so I began to feel a lot happier with my new vocation. I had a fortnight there at Babbacombe, and then I joined a party of about thirty other would-be observers on a train to Penrhos Aerodrome near Pwllheli, in North Wales, for a bombing and gunnery course.

What a journey it turned out to be! In all, it took us a full two days, in which we had several stops of varying durations, the longest of which was half a day spent standing in a siding at Barmouth. When we finally arrived – as a very weary and bedraggled mob – at Penrhos in the early hours of a Sunday morning, we were promptly marched to the village of Llanbedrog, where we had been assigned billets with the local populace.

Once again I was fortunate, being billeted along with five others with a Mrs Williams – a local schoolteacher – and her fifteen-year-old daughter Gwyneth. Mrs Williams was a charming, motherly lady who made us very welcome. The beds were extremely comfortable, and we were given the free use of a big lounge where we could chat, play cards or whatever, and generally had a free run of the house. Mrs Williams and Gwyneth often joined us in the evenings, and we all got on very well together.

Our bombing and gunnery exercises were carried out in Fairey Battles – a whole squadron of rattle-trap aircraft that none of us would have wanted to fly in, had we been given the choice! When practising bombing, we had to lie flat in the nose of the aircraft, over the bomb hatch but directly under the engine, and we usually emerged from that position smothered in oil. The pilots were mostly Poles or Czechs, and as a result, they weren't always easy to communicate with.

My regular pilot was a Czech by the name of Jen, who fortunately spoke very good English, and was always very cheerful. He believed in making life as easy as possible for us when we were flying, and his method was simple. The bombing targets were floats and pontoons that were anchored in the sea off Pwllheli, and to obtain good results, we were supposed to move towards the targets flying straight and level, but from different angles of approach each time. Not our Jen! He always made his run from the same angle, keeping to exactly the same track each time, telling us that it was far easier to fly straight and level that way!

When practising machine-gunnery, one had to stand up in the rear half of the cockpit with the canopy propped up, and then shoot at drogues towed by other aircraft. The only security one had was a safety strap attached to the waist to prevent accidental bail outs! It was never a very reassuring stance, nor was it comfortable, but one got used to it after a time.

We also learned how to dismantle and reassemble Browning machine guns, and practised with them in the sand butts. There was bombing theory to be understood, too, plus a modicum of the usual PT and foot drill, so there was rarely a dull moment. We went into Pwllheli on occasions, and at the weekends the town was packed with people. Apart from us RAF boys, there were two naval training stations just along the coast, and although brawls were a fairly common occurrence, I never heard of any serious incidents; three sets of military police prevented that!

The course lasted three months, and our first instructor was RAF regular Corporal Costain, a cheerful cockney that we all liked. I had my usual slow start, but it didn't take long to catch up. When Corporal Costain was replaced by Sergeant Ainslie, he took me to one side and said to me, 'Corporal Costain tells me that you're not doing too well. Any particular problems?' I was able to laugh lightly and tell him, 'No, none at all. As a matter of fact, I'm helping the other five at my billet now!' This was quite true, and when our final test came at the end of the course, I finished sixth out of sixty trainees.

One more course remained – the vital one of navigation itself (the practical side, not the theory that we'd completed at Newquay). Accordingly, we were split up once again, and I found myself posted to an airfield at Bobbington, near Stourbridge in the Midlands. Once again, I had to go through the process of finding new friends, and I teamed up with an Irishman named Bob Miller, who – like all the Millers in the services –

was commonly known as 'Dusty'. We did our navigation practice in the same group, and I found him excellent company throughout the course. He was an enviously tall, handsome, well-built lad who'd lived in England for most of his life; he only adopted an Irish brogue when it seemed to be either convenient or advantageous. He was very popular with the ladies, and I often set out with him for an evening's socialising, only to return alone!

At Bobbington, I experienced a substantial boost to my confidence when I discovered that the arts of navigation seemed to be right up my street (if you'll pardon the pun). I had none of my usual slow-starting difficulties, and I sailed through the course very comfortably. The only area of initial discontent was with our aircraft, as – in the early stages of the course – we flew in Blackburn Botha aircraft, so-called 'bombers' that were so unreliable and unpredictable to fly that even the pilots disliked them. As for us navigators, we found them cramped, and given that there were always four of us on each trip, that wasn't perhaps too surprising. We never felt safe flying in those planes and, finally, after the 'squadron' suffered three crashes in just two days (in which no one, fortunately, was badly hurt), the aircraft were withdrawn, and quickly replaced by much more comfortable and reliable Avro Ansons.

I really enjoyed those three months, largely because it all went so well for me, but then it was over. At the passing-out parade, we were all presented with our sergeants' stripes and observers' brevets, following which we had one day in which to sew them to our uniforms, then we were off for a week's leave prior to our final course, which was essentially just a last-minute act of polishing before being posted to squadrons and getting into the real action.

On that week's leave I returned home, and I can vividly remember walking up Grey Street in Newcastle early that Sunday morning, on my way from train to bus, when a police sergeant cycled past me. 'Morning, sergeant!' he called – and I found myself looking around to see who he was addressing!

That leave passed too quickly, as all time off did, and I was on the move once more, this time to 23 OTU (Operational Training Unit) at Pershore, near Worcester. This final 'brush-up' course was to be another three-month affair, and an extremely hectic one at that. All I can remember of it today, however, is that, working as an individual navigator now and teamed with pilots who were also on their final training stint, I never once got us lost, and we always reached home safely.

It all came to an unexpectedly abrupt halt one day when I was called into the squadron leader's office and was told that I had been posted to 101 Squadron at Oakington, in Cambridgeshire. This was after only five weeks – not the usual three months that I'd been briefed about and prepared for. The reason for this, I learned a little later, was simply because navigators were in short supply at that time, and not, as I'd initially thought, because of my individual brilliance! Under normal circumstances observers' training spanned two full years, but I was being thrust into the thick of the action after just over one year, so my initial 'chest-puffing' reaction to my early posting was perhaps excusable, after all!

The rest of that week passed in a haze of nervous excitement and, finally, I packed my kit bag and set off for Oakington.

Chapter 2

Battle-hardened

When I arrived at Oakington – which lies about 8 miles north-west of Cambridge – I discovered that there were two squadrons sharing the base: 7 Squadron, with their four-engined Stirlings, and of course 101 Squadron, who were equipped with twin Pegasus-engined Wellington Mark 1C bombers.

As soon as I had settled into a barrack room, I was introduced to my first crew – and what a mixed bunch we were! The pilot, the front gunner and the radio operator were all Canadians, the tail-gunner was a Londoner, and with myself from the north-east of England, we had a rich variety of accents between us.

The pilot, Al Moran, had been a school PT teacher at home, and was a tall, well-built and athletic-looking chap (as befitted his previous vocation), who was always good-natured and very cool when in action. The front gunner was Bob Oxendale (known to everyone as 'Oxy'), also tall, but slim and very pale-faced, with a dry wit and an extremely good sense of humour. Jake Daniels was the wireless operator, although, sadly, the only thing I can remember him for was the constant stream of thousands of cigarettes that he received from home and sold to anyone on or near to the aerodrome, as the luxury was rationed by then. Last, but not least, the rear gunner was the chirpy cockney, Pat Wade, always cheerful and seemingly quite happy with his job, in spite of the danger from sudden night-fighter attack.

Once I had become acquainted with them, we settled down to the business of thinking and acting as an operational crew. We spent the first few weeks getting to know one another, familiarising ourselves with the countryside to memorise 'homing' landmarks and the like – in fact, essentially, we were doing a little extra training until we were ready to go on operations. Finally, we were prepared for battle – but as a crew, we didn't stay together for very long. Despite that, however, we still managed to share several dangerous – and sometimes hilarious – experiences.

Our first 'op' – on 26 November 1941 saw us take off from Oakington at 17.15 hours to attack Ostend, on the Belgian coast, although it was to prove to be little more than yet another training exercise. It was – oddly – something of an anticlimax as there was very little there in the way of defences, and with cloud cover a 'full blanket' at 10/10ths (in navigators' parlance) we simply flew there, but couldn't see anything to hit. We were ordered to keep our bombs and returned home for debriefing – which we were all actually thankful for, as it was a somewhat soft 'baptism of fire'! At least we all knew we could now carry out a mission as a working team.

The second 'op' just four nights later was a little more serious, if highly amusing on our 'home run'. We had had a long but uneventful flight across the North Sea to reach Emden, dropped our bombs right on target – again, fortunately, meeting very little resistance in the way of flak – but when we were about halfway home, 'Oxy' called me up to the front turret. There was a hint of anxiety in his voice, so I hurried forward – not an easy task in the Wellington, due to its cramped passageways and differing levels.

'See that, Jack?' he asked, pointing forward.

'See what?' I queried, rather puzzled that I could see nothing.

'That little red ring, quite a way out ahead,' he replied. 'I can't make it out.'

I followed the direction in which his finger was pointing, but from where I was leaning over his shoulder, I still could not see anything ahead but brightly moonlit clouds, and I told him so.

'There!' he insisted. 'Right there!' He jabbed his finger hard at the Perspex.

I peered more intently this time, but I still couldn't see what he was becoming vexed about … and a moment later, he slapped his thigh and muttered, 'Oh, hell! I've left the Goddamned gunsight switched on!'

What he was seeing – and I couldn't from my position – was the targeting ring that the reflector projected on to the turret's screen, and not some new 'advance' in German airborne navigation lights or some-such device, and as a result he spent the next half-hour in a rosy glow of embarrassment while the rest of us had a good laugh and pulled his leg unmercifully!

That jollity soon changed, however. By now we were fast approaching the Norfolk coast. Oxy called out to me once more, and when I answered him, he asked if we were supposed to be flying over a small cluster of islands.

'Not according to my calculations,' I replied. 'Why? What can you see?'

'You'd better come up and take a look for yourself,' he answered.

Naturally I was concerned, but before I left my table I consulted my maps once more – and I admit that I did allow myself a little frown, for there were no islands shown at any point near our plotted route. I was beginning to worry that I might have slipped up somewhere in my calculations, and had perhaps taken us a long way off-course by accident.

As I struggled forward once more, I felt that my 'professional pride' might be about to be shot down in tatters – but one glance out of the turret had me laughing once more, and Oxy's face dropped yet again; his 'islands' turned out to be no more than images of the clouds above us, reflected on the surface of an almost glassy-smooth sea! Perhaps it might have been Oxy's attempt at gaining revenge for my pulling his leg, but if it was, it backfired on him severely, as he was often ribbed about his 'islands in the sky' afterwards.

Following that comically underlined raid, we were briefed for the first of two successive attacks upon Brest Harbour, where the German battleships *Scharnhorst*, *Prinz Eugen* and *Gneisenau* were being bottled up by the British Navy. Our job was to help keep these feared battleships in the harbour, and to try to sink them in place by bombing them; it was to prove no easy task, however.

On our first trip, the Wellingtons of 101 Squadron were set to arrive at Brest half an hour before the Stirlings of 7 Squadron, who would then lead the attack with their bigger bombs. Our initial task was to 'stooge' around the target area for the half-hour in an attempt to disrupt the German sound locators, which – in theory, at least – should have made the job of penetration of the mark much easier for the Stirlings.

There had been a slight miscalculation in the planning, though, for it was still daylight when we arrived over the target, and long before we reached Brest we could see a dense smokescreen being put up by the

German defenders. And so, when we began our 'stooging', all we could subsequently see was a thick white fog of smoke blanketing the entire harbour, and with a very strong barrage of flak our 'mad' half-hour turned into an uncomfortably long wait.

It seemed that we were circling Brest for an eternity, listening apprehensively to the 'crump, crump, crump' of the flak shells exploding all around us, with accompanying rattling noises along our fuselage … and, then, I had the fright of my life as a shard of metal punched through the fuselage fabric at my back, then clanged off my overhead light before landing in the dead-centre of my map table! I quickly flicked it off for fear of it burning a hole in the map, and as it clattered on to the floor, I stamped my boot over it to stop it sliding elsewhere to possibly jam some vital control rod or something. I shook like a leaf for some time – that had been far too close!

All the while that we were 'stooging' around, we were also worrying about fighter interception that could so easily happen, the longer we loitered – but finally 7 Squadron arrived, so we hurriedly dropped our bombs into the thick smoke and beetled off home as quickly as possible.

We arrived back at Oakington without mishap, but when we went to look at our 'Wimpy' the next morning, the ground crew showed us dozens of shrapnel holes in the skin and even the airframe of the poor aircraft. We'd been luckier than we'd thought – the Wellington's geodetic structure had indeed saved our own skins, and I had picked up that piece of shrapnel for a keepsake, to remind me just how lucky I had been!

A second raid on Brest followed two nights later, this time a straightforward bombing attack without the 'stooging' preamble, and all went well … until we were on our way home.

On the flight out, our plan had been to reach the coast a little to the west of Southampton, then take the shortest sea-route directly to Brest. That part of the flight plan had worked fine, but by the time we reached the target, thick cloud had blocked the land from our elevated view (10/10ths cover, in our jargon), so we were forced to drop our 'eggs' blind into the murk in the hope that they'd hit something worthwhile, then we turned for home.

I plotted a more direct course for Oakington, gave the bearing to Al, and we settled down for a (hopefully) quiet run home. When my calcu-

lations showed that we should be over the south coast, I told Al to steer
076 degrees, and to lose height so that we could break cloud cover and
so assess our position more accurately.

I made my way forward to the bomb-aiming position once more, but
when I squeezed past the pilot's seat, I noticed that Al had set 086 degrees
on the compass, not 076. I pointed this out to him and he altered it
immediately. Just then, Oxy cried out from the front turret.

'Breaking cloud now, Jack!'

I dropped to my knees behind the bombsight and pressed my face against
the sighting window in the forward floor – and the first thing I saw was
a clutch of barrage balloons drifting by below us, incredibly close underneath, and my mouth went oddly dry as I realised what I was seeing.

'Christ! We're right over Southampton!' I gasped, and then I called to
Al, 'Emergency climb now, Al, and keep going due north until I tell you
to stop!'

The engine note changed as he threw the throttles forward, and the
sudden swing to the left told me that he had complied, so I squeezed my
way back to my navigator's table and stood for a while with my head inside
the observation dome, trying to spot a landmark or something else to act
as a reference point. I dropped back down and moved to the starboard
-side waist gun window and soon spied one of the flashing beacons far
below, and once I knew precisely where we were I scrambled back to my
table, plotted our new course very quickly and gave it to Al.

Thankfully, we arrived home without any further excitement, and we
shrugged it off as 'just one of those things', accepting the incident as yet
another lesson learned the hard way. I dare say we had been very lucky,
too, that Southampton's flak crews weren't 'trigger-happy'; perhaps they
had been taking a tea break, or maybe even asleep.

Life was relatively good in those days, in spite of the operational stresses.
There was a tremendous sense of camaraderie among the aircrews, and
although we were kept busy, we mostly enjoyed our flying – either on
'sorties' or just training flights – even if the danger did play on our minds
from time to time, as each different scenario unfolded.

We visited Cambridge in the evenings when no operations were listed,
frequenting such places as the Criterion – which was 101's favourite water-

ing hole – and a restaurant we named 'The Greek's' (I never did find out the owner's real name, although Stavros was often bandied about) where we could buy a smashing mixed grill for half a crown. Back at Oakington, the sergeants' mess was always full of life and good cheer, which was only dampened occasionally by the loss of an aircraft from either squadron. We accepted the losses fairly stoically, knowing that casualties were inevitable in war, and we mourned only the men who had been close friends; rarely for long, however, as we had to maintain morale and sanity, or else crack under the strain.

My part-Canadian crew didn't stay for any length of time; they wanted to see the world, so they volunteered for the Middle East, and I was transferred across to become a member of D-Donald's crew. The pilot then was Willie Williams, who had already completed twenty-six 'ops', and since thirty operations completed a tour of duty, he left us soon after his remaining four ops for a rest period.

The remainder of the crew were: Henry Hanwell (front gunner), Stan Bradley (wireless operator, known to all as 'Brad'), and one of the squadron's ace marksmen, the wee Scot Alec Crighton (tail gunner). We also had a 'second dickey' (or co-pilot), on each sortie, but it was squadron practice to move them from one aircraft to another in order to increase their operational experience, so we rarely had the same man twice. As a consequence of this 'musical chairs', and for a very important reason, I can only remember the name of the one co-pilot, John Beecroft, who was eventually to become our crew skipper, taking over from Willie Williams. At 6ft 4in, Beecroft was a giant of a man, and his strength proved to be our lifesaver on more than one occasion.

Around the middle of January 1942, we witnessed the first of a few major changes within 101 Squadron. Our commanding officer, 'Wingco' Biggs, left us for another command, and in his place came 'Wingco' Nicholls. Shortly after his taking up the reins, we were re-equipped with Wellington Mark IIIs, and we had to fly our older Wimpys up to Dumfries in Scotland to exchange them for the new aircraft, then fly back south – this time, to Bourn, a satellite airfield of Oakington, which was to be our new home within the next month. The collection of new planes didn't quite go as planned, however; we were snowed in at Dumfries for two days – and a very pleasant time we had of it, too!

The Wellington Mark IIIs were a great improvement over the Mark Is; with their Bristol Hercules fourteen-cylinder engines, they seemed much smoother-running, were a little faster and more manoeuvrable. More importantly – to me, at least – they were fitted with the latest thing in airborne navigation equipment (a device known as 'Gee'), which was to prove extremely useful on more than one occasion.

After collecting X3472 – which, having been built in the Blackpool factory had already had a bit of a 'round-the-houses' fly about and was effectively (in motor car terms, at least), 'run in' – we had a short spell of training to familiarise ourselves both with the Wimpy and my new navigational 'toy', and soon, we were once more ready for action.

Although we were occasionally prevented from carrying out some operations due to bad weather, we added steadily to our score of completed 'sorties' with attacks on Wilhelmshaven, Essen, Duisburg and a number of other German cities including Cologne, which was always a real hotbed of Bomber Command activity.

By this time, we had completed our squadron move to Bourn and had settled in comfortably – but then came the raid that had us wondering for the first time if we might never see home again.

Rostock was the target. It was the longest 'run' we had yet undertaken – long enough to necessitate that I should plot the shortest possible route there, and to make doubly sure that we would have enough fuel to 'bimble' about over target, but far more importantly, that we should still have sufficient for our return flight. I reckoned that we would have just about enough provided that we had a clear run in, without diversions – but, as so often happened when calculations were so finely balanced, fate seemed to conspire against us that night, and we met with just the diversion that we could have done without.

About half an hour from reaching our target, we suddenly ran into a tremendous barrage of flak. With the crump of shells exploding around us once more (and they had to be really close for us to hear the explosions over the noise of the engines), we droned onward, each of us thinking private prayers – and then abruptly, the ack-ack stopped. We knew that this was usually a sign that there might be hostile aircraft close by and we prayed even harder, hoping like mad that the night fighters wouldn't find us.

'Keep your eyes open, gunners,' warned Beecroft. 'There might be one or two fighters about!'

It seemed such an unnecessary thing for him to say, as I knew that both Hanwell and Crighton would already be swivelling their heads this way and that, while I had my head in the observation dome again, adding my eyes to the task – but hardly had Beecroft finished speaking than our hearts leaped into our mouths as our fears were confirmed.

'Bandit above, ten o'clock!' yelled Hanwell from the front turret, and we heard and felt his guns begin to blaze away. To make matters worse, it was at that precise moment that the enemy searchlights caught us in their beams and 'coned' us. Then Crighton yelled 'Corkscrew, Skipper!' as he, too, began blazing away at something behind, and Beecroft went into swift action by hurling us into the most incredible evasive manoeuvres. He flung D-Donald about the sky as though it was a fighter aircraft and I hung on tight to anything that I could grab, spreading my legs to stop myself being catapulted about, but although we quickly shook off the night fighter, those blinding searchlights held us in their grip like torch beams tracking a moth. Beecroft continued to throw the aircraft around into the most violent yet amazing aerobatics for what felt like half an hour – then at last we broke free from the dazzling glare, steadied down, then began climbing back to our operational height and pressed on toward Rostock, each of us gasping for breath and calming our pounding hearts, as well as uttering thankful prayers for our continuing existence; it had been a very hectic, terrifying, seemingly never-ending episode – yet we were amazed to discover that the whole thing had lasted just a couple of minutes!

With sighs of blessed relief we settled back into our routine, I eased my way back to my table, and in a short while we were over Rostock, dead on target in spite of our 'diversion'. We dropped our bombs, thus adding more to the orange glow far below us, then turned for home, each of us wondering what the return journey might have in store for us. We needn't have worried; nothing untoward happened and my pre-plotted 'shortest possible route' saw us safely home at a gentle cruising speed. As the wheels kissed the runway at Bourn once more, we chalked up another successful – if not a little hair-raising – operation.

Our respect for John Beecroft's ability as a pilot was immensely increased by that episode, as we would never have believed – even in our wildest dreams – that a Wimpy could be thrown about the sky in such a fashion, or that we would live to tell the tale. It was quite simply an incredible piece of flying – and we later also raised a glass to the Wellington's designers, Barnes Wallis and Reg Pierson, for creating such a strong airframe with the geodetic structure invention; both they and Beecroft had undoubtedly preserved our lives that night.

Two nights later we were back over Cologne – and what a scare we had on the return journey! Just as we were recrossing the Channel coast, tired, yawning and looking forward to a good breakfast of bacon and eggs and all the trimmings, the port engine coughed and died, and Beecroft quickly adjusted his controls to compensate. We had, of course, practised single-engined flying for just such an occasion, and thankfully, D-Donald rumbled on for a while longer at a slower, steadier pace, until the port engine coughed back into life once more, coaxed by Beecroft and his 'second dickey'. All of us had had our hearts in our mouths while they were juggling with switches and throttles; no one yawned again on the remainder of that trip!

Once home safely, we left the Wimpy in our ground crews' very capable hands for repair; it was apparently a tricky fault, but they did their homework and fixed the engine, and several air-test flights later, D-Donald was declared fit for operations once more.

After that raid and the test flights, we had an extra period of night-flying training, followed closely by a 'soft' raid on the Dunlop factory in Paris. The whole squadron had an easy time on that last op because of the lack of flak defences, and upon our return I overheard one gunner telling his debriefing officer that 'There were just four machine guns firing at us' (which was a very ineffective way of defending a target, considering the great height from which we dropped our bombs), and yet another gunner was heard to claim that he 'Could smell the rubber burning', which raised many a smile when the comment was remarked upon in the mess, afterwards!

There followed yet another spell of night-flying training – and then we had a minor calamity when Beecroft sprained his ankle one night when leaving the mess after a celebratory party, and we were dropped from operations until he was fit to take control of D-Donald once more.

I managed to while away some of the time playing football, but soon Beecroft regained his fitness and we were given the task of training one or two 'sprog' navigators, for whom I acted as a 'screened' instructor – and what an interesting event that turned out to be!

We were detailed to fly out to St-Nazaire, in France, and the outward trip gave us no bother at all. On our return, however, I noticed that the coastline looked different from that shown on the map at the point where our marked route crossed it, so I used the navigation receiver to double-check the 'sprog's' dead-reckoning – and I soon found that, instead of being somewhere over Salisbury Plain, we were in fact almost directly over the Bristol Channel! It was an excellent demonstration for the new boy, although he took the ribbing in good heart; he then made amends by plotting an accurate course for home – which I was obliged to double-check for him again – and we arrived safely back at Bourn, none the worse for the experience, but a little wiser than before.

A few nights later, we had another session of night-flying training with the aid of the navigation receiver, and after that we were back in the swing of things and fit to rejoin operations.

By now, we were a fairly battle-hardened crew, and we had shared eleven successful operations, each of which had had their moments of excitement, laughs, danger and relief. That raid on Rostock, however, was the one that stuck most vividly in our minds – but the operation that we would never forget was yet to come.

Chapter 3

A piece of cake

The morning of Tuesday, 19 May 1942 dawned bright and clear, seeming to instil an uncannily peaceful atmosphere across Bourn airfield. I awoke to a cheerful birdsong just outside my barrack-room window, and I felt as if I was on top of the world. Life seemed very good indeed at that moment. I had notched up twenty-two operations in my navigator's log, which left me with just another eight to go until I could qualify for a well-earned rest – and a glance at the DROs (Daily Routine Orders) revealed that we were listed for another operation that coming night. The briefing was set for 16.45 hours, so it was obvious that the op would be a 'late show', and equally obvious that it would only be a short one. 'A piece of cake', as the fighter boys would put it, and a step nearer that long break.

Nothing could mar my feeling of joie de vivre, and to lay some gilt on the gingerbread, we'd be returning to start a week's leave – always welcome to us. To complete this happy picture, I'd just recently met an old friend from Ashington who was also in the RAF, and – lucky laddie! – he was in a civvy billet in Cambridge. During a visit to his digs, I had arranged with his landlady that – on return from leave – I'd bring my wife and son to stay for a week, perhaps longer. No wonder, then, that I harboured not a single thought of danger, but looked forward instead to the fortnight of happiness before me.

Little did I know that the events of the coming night were to drastically alter not only my immediate joyous plans, but in fact, my whole life.

At 16.30 that afternoon, we all trooped into the briefing room, the air filling with the usual ribald comments from friendly rivals. We were a complete squadron, a well-trained and fairly close-knit group of healthy, fit men – 'The cream of the nation's youth'. At least, that's what the newsreels kept telling us.

All joking stopped as 'Wingco' Nicholls took the stage and, instantly, we settled into an expectant silence; we were 'all ears', as the saying goes. Without further ado, he swept his eyes across us all, then cleared his throat and nodded.

'Tonight's target, gentlemen,' he announced, 'is Mannheim.'

There came a few murmurs from crewmembers who knew the target of old, but 'Wingco' got straight down to business as though no one had spoken and went on to give us other vital details: the kind of opposition that we could expect from both flak and possibly night fighters; the best route; take-off time; time over target; and so on. Then came the meteorological reports and, next, we were left to confer with the heads of our various sections. Pilots huddled with their flight commanders, wireless operators and air gunners with their respective seniors and, as a navigator, I joined with my fellow observers in a meeting with our senior navigation officer, Canadian Flight Lieutenant Pilkington.

After that, Beecroft and I plotted the route as usual. As the 'Wingco' had told us, we were to avoid at all costs the industrial Ruhr Valley, which was known throughout Bomber Command as 'Happy Valley' because of its tremendous concentration of searchlights, ack-ack guns and night fighters. If you were ever once caught in those searchlight beams, you had to be extremely lucky to break free and escape safely; therefore, our route would take us south of the Ruhr, then we would attack our target from the west. Mannheim, we had been told, was not heavily defended; eyebrows were raised at that, because we had all heard similar intelligence claims before, regarding other targets.

Hanwell and Crighton went off to check their guns, and Brad joined the 'dit-dit, dah-dah' boys to consult with the officer in charge of the radar and communications about such things as signal codes and frequencies, and the designated operation call-signs.

As well as navigation, I had of course to check the bomb bay and the sighting mechanism on D-Donald to ensure that everything was in perfect working order, even though we felt that this wasn't really necessary owing to our confidence in the skills of our ground crew. I'd never yet heard of any 101 aircrew having trouble through careless maintenance or forgetfulness – and, besides, wasn't our ground crew sergeant a Geordie, like myself? I felt that I could trust all of the crew with our lives, but, nevertheless, I performed my duty carefully, every time.

There was one significant change from the usual set-up; for the first time ever, each crew was to be comprised of only five men, leaving the customary sixth – the 'second dickey' (co-pilot) – to twiddle his thumbs in the ops room while we went to 'work'. That alteration, we were eventually to discover, might just have made all the difference to the way things were to turn out for us, that night.

With our chores completed – including packing our kitbags, ready for that other 'take-off' for home and beauty when we returned – we whiled away the remaining few hours in various ways until take-off time approached. This was set for 22.50, and at 20.00 we met up and descended as a crew upon the sergeants' mess for the obligatory pre-flight meal. From there, we took an almost leisurely stroll to our crew room, joking and teasing each other as usual along the way.

'That redhead will miss you at the Criterion tonight, John!' called Hanwell.

'You should talk!' countered Beecroft. 'What about that blonde WAAF you've been seeing lately? Have you told your fiancée about her, yet?'

'I'm thinking about it,' laughed Hanwell, by reply. It was all fictitious banter, but such exchanges always helped to raise spirits as our nerves began to tingle in anticipation of the coming operation, no matter where the target. After the jesting our thoughts turned to the job in hand as we settled down to real, far more important, matters.

We reached our crew room, kitted ourselves up, and eventually left there either wearing or carrying a veritable mountain of equipment, all of which was vital to our well-being in the air. We all had Irving suits, flying boots, parachutes, Thermos flasks – I also had my maps and other notes – everything but the kitchen sink, as the saying goes, and as well as these essentials, Hanwell had made sure that he had his 'lucky' rabbit's foot (although it hadn't been so lucky for the poor rabbit, obviously!), and Brad wouldn't dream of setting out on an op without his black cat mascot.

Myself? I made sure that my Pegasus (winged horse) tie-pin was in my pocket – a little personal memento that Evelyn had bought for me when we began flying in the earlier Wellington Mark IC, fitted with Pegasus engines (slightly under-powered, but quite reliable); my tie-pin, therefore, was more of a personal keepsake than a lucky charm … and, anyway, I had no doubts whatsoever that we'd all return safely, and then take off for home in the morning – our leave passes all said so!

A truck soon picked us up and, eventually, we alighted at D-Donald's dispersal point. By 22.30 hours, we were settled in and had everything ready, with the engines ticking over as we waited for take-off, fourth in line. The green light was flashed, the three Wellingtons ahead of us moved off into the darkness one by one, then – at 23.00 precisely – it was our turn, and we trundled forward, then accelerated down the runway with a thundering roar.

The two Hercules Mark XI engines were deafening under full take-off power, and D-Donald jolted and rattled a little and occasionally seemed to sway a touch, but despite all that I experienced once more the sheer thrill that never deserted me, no matter how often we flew; that same noise-filled, breathlessly anticipated start had excited me from the very first time I'd flown – seemingly years before – in that humble Tiger Moth, and, once more, I found my concentration wandering slightly from the maps on the table before me. We were 'back at work' – and the exhilaration felt marvellous!

Very soon, the jolting and rattling eased and then stopped as we became airborne, and I gave my first instruction to Beecroft. 'Steer 130 degrees for the first leg,' I told him. 'About two hours will put us in line for the turn on Mannheim.'

I heard his acknowledgement, and then I settled down to pore over my maps. We were carrying close to our maximum bombload – around 4,500lb – on this sortie; this meant that our all-up weight (including all fuel, supplies and crew) amounted to around 15½ tons, so we were in for a slow, steady climb for an hour or so to reach an operational height of around 20,000ft, which was literally as high as we could expect to get with such a heavy burden aboard – so, to begin with, there wasn't an awful lot for me to do, except check and re-check our route.

Eventually, we levelled out. It was a fine, clear night with occasional cloudbanks and just over a half-moon or so, and we had no difficulty at all in seeing the south coast of England slip by far below us. As the coast of France came into view, there came the brief hammering from both the nose and the tail as Hanwell and Crighton tested their guns (I also saw a few tracer-bullet flashes around us as other crews did likewise), and once again, I set about checking my navigation, this time using the radar unit.

This device – as I have mentioned already – had by now proved to be an extremely useful (if not a little belated) 'Christmas present', and as I began to set it up, I couldn't help but feel a heightening of pride in British ingenuity. It was a huge advance over anything the Germans had yet achieved (so we had been told), but it was simple to operate. The TR1335 (to give it its official equipment number) was essentially just a radio frequency receiver that picked up separate signals from two or more transmitting stations in Britain, which would then be displayed upon a small television-type screen as a pair (or more) of intersecting lines. The navigator would adjust these until they all crossed at one point, then push a button and be rewarded with a set of coordinate figures, which he would then apply to a specially marked map, and thus obtain an exact position through signal triangulation. The system became progressively less effective the further you flew from Britain, but as I had already used the unit to guide us to and from several other targets deep inside Germany, I had every confidence that it would see us to Mannheim and back home safely.

For just a fleeting moment I smiled to myself as I remembered that recent 'sprog' training flight, then I concentrated all my thoughts on the job immediately at hand, and I found that we were nicely on course and keeping good time. We knew that we could expect little in the way of trouble until we reached the target, so we prepared to just stooge along at our pre-planned airspeed, but all the while keeping a weather eye out for the ever-present threat of prowling enemy night fighters. There would be no relaxation for either of our gunners.

We had been briefed that as we were crossing France for the bulk of this trip, there was less danger of suddenly being caught by anti-aircraft fire, so a general feeling of contentment was present ... until, abruptly, we were bracketed by a cluster of popping smoke puffs – not too close, but near enough to scare us with a little buffeting – and we heard the rattle of shrapnel clattering off various parts of D-Donald as we took evasive action, hoping that the rest of the squadron was also dispersing slightly. It was a very nasty moment that set our hearts into our mouths, but the barrage was over as quickly as it had begun – just a token flurry, apparently – and we settled back down to our individual tasks, checking for damage and reporting back to Beecroft.

After a while, the steady, throbbing drone of the twin Hercules engines was like a comforting, reassuring background 'music' to my ears as we flew through the night, ever onwards to our target. As I raised my head into the observation dome it seemed as if the engines' roar sounded a little louder – even with my flight-hat's earpieces damping the din – but I knew that it was a figment of my imagination as there was little difference between the acoustic properties of the Perspex dome and that of the fuselage skin. As always, though, I was captivated by the sight that met my eyes.

The top of the Wellington's cockpit canopy gleamed in the moonlight while the fuselage showed dully ahead of me, intersected by the shadow of the radio DF pod on its stalk. As I admired the heavens above, I felt awestruck once more; it was always quite a majestic image, and the sight of all those millions of stars above us never failed to amaze me – a view that we could rarely see from our homes and cities because of the usual clouds in our atmosphere (and sometimes the smog, it has to be said), and was therefore something that I treasured with every flight above the cumulus.

I brought my wandering mind back to the task at hand and set about confirming our position from the stars that showed brightest. Having already checked our course by compass calculations I was confident that we were on the correct heading, but it didn't hurt to double-check – and besides, it was a rare 'treat' to enjoy such a clear night.

Ahead and slightly to starboard of our nose – once my eyes had adjusted – I could just discern the glint of the tail turret cupola of our lead aircraft, and as I turned my head left and right, I saw another couple of Wellingtons in a loose but reassuring formation around us. I couldn't help but feel a surge of pride (and a little comfort in numbers) as our aircraft rumbled onward to Germany.

We were about to graze the top of another long cloudbank that was brightly lit by the moon, and with that came the heightened danger of being spotted by any night fighters that might be prowling above us. Given that it was such a clear night, we were all somewhat fearful of the likelihood of their presence – if we could see so well, then so could they, obviously – and given that our ground-schemed camouflage meant nothing against a glaringly blue-white blanket beneath us, every aircraft would stand out like flies skimming a rice pudding, presenting an easy sighting for an enemy.

Beecroft's voice crackled in our earpieces once more. 'Going over cloud … now! Keep your eyes peeled, lads – we don't want to be "bounced" now, do we?'

Almost on cue, as I thought about that very danger, a Glaswegian brogue crackled in my headphones. 'Aye, 'tis a braw, bricht, moonlicht nicht, t'nicht, laddies!' It was little Alec romanticising from the rear turret, almost as though he had read my thoughts, and we all managed a few chuckles at his fine attempt to break the tension.

Right at that moment, the port-side engine spluttered, ran on again, then cut out altogether. My heart lurched again as I watched the propeller falter and then carry on windmilling, and then I heard the starboard engine begin to strain as Beecroft juggled the throttles. I had to grab the rim of the astrodome with both hands to stop myself from falling as we swung a little sideways, then I felt the Wimpy yaw slightly as Beecroft rapidly fought for control, throttling-up the other engine to compensate. Normally a very cool man under stress, it was most astonishing when we heard a string of loud profanities escape from the cockpit over the intercom system, of which 'Damn and blast it!' were the only printable ones!

'Trouble, Skip?' I heard wee Alec ask; he probably couldn't turn his head enough to see the dead port engine, though from the tail turret he would obviously have felt the movement more and known there was something wrong, even if Beecroft hadn't cursed aloud … and, of course, he wouldn't have been able to rotate his turret either, as that engine also powered its hydraulic motors.

'That bloody port engine – I can't believe it's cut out again! Either that flak's got it, or perhaps the erks didn't fix it, after all,' Beecroft replied, reining in his temper. 'I can't feather the prop, either, so something's a bit amiss.

I'll try a couple of tricks – see if I can get it going again. Carry on, lads.'

Quite gently, we felt D-Donald's nose drop then heard and felt the noise and vibration from the starboard engine's increase in revolutions as our pilot put us into a shallow dive – presumably to try to use the air pressure to rotate the port propeller a little faster and thus attempt to get it to restart the engine – but in spite of his assurances, my heart began to race with fear. In my mind's eye, I could 'see' him trying to fly D-Donald with the joystick clamped between his knees while struggling to reignite that swine of a port engine; we already knew from that last raid that it would normally take the pilot and a co-pilot to achieve this as the procedure was complicated, but Beecroft was alone in the cockpit on this run, so it would be a doubly difficult task.

We all had faith in him and his piloting abilities, but we had already dropped some way out of the formation, and our remaining engine roared louder than ever as it struggled to keep us flying.

Chapter 4

Crash stations now!

As perturbing as this situation was -— but ever confident in Beecroft's flying skills – we did as he recommended and 'carried on'. I dropped down from my dome and returned to my table to check our location and to start replotting an emergency return route – just in case.

Returning to the dome once more for a quick star fix, I cast my eyes down at the port engine, but even though I could see the propeller spinning and stuttering around in alternating doses as he tried several times to restart it, no roaring, revving or cries of relief were forthcoming.

I sat back down at my table, reading and working with my maps, and my heart sank further when there was still no joy from the cockpit some minutes later; it became gradually and worryingly obvious that we might have real trouble on our hands. Our fears were confirmed when Beecroft next spoke.

'I'm sorry, lads,' he said, 'but I'm afraid we'll have to turn back. The engine's as dead as a dodo, so it's no good trying to carry on to target. Give me a course for home, please, will you, Jack?'

In anticipation of such a request, I quickly gave him the return bearing. At that moment we were – frustratingly – only about 35 miles short of the French–German border; so near to the target, yet unable to reach it! By now we were flying at a little under 20,000ft, and were all far from happy at the prospect of bumbling off home fully laden, one engine short and the other struggling against that windmilling propeller (we knew from various briefings that the drag of unfeathered propeller blades increased air drag significantly, and although the Wellington had been designed to fly on one engine in the event of such a failure, it could only do so for any length of time if the 'dead' propeller's blades were turned into the slipstream like knives, thereby lessening the load on the work-ing engine).

It was now clear that we were in dire trouble, for not only did the port engine provide hydraulic power for both of the gun turrets, it also pres-surised the landing gear. We weren't too concerned about the under-carriage side of things right then, but the prospect of flying over enemy-occupied territory without any real means of defence (with our guns effectively disabled) worried us all greatly, and we fervently prayed that our skipper would get the engine going again. We could fret later about the undercarriage, as we knew that we could jack the wheels down, should we need to, with a manual pump fitted close to the port wing root, just behind the main spar – but first, we had to get home.

For the second time, I felt a small chill of fear that I might not see my wife and son again – a fear most likely because this was happening in the wee small hours of the morning, and we were so far from home and safety.

Dishearteningly, just a few minutes into our return journey, Beecroft called again. 'It's no good, lads, it just won't fire up,' he said. 'Something's wrong with the ignition circuit, I suspect, as well as the feathering mech-anism – maybe it was that flak, after all. We're still losing height and the starboard engine's beginning to overheat now – we'll have to get rid of some weight, at least, if we expect to carry on any further.'

'The bombs,' I said immediately, stating the obvious. 'We're well away from any towns or villages.'

'Right,' he agreed. 'Let them go, then.'

I clambered forward and down to the bomb-aiming position, made doubly sure that none of the bombs were fused, checked that the 'bomb doors open' lamp was illuminated, and I pressed the button.

'Bombs gone!' I called as the Wimpy gave its usual upward lurch. Although we all knew that jettisoning the load could possibly help us out of our predicament and all being well see us safely home, I fervently hoped that I hadn't unloaded them on top of a farmhouse or a peasant's cottage, or similar.

Thus lightened by about 4½ tons, I made sure that the bomb doors were closed properly and then made my way back to my table. We trust-ed that all we had to do now was to concentrate all of our attention and efforts toward getting back to Bourn, or at least an English coastal airfield – but no sooner had the dream of bacon and eggs crossed our minds than Beecroft put the dampener on things yet again by informing us that we were still slowly losing height.

'Hate to say this, lads, but I can't hold her up much longer – you'd better get your parachutes on and get ready to jump!'

This was something that none of us wanted to do; I wasn't sure about the others, but I had to admit to being terrified at the prospect. Jumping out of an aircraft was daunting enough in broad daylight – at least you could see where you were going to land – but to leap into the darkness to drop on to Lord-knew-what, and in enemy-occupied territory? Most definitely not my idea of adventure! It very quickly proved that I wasn't alone in my fears – and not surprisingly, Beecroft was nearly swamped by our chorused reply.

'Of course not, Skip! You'll get us back all right!'

'Thanks for the vote of confidence, lads,' he said, 'but there doesn't seem to be anything else that I can do – I really think old Donald's done for.'

There was a silence on the intercom for a few moments as I suspected he was thinking what we were all dreading … then he declared, 'Oh, bloody hell! All right, then – the temperature's stabilised again … let's give it a try for a bit longer – but we still need to lighten the load a bit more. See if you can get rid of anything that isn't bolted down, and I'll keep trying with the one engine.'

We embarked on a mad spree of weight loss; first to go were the fore and tail guns, useless now that the turrets themselves couldn't be operated, and with the guns went their belts of ammunition. They were followed immediately by the waist guns and their ammo belts – a trick involving passing them through to Alec in the rear turret and out through his cupola – and then went a host of other sundry bits and pieces that would be of no use to the enemy once they'd smashed into the ground from that height – and then we waited … and waited. …

The engine note hadn't changed, and we were still struggling along. My hopes were beginning to rise again with every second that passed without comment from Beecroft, and I imagined that the other lads were feeling just the same; none of us would have wanted to just give up and jump into the unknown. I had that feeling that there just had to be something else that we could do – possibly something that Beecroft might have missed in the restart procedure, assuming that the fault wasn't flak damage, after all – but how should I approach the point tactfully? He was the skipper, after all. I thought very carefully for a few moments, then cleared my very dry throat and spoke to Beecroft.

'Er – Skipper,' I interjected, 'is there anything that might work better with an extra pair of hands?'

'Such as?' He retorted.

'I don't know, Skip – I've no idea what your start-up routine is, but I just wondered if there might be something that a second dickey might have done for you – like the last run? Maybe one of us can help, there, if you say what you want done and when?'

With nothing to lose now, Brad piped up. 'Would it help if I come forward and help with the switches and things?'

'Why not, indeed?' Beecroft agreed immediately, and Brad quickly unstrapped himself and twisted out of his seat, then squeezed his way forward from his wireless station to set up the 'second dickey' seat in the cockpit.

'Rather him than me,' I thought, but I crossed my fingers anyway and set about rechecking my compass and charts, yet again.

Even with Brad to assist, though, it was to no avail. Standing up and looking out from my dome once more, I could see the propeller spinning freely and then straining to rotate as they applied various techniques; the port engine would turn over, but it just would not fire up and run.

While they were struggling, I was praying – and thinking, 'Would a trained, experienced "second-dickey" have succeeded?' Would it have helped to know more about the actual technical aspects of flying D-Donald, even allowing for the increasingly apparent likelihood of flak damage in this instance? I wasn't sure – and we all had plenty of technical issues and aspects to remember in our own specialised crewing roles, so it would have been even harder to cram in such complex, higher-level cross-training in the time that we'd all had already, relevant to our positions. Sure, I had had gunnery training and had occasionally let loose in anger with the 'waist' guns, but none of us had undergone pilot training at Beecroft's level.

Right at that moment of impending catastrophe, however, all we could do was keep pinning our hopes on Brad and the skipper getting the engine restarted (praying that it hadn't been damaged after all), and if they were successful, then we'd be banking on Beecroft's skills to keep it going and get us safely home once more. The gunners must have felt especially help-less, sitting in what were now 'toothless' immobile turrets, but they still had their 'look-out' jobs to do, and I still had to keep track of our progress.

All too soon, Brad was making his way back to his wireless station, the port engine still silent, its propeller blades glinting in the moonlight, now defiantly stationary. I think we all especially began to fear for our lives at that point, when the intercom crackled again.

'Really sorry, chaps,' Beecroft apologised, 'but I don't think we'll get home in this bus tonight – the starboard temperature's starting to creep up again and the altimeter's dropping. What's our current position, please, Jack?'

Again, in anticipation of events, I rattled off our estimated location – now about 10 miles east of Metz – and my heart sank as I saw Brad begin tapping away at his Morse key, sending a situation report back home.

We all began to mentally prepare ourselves for either jumping or crash-landing – and whatever the outcome of either might be. Even if we were still high enough to bail out (and assuming that our parachutes would open quickly enough, in the event) we would probably be scattered over a good-sized area and it would very likely be 'every man for himself' to try to escape home. If there was to be a crash-landing, we knew that we couldn't risk hand-pumping the undercarriage down, because if the terrain was rough – like crossing a ploughed field, for example – we would nose-down and cartwheel to our deaths; therefore, it would have to be a belly-flop landing, and with the added danger of random darker spells now that there were clouds skimming across the moon.

We tried hard not to think about the consequences of finding poten-tial hazards like unseen trees, embankments, wide ditches or dykes in our prospective landing path.

Unbelievably, it seemed that another quarter of an hour had crawled by; in reality, however, it was probably only a couple of minutes or so, simply elongated by natural fear. I was just beginning to wonder if things had evened out, and to hope that perhaps the starboard engine had set-tled down to its task at last and that we might yet still have a chance of getting home at a crawl, when Beecroft's sigh and his apologetic voice sounded over the intercom. I knew, then, that it had indeed just been desperate, wishful thinking.

'I can't hold her up much longer, lads!' He broke the bad news as gently as he could. 'We're just over a thousand feet, and still going down. Stand by to bail out!'

'It's a bit late for that, Skipper,' came our collective reply. We knew that we would almost certainly all be seriously injured or killed by parachuting out so low, so a crash-landing was the only realistic option left open to us.

There was no way now that we could expect Beecroft to pull a miracle out of his hat to coax any more power out of the struggling starboard engine, to keep us airborne long enough to jump, and there was certainly no chance that the already overstressed, overheating engine would be able to climb to a safer jump height. We all felt that we had already stretched providence a little too far, and any extra stress on that cooking engine might seize it solid, flip us into a stall, and that would be very much that. Besides, we were practically gliding now, favouring the engine.

'Come on, John,' I called, gently, rapidly rescanning my maps. 'Time to put her down, I think. It looks like it's all pretty much flat fields around here, so we should get down okay. We'll be all right.'

Time was passing very rapidly now, but as much as Beecroft was reluctant to give up the fight, he was finding it just impossible to even maintain what little height we still had, so we were left with the most basic choice of all; either we found a good spot now and crash-landed while there was still some semblance of control, or we could bumble along further and literally wait for the ground to come up and meet us, with whatever consequences that might bring. Naturally, we all favoured the 'controlled' element – and it took Beecroft only an instant to decide.

'Right – crash stations now!' He called.

The die was finally cast, training took over, and – at a feverish speed, now – we all had final jobs to do. Brad had already signalled that we were in trouble, and it was my job to plot our final position as swiftly and accurately as possible. I used the TR1335 and my map for the last time, tapped Brad on his shoulder and handed him the coordinates, and as he began transmitting the updated information I turned to my next task, which was to make certain that no useable traces of the 'Gee' equipment would be left intact for the Germans to find if D-Donald wasn't destroyed in the crash. With that purpose in mind, a self-destruct mechanism was built into the device, and I set up the sequence of switches so that all I would have to do – in the last moments before impact – would be to push just one button to blow the whole plot into tiny pieces, internally.

Another gadget of a similarly destructive nature was provided in the shape of a long tube situated beside the navigator's table. All maps, radio frequency notes and code books and any other paperwork that might be of use to an enemy had to be shoved into this tube, and after a little scrabbling about to collect all such material on my table, Brad handed me his books, I jammed it all into the tube, pressed a button, and with a low whoosh it all disintegrated into ashes (I think it was done with a magnesium flare type of device, but it didn't matter; I was just gratified that it did its job when called upon). Brad went forward once more – this time to release the inner door for the front turret in readiness for Hanwell to make a rapid exit when he was ready – and I finished off my duties by stuffing my spare compass into one pocket, along with anything else that I could grab that might prove useful.

With these vital tasks completed, all that remained was to manoeuvre ourselves into our crash positions – a misnomer, if ever there was one! Officially, there were no really secure, safe positions in a Wellington in the event of crashing or ditching; however, it was generally established among the aircrews that the most likely safest (and strongest) spot in the aircraft was either behind or ahead of the central wing spar that crossed through the fuselage – but due to various pipes, brackets and other fittings in the way, there was really only just room for two crew members on both front and rear of the spar, so most crews allocated the spaces as gunners behind, observer and wireless operator in front (although we had prepared, weeks before, with an improvised webbing strap to act as a form of safety belt). So, I settled down quickly but somewhat uncomfortably with my back against the front of the wing spar. I had to leave my improvised strap loose in order to reach that last self-destruct button on the TR1335, and in a few moments, Brad slid down to sit beside me.

Hanwell and Crighton had to stay in their turrets for a little longer, though; their job had been to look out for a suitably lengthy field, which was no mean feat in the dark – even with the moon now bright enough once more to assist – but soon Hanwell spotted a likely looking field and told Beecroft. We felt D-Donald bank to starboard as we began circling around, then as Crighton clambered backwards out of his rear turret and struggled forward to seat himself with his back tightly against the rear of the main wing spar, Hanwell unlocked his turret's back doors, heaved himself out, latched the inner and outer turret doors and scrambled back over something resembling an obstacle course to drop down next to Crighton, climbing over the spar between Brad and myself to get there. We all settled down, in preparation for the impact.... This all sounds like it had taken quite some time, but as we had been drilled with the procedure several times, in reality, our ducking and diving had taken only a minute or two.

'All set, lads?' Beecroft asked.

I answered 'Okay' for all of us, as I was the only one with my headset still plugged in, and he gave us his final instructions.

'I'll go around once more, then I'll have a stab at landing. Looks like a ploughed field, I'm afraid, so it may be a bumpy landing. We'll obviously only get one chance at it – I just need to be sure of aligning with the furrows. Don't forget – as soon as we stop, let's get out as fast as we can, okay? Right, lads – hang on to your hats!' I relayed the information by shouting to the others and we felt the gentle movement as the Wimpy circled, losing that last bit of height; then we heard Beecroft shout, 'Here we go!'

I stretched up and jabbed the 'self-destruct' button, and as the detonators blew up the 'Gee' unit with a muffled whump, I dropped back down and tightened my strap hastily as we plunged toward the ground. I took a last look along the inside of the fuselage, praying fervently that the geodetic framework would keep us all safe, then waited.

It was – as one might expect – nothing like the carefully controlled and smooth landing that we usually enjoyed. There was a short, sudden, sweet silence as Beecroft shut down the starboard engine; then we heard the gentle whistle of the wind pushing at those front turret doors and sighing over the fuselage skin.

Beecroft repeated, loudly, 'Here we go', followed by 'Three ... two ... one ...'

And then, crash!, bang! clatter! as D-Donald crunched down on to terra firma, then bumped, shuddered and swayed a little as awful groans and shrieks sounded through the aircraft as we slid along at quite a pace. There was a lot of muck and dust flying around inside as the doped canvas skin tore away beneath us, and then there was a louder bang! as the front lower ventral hatch – the one by which we usually entered the aircraft – suddenly burst inward, and we cringed as Beecroft, Brad and I were showered by a cloud of loose soil being scooped inwards (Beecroft more so than us, as the hatch was right below his feet).

There came a few more bumps, shudders, squeals and bangs as we skidded gently from side to side … and then, suddenly, the nose dipped, the tail rose slightly and swung a little to starboard – and we halted; we had made it!

In the brief, eerie silence that followed, we spluttered and shook our heads to dislodge the soil, and we all drew deep breaths of blessed relief. I could just about hear the clicking and pinging of the overheated starboard engine as it began cooling, the erratic creaking of the airframe as it settled … and then came the very strong reek of spilling petrol; evidently, either the nacelle tanks had surged their contents over the engines (a common cause of forced-landing fires in Wellingtons, we'd been told), or one or more of our wing tanks had sprung a leak – and we came alive with a clatter of boots and a chorus of grunts as we struggled to stand upright, all trembling with fear and a strong desire to make extreme haste to exit in case of fire breaking out while we were still inside.

I was first up from my position, hoisting Brad upright as he unhooked his strap, then he reached back over the spar and hauled Hanwell to his feet in turn. As Brad scissor-legged over the spar, Crighton popped up beside him, then I heard a clank from the pilot's seat as Beecroft flipped open his own hatch to climb out, and I swung my legs over the spar to join the lads.

With everyone clear, I released the observation dome (our upper escape hatch), and as it swung down, Brad stepped on to the wing-spar and quickly pulled himself up, with Hanwell giving him a leg up as he wriggled through the hole. As he dropped over the side to slide down on to the port wing, Hanwell followed through the hole after him, getting a shove from Crighton. He went up next with a leg push from me, and as he stood astride the aperture waiting to help me, I finally clambered up and squeezed through with Crighton hooking his hands under my armpits to haul me up and out.

I'm sure that we each mentally cursed the useless collection of metal parts that was the port engine as we dropped from the fuselage on to the wing and then to the ground, but we had no time to stand around uttering profanities at it as the reek of leaking fuel was far stronger now. As soon as we had jumped down beside Brad and Hanwell, we sprinted away from the wreck until we had made safe distance.

Within moments, Beecroft rounded the port wingtip and joined us. We were huddled together about 100yds from the aircraft, on the edge of what seemed to be a very long field surrounded by a screen of trees.

'Anybody hurt?' Beecroft asked, ever responsible.

'All okay!' we chorused, almost laughing with the sheer joy of escape.

'Great work, John!'

'Wizard prang, old boy!' Hanwell wisecracked.

All thoughts now turned to what our next move would be.

'Well, there's one problem solved,' Beecroft commented, pointing at the wrecked Wimpy. 'Look! No need to worry about destroying the evidence.'

We turned to gaze back at poor old D-Donald as flames began to lick around the cowling of the overheated starboard engine – and barely seconds later, it ignited fully. As we watched, the flames grew from a flicker to an all-out blaze that spread rapidly along the wing, flaring brightly as it devoured the doped-fabric skin. The flames quickly engulfed the fuselage, rapidly crossed to catch the port wing and so began to consume the entire, mangled aircraft, and it was evident that there would soon be very little left worth salvaging of the poor thing.

'We'd better get out of here!' I urged everyone. 'That crash must have awakened the whole countryside. The first thing we have to do is get away as far and as fast as we can!' I took just a moment to get my bearings – firstly as a calculated guess, as the flames had messed up my night vision for a few moments – and I pointed in the direction I thought we ought to take. 'Come on, lads – this way's south,' I declared, then I led the way toward what looked like a gap in the trees; we had to get out of silhouette from the flames, just in case anyone was watching.

Sure enough, there was a gateway, so we hurried through it (not forgetting to close it behind us!) and found ourselves standing on a narrow country lane that seemed to lead directly south.

'Let's get as far away as possible, then we can stop and discuss the best way to tackle things, eh?' I suggested. Nobody objected, but just as we were about to step on to the road, I looked down and called an immediate halt. 'Hey! Look out – we'll leave muddy footprints! Better clean off our boots on the grass – quick!'

Everyone stepped on to the long grass at the roadside, busily wiping the mud from boot soles on the long broad grass-blades, then we pressed on, not talking, half-expecting at any moment to see vehicle headlights or flashing torches, to hear the excited voices of Frenchmen (or even the dreaded shouts of a party of Germans!) who might be heading toward the Wellington – but there wasn't a sound, nor a hint of light anywhere.

All was strangely quiet ... so quiet, in fact, that we actually felt a little peeved that no one seemed to have noticed our spectacular arrival! It was almost disappointing, in a peculiar way, until there came a dull thump as D-Donald's fuel tanks finally exploded. Oddly, there was no fireball as one might see in the movies, just a brief flickering glare that didn't last more than a second or two, but must surely have attracted the ears and eyes of any of the enemy forces that might have been within a few miles – and we passed quick, fearful glances at one another as we spurred ourselves away from the field.

Chapter 5

Je suis un aviator Anglais

It was by now about two o'clock in the morning. As there was no sign of life anywhere, we decided to keep on walking as far and as fast as we could until daylight, in the anticipation of finding somewhere to hide up for the day. We hoped, then, that we might see where we were – and also comprehend just what sort of a country this was, that was in the middle of a war yet everyone stayed in bed all night!

Oddly enough, the further we tramped along, the more the walk began to feel almost as casual as a stroll back to base from the village pub, albeit kitted out with flying suits, boots and the rest; we hadn't even spared a moment to pull off our flying hats in our haste to escape D-Donald, although we had done so before we left the field, and stuffed them inside our suits. By now, though, we all had our suits and jackets fully unfastened as our marching pace was beginning to make us sweat with the generated heat (this was in late May, so it wasn't cold).

When the first light of dawn began to creep across the sky we started to look for somewhere to hide, for we had by now agreed that the obvious thing to do was to walk by night and hide by day; we felt – logically – that a party of five men dressed in RAF flying kit and uniforms strolling through the French countryside just might be a trifle suspicious.

As the light increased, we began to appreciate why everything was so quiet; for as far as we could see in every direction, there was just wide open space – no houses or buildings of any sort, no hedges or fences marking either roads or field boundaries, no crops. Nothing but a great emptiness. The only sign of civilisation was that the road that we had been following had a metalled surface, and it just kept on going right through this strange wilderness.

Eventually, just as the sun began to show its upper curve, the one and only feature of this otherwise bland landscape came into view – it was a tiny but seemingly dense copse, away off to the right of the road, about half a mile distant. We all stopped and exchanged looks, and I shrugged.

'That looks like our only choice for a good hiding place,' I observed, rather stating the obvious. 'Shall we see if it'll do us until dusk?'

With nothing else between us and the horizon in any direction to offer any other prospect of shelter for the day, the others agreed after a brief scan about, and we set off to investigate the wood, being careful to walk only on hard surface and grass where possible, to cut down on traces of our passing, just in case any German patrols came looking for any stray types like us.

Sure enough, we found that – although the copse was quite small – it was indeed very dense inside, but we managed to carefully push our way into the centre (still being mindful of setting the undergrowth back in place, in case of prying eyes!), until we found a tightly clumped group of trees that would provide us with good extra cover. We made ourselves comfortable, then settled down to take stock of our precarious situation. As he was our skipper, Beecroft set the ball rolling.

'First things first, we have to determine exactly where we are, and just as importantly, where we'll aim to go.'

'Well,' I spoke up, taking his cue, 'I think I can help, there. From what we've seen so far, we seem to be in the middle of some sort of uncultivated wilderness. Now, if my navigation was correct before we pranged' (surprisingly, there were no playful jeers to greet that statement!) 'we must be in the Marne area. In fact, I'm pretty sure we're in the actual place where the great battles of the Marne were fought in the Great War. That will no doubt go some way to explain the apparent lack of human occupation around here.' No one disputed my reasoning so far, so I continued. 'It seems to me, then, that the obvious place for us to aim for – without a doubt – is Switzerland. It's no good heading north – we want to steer well clear of any large towns like Reims, because that's obviously where the Germans will be concentrated. We should keep to the country areas as far as we possibly can.'

Still no one disagreed, so with our target thus decided by everyone nodding sagely, we got down to practicalities.

'Okay, that's settled, then,' Beecroft confirmed. 'Now, to begin with, I think that we should not try to get help until we are well away from the scene of the crash. Are we agreed on that?' He glanced at us all, one at a time as we nodded in turn, so he added, 'Right – so, what provisions do we have between us, then?'

We should each have had the usual survival tin, the nutritional side of which comprised of a dozen Horlicks tablets (very concentrated 'food'!), barley sugar sweets, energy tablets (Benzedrine, or something like that), a thin bar of chocolate, some water-purifying tablets – and that was all! Not a very edifying collection of tidbits upon which to set out on a journey of nearly 300 miles, we felt – but what was worse was that Alec had accidentally left his ration kit in D-Donald as we jumped clear, so we only had four kits between the five of us. Nobody complained at that, though – it would have to be share and share alike, and that was that. We had to just grin and bear it, and hope that we could find some proper food and water soon.

'Right, then,' Beecroft declared, 'we'll just have to tighten our belts for a day or two, until we can hope to contact some friendly French folks, eh?'

We all grimaced at the thought of having to eke out our meagre reserves, and Hanwell – the gourmet of our crew – looked a little gloomy at the prospect of the enforced diet, but there was no dissention on the point. It was to prove a little longer, however, before we could savour the taste of proper food.

'Next, then – who speaks French?' Beecroft asked.

No answer – just a few searching glances. Reluctantly, I broke the silence.

'Well – I know a little,' I offered, realising that it was very little indeed, considering that I hadn't practised the language since I'd left school in 1930! However, even rusty Grammar-school French was better than nothing, right then; I was immediately and unanimously nominated 'official interpreter' for the party. Far from being nervous at such a daunting prospect, I immediately set my mind to try to recall those school lessons by attempting to mentally translate our chat from that point onward, as a form of a refresher.

With these main details thus settled, we made ourselves more comfortable between the trees and prepared to 'bed down' for the day. To be on the safe side, we arranged that each of us would take a two-hour watch, so that (in theory, at least), we should all benefit from an average of eight hours' sleep – and that was something that we all desperately needed to catch up on, considering that we had been awake for the best part of twenty-four hours by now, with a high dose of excitement and adrenalin to wear us down even further still.

The day passed uneventfully, and I found that I slept as soundly as if I had been in my own bunk back in Bourn, as snuggled-up in my flying suit as I was. I think the others slept as well as I did, too, because all I could hear during my spell on guard was deep breathing, interspersed with occasional snores and grunts. It was amazing what a bit of excitement and a little walk could do!

We roused ourselves just as evening was setting in, and 'breakfast' consisted of four Horlicks tablets each, but without water to wash them down they took some chewing. While there was still just enough light to see, we checked our tiny survival kit compasses against my spare navigator's compass (I'd managed to grab it just before the crash) to confirm that all were pointing in the same direction – a useful check, in case we became separated for any reason – then we reluctantly decided that we would have to leave our flying hats and suits in the trees, both to travel lightly and to avoid being easily spotted (Alec and Henry's extra-insulated flight suits were a light 'cream' in colour, whereas our Irving jackets, although distinctively British, were dark brown, and our uniforms beneath those were dark blue – fortunately more difficult to spot in the dark). Brad and I removed our fleecy overtrousers and braces, and they were buried along with the gunners' suits. After that struggle, we scanned the horizon to check that the coast was clear, before making our way back to the road and setting off once more.

The scene as we travelled further was still the same bleak, apparently uninhabited and desolate area, with very few trees once we'd left our wooded refuge well behind. We were beginning to feel somewhat exposed and vulnerable, and very hungry indeed now, but we steeled ourselves to ration out what little we had and marched onward in the moonlight.

This was to be our pattern for another two nights – walk as far as we could, then find another hiding place for the next day; sleep on shifts, eat another Horlicks tablet or two, then wash them down with water extracted from any handy streams, ditches or puddles – as long as they were clear, we used the water (with a purifying tablet, of course).

On we plodded, our nightly pace slowing gradually but very definitely, while the roads and tracks that we followed in a generally southward heading seemed to dwindle ever narrower until they became little more than the width of a path, but as we still seemed to be going in the right direction, we decided to stick with it until we could ascertain precisely where we were. The terrain through which we were passing seemed to confirm my navigation, so at least I had something to feel slightly pleased about, and further corroboration of this arrived when we eventually came upon a piece of metal stuck in the ground. Balanced on top of this was a German helmet, green and rusty with age, its tattered strap just about hanging on to the post; it looked and felt to us as if the French had decided to abandon the whole area, as a kind of memorial to the thousands of men who had died there in the First World War.

We all looked at each other at that point, our thoughts unspoken; I know that I felt a cold shiver up my spine – I don't know if the others did – but we turned away from the post without a word passing between us, just plodding on, deep in thought.

All the excitement of the crash had now long gone, and as we trudged ever onward we each became lost in our own reflections, hoping that we would all get home safely. We found ourselves remembering even the most simple pleasures of our family lives, sometimes discussing them at a mumble after taking a furtive glance around – and then we would lapse into silence once more as the miles slowly passed.

I couldn't help but wonder if anyone had yet informed my wife that we hadn't returned, and if someone had, I wondered how she would take the grim news; I felt that – such was her strength of character – she would take it all in slowly, but hold out hope that I was still alive, until she heard otherwise. Our son, John, would no doubt be confused, but he was just ten years old and full of 'hero worship' for his Dad, and would carry on as normal; I was sure that he would 'muck in' and help Evelyn with her housework, just to keep her spirits up – and as she had great faith in spiritualism (she attended the Ashington Spiritualist Church), I gave myself a little mental 'exercise' to try to 'send her a message' by concentrating on a memory of her face as we marched along, hoping to convey positive thoughts that might let her 'feel' that I was still alive and trying to get home. A romantic notion, but worth a try, I thought!

We were yet determined to stick to our plan of avoiding people for at least the immediate future, and we'd certainly 'picked' the right place for such a plan to work, for there were still no houses or buildings of any kind to meet our gaze when the dawn finally broke.

Deciding to call a halt, we searched the ground close to the path in the hope of finding another refuge, and eventually we settled for a saucer-like depression in the ground about 50yd away from the path; it was probably an old shell-hole, but it suited our purpose perfectly – as long as it didn't rain during that day! Wearily, we sank down into the depression and rested for a while, then after a few jokes about 'breakfast', we tried to sleep. It was a lovely spring day, however, and tired though we were, sleep just wouldn't come.

At last Hanwell, the impatient one, said, 'Why don't we just push on? We haven't seen a living soul, yet – and we could be getting nearer to Switzerland all the time!'

That caused some wry laughter, but after a lengthy rest, we decided that it was a good idea after all. As Hanwell pointed out, even if anyone approached, or if a house or a farm appeared, we'd spot them from miles away – although, equally, any observers or occupants (but more fearfully, any Germans) would also see us, so we would have to be extremely careful.

Back to the path we trudged, then pushed on once more, almost like a casual stroll again – then about four o'clock in the afternoon we saw smoke rising in a narrow plume, almost vertically from a horizon that appeared to be many more miles distant than usual. It wasn't quite that far, obviously, but it still took us the best part of an hour to cover the distance to what turned out to be a small farm – and with every step nearer to that farm, our nerves were getting decidedly shakier. Finally we stopped and crouched down by a very slight rise in the ground between us and the farm (although we had been in full view of the roof for some time by now, so our crouching might well have proven futile, had somebody already observed us).

We approached the farm very warily, until we reached a point where we could squat down again, but see enough to 'scout' the buildings. Apart from the rising smoke, though, there didn't seem to be any other sign of life. There was a small house and an old barn that stood well away from it, but that was all; no chickens or animals running loose, no noises. We sneaked into the barn, and went into conference mode again.

'I reckon it's time for you to do your stuff, Jack,' urged Beecroft, instantly setting the butterflies loose in my stomach.

I swallowed hard, glancing from face to face. What if the owners turned out to be collaborators? What if the farm had been taken over by Germans? (Just because there were no military vehicles in the yard right then, didn't mean that some might not turn up at the wrong moment.) Finally, I nodded, accepting my nominated role.

'Fingers crossed then, boys!' I whispered, giving them a slightly shaky thumbs-up gesture as I turned and crept out of the barn. Then with some serious trepidation, I stepped lightly round to the back of the house. For just a few moments I stood very quietly near the door, listening intently for signs of movement inside, without success. Finally, I drew a deep breath, summoned my courage, hesitated as I raised my knuckles near the door and then knocked on its rough planking. Instantly, I heard the scrape of a chair being moved – and I have to confess that I almost panicked and ran, but I calmed myself, swallowing hard again as I heard slow footsteps approaching. My heart was pounding in my chest as the door opened, and an oldish-looking man peered out very cautiously. He was shabbily dressed and smoking a blackened pipe, and he squinted at me, evidently very puzzled. I took another sharp breath and tried to give what I hoped would be a reassuring smile.

'Bonsoir, Monsieur,' I greeted him, making my best efforts at a Gallic inflection.

He looked even more surprised, but said nothing. 'Now for the real test,' I thought.

'Je suis un aviator Anglais,' I gabbled. 'RAF. ...'

Behind his straggly moustache, his face broke into a wide smile as he held his arms open wide.

'Ah! RAF!' he exclaimed. 'Vous ete bienvenue! Entrez, mon enfant – entrez!' He clasped my hand with both of his rough-skinned ones, then shouted over his shoulder into the house. 'C'est le RAF, Maman!' he declared, then turned back to face me, gripped my arm and bustled me into the house with an enthusiastic 'Venez! Venez!'

His wife, dressed in black from head to foot, was standing with a look of total bewilderment on her face. 'Le RAF?' she stammered, then she recognised my uniform. 'C'est vrai!' she cried, 'le RAF!'

Up until now I had understood them without much trouble, but then they began to gabble and twitter on in what had suddenly become a very foreign language to me.

'Excusé moi,' I interrupted their flow of words. 'Voulez-vous parlez plus lentement? Je ne sois parlez Francais que peu.'

'Oh, pardonnez-moi,' the old man apologised, 'et nous ne savons parlez Anglais!'

By now, I thought I'd almost exhausted all of the French that was familiar to me, but when he ushered me to a chair and said 'Assez-vous', he triggered yet another spurt of my limited vocabulary.

'Mais,' I interrupted again, 'Je ne suis pas seul. Il y a cinq de nous!'

'Cinq!' exclaimed the old chap. 'Ou sont les autres?'

'They're in the barn,' I answered, momentarily stumbling for the right words. 'Dans la grange!' I eventually translated.

'La grange!' he repeated, then pointed to the other seats around the kitchen table. 'Apporter ici!' he proclaimed.

Without further ado, I returned to the barn, collected the rest of the crew, and once back in the tiny kitchen, I introduced the others one by one, stumblingly. When I had finished, the old man pointed to himself.

'Monsieur Duchamp,' he said. 'Et ma femme,' he added as he introduced his wife. He waved at the chairs, and said, 'Asseyez vous!'

Hardly believing our good fortune at finding friends so soon, we each took a seat around the table and, true farmer that he was, he pointed to his mouth and made eating motions.

'Vous avez faim?' he asked, and the boys all nodded their heads vigorously, while I showed off a little by saying 'Mais oui, Monsieur!'

In an instant, they produced a large loaf of bread, some butter, a huge lump of cheese, five glasses and a jug of wine; no tea, of course! While his wife sliced the bread and prepared this most basic but so eagerly anticipated meal, M. Duchamp poured the wine, chatting away slowly all the time – and as far as I could make out (his accent was quite strong), he was actually apologising for the 'poor fare' that they were about to offer us; we soon showed him just how welcome it all was by devouring the lot, and by a mixture of sign language and rusty French, we let them know just how much we had enjoyed it all!

'C'est très bien, Monsieur!' I assured him, patting my now-full stomach and smiling. 'Lovely,' contributed the others, all smiling, nodding and also rubbing their stomachs.

Now it was time to get down to the nitty-gritty, and although I struggled a little with my limited vocabulary and a good deal of sign language on both sides, I managed to answer our hosts' questions and inform them what had happened. We all chipped in and had a go at telling them why we'd had to make a forced landing, illustrated by hand signs showing a plane crashing.

'Ah, vous êtes encraser,' said the old chap, and I mentally added yet another word to my vocabulary ('encraser' – to crash). When we managed to assure them that none of us was hurt in the crash, Madame Duchamp crossed herself and murmured, 'Vous êtes protégés par le bon Dieu', to which we all heartily agreed, all of us understanding the gist of what she'd said, right away.

At that point, we steered the conversation toward our need for rest, now that we had eaten our fill and were feeling the pull of chronic fatigue. I asked if we might retire to the barn for the afternoon for some sleep – again by broken French and sign language – and M. Duchamp agreed that although there were very few Germans in the area, it would be best for us to be out of their house in case any did turn up, out of the blue; if we were captured thus, we could do our best to deny that our presence in the barn was known to M. Duchamp, in the hope that they would not be punished – or so we naively thought, anyway.

As we made our way back to the barn, M. Duchamp told us that we were just outside the village of Hans, in the Haute Marne province, and he confirmed that we had just tramped through the old Marne battlefield.

'Un region sauvage' he called it. 'Beaucoup de Français et Anglais mourivent la-bas,' he added, shaking his head sadly.

By this time, my understanding of French was improving almost by the minute. I managed to convey to him that we were hoping to reach Switzerland, and that we would walk by night and hide up by day, and as we stopped beside the barn door he brightened up, for that had given him an idea. Speaking excitedly, and so quickly that I struggled once more to keep up, he squeezed my arm.

'This afternoon,' he said, 'I shall go down to the village and bring the schoolmaster. He is sure to speak English, and he will advise about the best way to go, and the safest things to do on the way!'

I smiled – perhaps a little dumbly – as I took a few seconds to mentally translate what he'd said, then I nodded and said, 'C'est grande, Monsieur! Merci beaucoup!'

With his idea formed, M. Duchamp returned to the house, and I joined the boys on a pile of hay and told them of the old man's intention.

'Well,' Beecroft said, with a shrug, 'they've been very decent so far – I suppose we'll just have to trust them now and hope for the best, eh?'

We had taken a dangerous chance here but it seemed to be paying off, and so we settled down in the barn to spend the afternoon either sleeping soundly (in shifts, still, just in case), or talking quietly as the hours passed.

Crighton sneaked out to the toilet at the back of the house, and when he returned, he was chuckling to himself.

'What's so funny, Alec?' I asked him.

'Go see for yourself,' he replied, with a wink. 'Have a look in the "oot-hoose".'

At that moment, I discovered that I needed to 'go' anyway, so off I sneaked, as he'd suggested (taking elaborate care to look about as I slipped across the yard – though I needn't have bothered), and I found what must have been the most primitive yet effective of sanitary arrangements that I'd ever seen, barring a stone drop-hole in an ancient castle. The Duchamps' latrine consisted of a small hut, in which I found a fair-sized hole in the centre of the floor, with floor-boards all sloping steeply down toward the hole – and that was that! There didn't seem to be any means of disposing of (or flushing away) the effluent – as I think we'd politely call it now – and it was rather smelly, as I'm sure you can imagine, so I didn't bother to inspect further, just prepared myself and squatted somewhat precariously.

In no way did this arrangement belittle the old couple (our 'saviours', as I thought of them) in my mind, for it was quite likely that the hole drained into an underground stream (or something of that nature), in which case, they were cleverer than we might have given them credit for, by making best use of Mother Nature.

As I left the latrine, I saw something else in the back garden that intrigued me, and after casting glances to either side (it was becoming a furtive habit!), I wandered a few paces off-track to investigate. I'd read of the French eating snails – even of snails being regarded as delicacies in this country – but now, I could see them 'in the flesh', so to speak. A wire-netting enclosure, not unlike a pet rabbit's run – measuring about 6ft long, 3ft wide and 3ft high – was full of the biggest and fattest snails that I'd ever seen! It reminded me of how – in my youth – we used to collect whelks ('willicks', as we called them in north-east England) from the rocks of Newbiggin-by-the-Sea, then take them home, boil them, then extract them from their shells with a pin and eat them – and thus enjoy them as a treat! These French snails, however, were something different, and it wasn't hard for me to guess just how tasty they might be. After seeing those monsters I stepped away, and I just knew that 'willicks' would never taste the same, to me.

When I returned to the barn, we discussed our circumstances and the conditions in which the Duchamps lived; we'd all realised by now that the old couple were not very well off, as the farm – as we were calling it – was very small, no bigger than what we'd call a smallholding back home. They probably lived mostly off the produce of their farm, which made their very warm welcome and their proud efforts on our behalf far greater than they might appear at first glance. Add to that the probable harassment from their German invaders, and you can see that we were immeasurably grateful to them for everything so far.

Not long after this discussion, we heard footsteps outside the barn door – and we all froze, glancing at each other in the dim light, each of us swallowing hard … then the door creaked open slightly – and M. Duchamp poked his head around it and smiled, then mimed that he'd brought us some more food!

He perched on a small wheelbarrow beside us, and unravelled a rolled cloth on the ground, gesturing for us to 'tuck in'. We didn't need a second invitation, although we did protest at the inclusion of meat in this little feast; we felt that they shouldn't have given it to us as it was probably their whole meat ration for the week, but M. Duchamp insisted, so we demurred and got stuck in, gesturing our humble appreciation as we ate.

He told us that the schoolmaster would come to the farm at about seven o'clock, and as that time approached, we became very nervous indeed; what if someone had betrayed us to the Germans instead, we wondered? There was no point in worrying too much about it, though, so we decided to simply wait and see what transpired, for good or bad. We just had to trust these simple folks – after all, they had already taken a huge risk in sheltering and feeding us.

Seven o'clock arrived, and with it came the schoolmaster, right on time. He was a short, thick-set man, wearing spectacles with heavy lenses ('jam-jar bottoms', as Hanwell later called them), and carried a huge, bulging hessian sack. But when he began to speak – to our enormous disappointment – he rattled off in his native tongue, not the suggested English that we'd hoped for; it turned out that his second language was in fact German! He congratulated us on our escape so far, listened while I translated for the lads, then he tipped up the sack and out tumbled a motley collection of donated everyday coats.

He waved a hand across the heap, then told us that we must (obviously) cover our RAF uniforms when travelling – even at night – and with a grin and a flourish, he produced two pairs of shoes from the cavernous outer pockets of his own coat. One pair of shoes fitted Crighton nicely, but the rest of us would have to make do with our flying boots, as the other pair of shoes were only just big enough to fit an adolescent. My boots were only the canvas-covered type, lightweight but comfortable, but the others had the style of boots with the top section detachable, leaving a pair of black shoes, so there was no problem for them. Having ditched our flying suits and Mae Wests back in that first wood, and now equipped with a coat apiece, we felt ready to move and hopefully merge with the population, if seen.

The schoolmaster then produced his pièce de résistance (if you'll pardon the pun) – a map! Not a very good map, mind; in fact it was a pretty poor one, having been the back sheet of a calendar (apparently a standard issue in the province). However, it was better than nothing but guess-work, although it showed very little detail – only the main roads and the names of any fair-sized towns that we would have to either pass through or avoid – but the important thing was that at least it did show us the way to go.

The nearby village that M. Duchamp had told us about – Hans – was too small for such a map, but the schoolmaster pointed out approximately where the village was in relation to some bigger (marked) towns, and the direction from there that we should take in order to reach our goal.

So, with final farewells, goodwill and blessings from Monsieur and Madame Duchamp as darkness fell, we left the farm and started on our way, full of deep gratitude and much more hopeful than when we'd arrived at that barn. The schoolmaster escorted us through the village – oddly, there didn't seem to be a single soul in the street as we passed through – and then he set us off on the right road.

'The next place to look for will be Rimacourt, about 30 kilometres away,' he directed (in French), slowly and thoroughly. I nodded my understanding, and he continued: 'This is not a main road and there are very few Germans in this area, so if you are careful, you should not meet any trouble.' His departing words were 'Bonne nuit, mes amis, et bonne chance!'

We all smiled and took turns to shake his hand, then he waved us on, turned and strode back into the village. We watched him go for a moment, then looked at each other and began walking toward Rimacourt, highly buoyed up by this first encounter with the native populace. I couldn't speak for everyone, but I certainly felt that if we were to receive help like this all the way to Switzerland, then with luck on our side, surely we must reach freedom? Well, given this most encouraging start, we could but hope.

We'd been marching at a steady pace for more than an hour when we began to hear the first mutterings of thunder way off in the distance. Gradually, the skies that had been clear when we'd set off into the dusk, became filled with black, threatening clouds. To make matters worse, we found that preparations were being made to repair the road surface on which we were travelling. It wasn't a very wide road, and the work thus far had apparently consisted mainly of laying piles of chippings all along one side, almost halving the width.

It became darker and darker – not just with the fall of night, but also from the density of the thunderclouds – and we began to stumble and slip on the gravel piles until eventually it became so murky that we were forced to walk in single file, each of us keeping in touch – literally – by touching the shoulder of the man in front of him.

The chipping piles were now a little haphazard and scattered across the road in untidy and irregular humps, so to avoid stumbling over them we put Hanwell up front, as he was acknowledged as having the best night vision of our crew. He had by now found a stick from somewhere along the verge, and he went tap-tapping along the road, with the rest of us tagging him in line; talk about the blind leading the blind! If it hadn't been so serious, I'm sure we'd all have had a good laugh!

The night had become eerily still, the silence only punctuated by the deepening rolls of closing thunder. It was now so black that we literally couldn't see a hand in front of our faces; only occasionally vivid lightning flashes lit the scene, but although we were presented with very brief glimpses of any obstacles in our path, each searing flash destroyed our night vision every time, after which it then seemed darker than ever – almost like walking into an unlit coal mine. The lightning flashes became more and more frequent, the thunder rattled and banged louder and louder – then just as we were hoping we'd get away with it, down came a colossal deluge with frightening suddenness!

I don't think I've ever seen or experienced rain like that. With no wind to drive it, we were soaked to the skin in seconds flat, and we felt thoroughly demoralised in an instant. Being caught out in the open in this atrociously heavy downpour, we anxiously cast glances from side to side, hoisting our collars over our heads as we saw that the trees were taller in the hedge on the side of the road opposite the bulk of the chipping piles. We sought shelter under one such tree, crowding together underneath it, but soon found that we'd made a bad mistake, for in addition to the rain itself, we now had huge globs of water dropping on us from a great height! After a few minutes of this bombardment, as we became more and more miserable, I said, 'Why don't we just push on? We can't get any wetter, can we? We may as well cover some more distance.'

So, off we trudged again, finding walking easier now, for the lightning was so frequent that we could see well enough to pick our way a little better, without that annoying pitch blackness of lost vision between flashes.

At last – after what seemed like hours – the torrential rain began to ease, slowly dropping to a steady drizzle, and then a gentle spotting, until all we could hear was the gentle trickle of water running down the side of the road. We stumbled and squelched onward, drenched and thoroughly cold and miserable, nobody attempting to talk now, but just praying for the dawn and the hope of drying out in the sun, when it might eventually show itself.

Mile after mile we trudged onward, taking left and right turns in an increasing zigzag of connecting lanes and tracks. We neither saw nor heard any life at all – not even wildlife, which I thought odd – but at least with each step, we were working up a little frictional heat, which – along with our movement – was slowly squeezing out the worst wetness from our saturated clothes; it was most definitely a horribly clammy experience that I didn't want to repeat, and I think we were all a little worried that we might catch chills as a result of the tremendous soaking.

The clouds gradually broke up and dissipated, the sky cleared into a starry dome, and eventually the sky began to lighten in the east (about 70 degrees to our left, I was glad to note, as it meant that we were still going in the right direction!). When the sun finally appeared, it was marvellous! A few birds awoke and began singing to greet a glorious day, and very soon it became warm and cheerful, with the storm now forgotten – well, almost, anyway as we were still decidedly soggy!

There were more trees around us now, so we plunged into a fair-sized wood and started looking around for shelter. The gods must have been smiling upon us (or perhaps feeling sorry for us), for – well into the heart of the wood – we found an enormous pine tree, its lower branches and fronds spread out like a huge umbrella, and when we crawled in beneath it, we found that it was a perfect hiding place. The ground under the 'umbrella' was soft and littered with old, dried leaves and pine needles (now softened with age from the last year's fall) – and best of all, it was amazingly bone dry. We discovered that we could all lie down there, and be completely hidden from anyone passing by. The sun was by now quite high, and everything was basking in its warming rays.

The pine tree seemed to enjoy a semi-clearing all to itself, and the sunlight splashed across the ground in large patches, unimpeded by other trees or branches, so we took off most of our clothes and spread them to dry on the ground around the fringe of the tree's branches. Crawling back under the pine, we lay down to sleep once more. We didn't discard all precaution, however; we maintained the system of two hours on watch, each.

The day passed surprisingly quickly, and we neither saw nor heard a single human soul, although we could hear plenty of birdsong and rustling of leaves and other undergrowth as woodland creatures went about their daily business, obviously very wary of our presence, but nevertheless still needing to forage for their food, as normal. It was altogether quite a pleasant scenario; one wouldn't know that this country was in the middle of yet another war!

We'd eaten the sandwiches that the schoolmaster had given us – all donated by the very kind (but apparently shy) villagers – and as soon as dusk began to fall, we prepared for our next night's march.

The slowing pace caused by the storm meant that we should aim straight for Rimacourt now; it had put us back by one day, but we also began to feel that perhaps it might prove better not to rush the trek, anyway. Who cared? We had all the time in the world!

Our clothes were thankfully dry (if smelling a little mildewy), so, keeping to the roads that apparently led toward Rimacourt, we stepped out cheerfully.

We'd had some time to talk, and I think we were all surprised to find how little we knew of each other's personal lives. As a crew we'd shared twelve ops together, having been in different crews before and seen one or two other changes of squadron personnel before that, too – but we knew very little outside our flying 'team' duties. Now, in the course of our casual 'strolling' chat and long rests, we soon found that we all had very diverse hobbies and interests.

Crighton and I were the married ones, and we each had a son. Alec lived in Glasgow, where he had been the manager of a large grocery store. He was a country boy at heart, though, born and bred in Meigle, in Tayside, where his hobbies had been fishing and shooting – so that was why he had a reputation as one of the best gunners on the squadron! He'd come to the big city of Glasgow to improve his chances of rising in the grocery trade, and he'd met and married his wife there.

Hanwell lived in King's Lynn, and had worked as a salesman in a shoe shop. He'd no particular hobbies, but after this spell in the RAF, Henry had decided that he wouldn't be going back to any shoe shop after the war – it would be too boring!

Bradley expressed similar sentiments. He had been a clerk in Liverpool with Wills, the tobacco firm; he declared that he, too, would be looking for something much more exciting after the war was over. He was an unusually quiet man, for someone born in Liverpool; I'd met many 'Scousers' during my spell in the RAF, but while they waxed lyrical about their home city, Brad was the least vocal about the glories of Liverpool. However, it was Beecroft, our quietly spoken pilot, who surprised us the most. He was easily the biggest of our crew; a round-faced, happy-go-lucky type, but an excellent pilot. In his early twenties, he had lived in Cheshire, and was training to be a veterinary surgeon. From the way he talked about it, it seemed that it was not only his job, but his hobby, too – his whole way of life, in fact. He was dedicated to the ideals of caring for animals, and we all respected him higher still for that.

At twenty-nine, I was the oldest of the party. As previously mentioned, I had been a bus conductor, waiting to become a driver. In the time before the war, my grammar school education hadn't been much help in getting a decent occupation in a particularly depressed mining area of North-umberland, but that bus conductor's job just happened to be one of the better-paid ones around; at least it was an improvement on the risky coal-face slog in the mining industry – and it was clean!

This war – although I hate to say it – had actually come along at the 'right time' for me, and had given me the chance to show what I could do – and I loved the 'work'! I found it so exciting to fly that I just wanted to make a career of it – always assuming that we all got out of this current mess!

Sport was my hobby, and I played football, cricket and tennis, and was a fair hand at snooker. However, when the squadron had been moved from Oakington to the new aerodrome at Bourn, I was very disappointed; at Oakington, we'd had a football team and a snooker table! Oh, well.

And now, here we were, forcibly separated from all that fun and luxury, foot-slogging somewhere in France, hoping to land up somewhere in

Switzerland and thence be whisked off back home to return to flying duties – just like that! Oh, for a magic wand, right then.

It was by now a fine, clear night, and the only snag was that we were all very hungry once more. However, after that very fortuitous first encounter with the French, we were optimistic for such continuity, and that our hunger would soon be sated.

On this, our second night heading towards Rimacourt, all went well; no alarms or side-tracking excursions, until, as dawn was once more beginning to break, we came – literally – to a crossroads. We consulted our map and decided from this that we must now be quite near Rimacourt, but as the day was becoming lighter we would have to find another hiding place very soon.

According to the map, we should take the left turn – but knowing that the map was only a basic one, how far could we trust its accuracy? To our relief, we then saw a silhouette against the ever-lightening sky – it was a very welcome signpost!

'Hold on,' said Hanwell, 'I'll climb up and see what it says.' With that, he immediately began to shin up the post – and then suddenly, to our intense shock and dismay, there came a hoarse shout.

'Halte!' came the cry – and we heard the unmistakable rattle of rifle bolts being worked.

Chapter 6

Papieren bitte?

To a man, we froze, all of us snapping our heads around in the direction of the voice. There, away to the right of the crossroads, we could now just about make out the parapets of a railway bridge – and just above that on a slight embankment stood two German soldiers, easily identified by their 'coal-scuttle' helmets. Frighteningly, their rifles were pointed very steadily at us, and I heard Crighton mutter, 'Christ, we've had it, now.'

We remained motionless, watching helplessly as the sentries scrambled down on to the road, still keeping their rifles levelled as they approached us very warily, and in that time, I had very slowly and carefully moved my hand out of sight, folding the map in my fingers and slipping it into my coat pocket as unobtrusively as I could.

'What do we do, now?' Beecroft mumbled.

'Just stand still,' I hissed, 'and let's see if we can bluff it out.'

The leading sentry came closer, raising his rifle in one hand, the other held up in a universal 'Stop' gesture, while his companion kept us covered, with his rifle held steady.

'Papieren, bitte?' he asked.

I swallowed hard, then took the lead.

'Nous navons pas des papiers,' I said, quickly adopting the role as leader. 'Nous voyagons á Rimacourt ou nous travaillons.' Then, as he squinted at my face in the poor light, I gave him what I thought was a Gallic shrug and repeated, 'Nous navons pas des papiers.'

I was trying to tell the sentry, 'We're working at Rimacourt, and don't need papers', but evidently neither of them had a clue what I was rabbiting on about – then, as they hesitated, another soldier appeared, this time a Feldwebel. He appeared to ask his sentries what was going on, then – when the soldier I'd spoken to nodded at me – the Feldwebel turned to me and demanded, 'Votre papiers, Monsieur!'

His French sounded very rough to me – and I was a rank amateur with the lingo, too! I went into the chat once more, speaking as quickly as I could, while waving my hands about, trying to gesticulate as I thought a Frenchman might, hoping to convince him that we were farm workers.

'Rimacourt?' He repeated, apparently recognising the name, anyway.

'Vous travaillez la-bas?' ('You work there?')

'Oui,' I replied, beginning to feel my confidence picking up. I went on to say (or so I hoped) that we were late now, and that work was hard to get, etc, etc, gabbling away in what must have been execrable French – then he held up a palm to stop me, and stood in thought for a minute. Finally, he lifted his chin slightly as he glanced at Beecroft, then back to me.

'Attendez ici – je chercherai mon Offizier. Il parlais Francais.'

My heart fluttered as he turned away slightly – we certainly didn't want him to fetch his French-speaking superior, so I repeated my previous act, injecting a little hint of pleading in my voice, and after another hesitation, he looked at Beecroft again, then back at me – then shrugged and growled 'Allez!' and waved us on our way with a flap of his hand!

I couldn't believe our luck! All this time the rest of the crew had stood there mutely, not a murmur coming from them; we had no papers to show – and they were letting us go! Just incredible!

Amazed – but trying hard not to show it – we departed in the direction of Rimacourt. I gave the Feldwebel a very grateful 'Merci beaucoup!' as we moved off, all of us holding back from the instinct to run, heads down to avoid eye contact, but not obviously so.

After about half an hour, during which we'd picked up our pace some-what once out of sight of the Germans, we stopped to consult the map once again – but just as we'd opened it out, we glanced back, and there were the two sentries, on bicycles now and observing us with great interest. Had they had second thoughts? Or had their boss simply sent them to check up on us?

We didn't wait to find out but pressed on, taking care not to look back and trying to act and walk naturally. We all had our fingers crossed for good luck – and at last, when I finally, very carefully, glanced back over my shoulder, I let out a great sigh of intense relief when I saw that they were no longer following us, and had turned back.

When we talked about the incident much later, we were very surprised at such sloppy behaviour. The occupying army in an enemy country, in complete control, yet they had allowed a party of five strangers (evidently foreigners) without any sort of papers to wander about freely at about five o'clock in the morning? I'll bet there were hundreds of German soldiers who had been shot for far lesser military 'offences' than that! So, the only explanation that we could agree on was that they were on such a 'cushy number' there that they wouldn't allow anything to disturb their idyll – or just couldn't be bothered with writing any resulting reports.

It was by now fully daylight, so yet again we had to find somewhere to hide for the day, but we still felt the urge to put as much distance as possible between ourselves and that sentry post. We marched onward at quite a pace, covering a good distance more before finally finding another small farmstead – very much like the Duchamps' farm back at Hans – and we slowed down and stopped short of it behind a convenient hedge, to confer on our next move.

We decided to try our luck again, just as we had back at the Duchamps', and after a quick glance about, I moved away from the hedge. This time, I decided to be a little bolder with my movements and marched smartly (but not militarily) down the garden path, and slipped around the back to the rear door. The place had a very neglected air and look about it; no smoke from the chimney, a garden that was untended and quite overgrown with weeds, and a general look of decay to the house. I began to have serious misgivings, but I tentatively approached the back door – and I found it to be practically hanging off its hinges.

I knocked, my heart lurching as I heard movement inside; no reply, so I knocked again, a little more firmly this time. Still no answer – so I pushed the door aside enough to see inside and my eyes fell upon an ancient-looking lady who was sitting in the sole chair at a rickety old table, the only other piece of furniture in this very dirty, messy room. The old lady herself looked no better, her almost white hair bedraggled and her general appearance very unkempt.

A half-emptied bottle of wine stood in front of her, and as I pushed the door just that little harder, she raised a filthy glass to drink, heard the door creak, and snapped her head up to snarl at me, rather unexpectedly.

'Allez!' she cried, flapping at me with her arthritic-looking free hand. 'Allez-vous-en! Vite! Vite!'

But I had to try, anyway. 'Bonjour, Madame – je suis un aviateur Anglais,' I began, but she cut me off with another hand-flap.

'Allez-vous-en!' she repeated, and so I stepped back, needing no further urging. Deciding discretion was the better part of valour, I eased the door back into its rough frame and retreated rapidly – but before I returned to the others, I cast a quick glance around. There was a large barn in a pretty tumble-down state, but still containing some straw, although there was very little else There were two apple trees, each bearing some ripe-looking fruit even if out of season, and among the weeds in the garden I could see a few carrots and turnips, but there was no sign that this patch had been visited recently by humans, so I had a few thoughts.

Back I went to the boys, and gave my report. After a short discussion, it was decided to risk settling down in a corner of the barn for the day, and there were those carrots and apples available, so we could pinch some food to keep the tummy rumbles at bay. It didn't seem to me that the old lady would be able to do us any harm, or would be in any condition to raise the alarm anytime soon due to the volume of wine she'd already consumed, so – almost reluctantly – we crept into the barn and settled down for a day's (watched) sleep yet again.

It turned out to be something of a disturbed sleep, however, for although we saw nothing more of the old lady or of any other life about the place, there was plenty of life in the straw! What with all of us rubbing or scratching or just moving about in feverish attempts to avoid the various pests (I'll swear that French fleas bite harder than their English cousins!), we did little more than doze the day away in very short bursts. The apples and carrots went down well – even though the apples were far from French Golden Delicious, being somewhat sour – but we were relatively pleased when it neared the time for us to be on our way once more.

Eager to get away from that noisome barn, we set off once more, best feet forward. Very soon – even though the light was dwindling fast – we were able to get quite a good look at Rimacourt, which turned out to be a fairly large village. We managed to find a reasonably easy route around the fields surrounding the village, rather than going through (and risking any encounters with German patrols), and once safely past it, a brief look at our little map showed Clefmont and Bourbonne-les-Bains should be our next points to aim for, so off we went as briskly as we felt comfortable with; far better to keep up a fair pace and conserve our meagre energy, rather than rush into fatigue and possible trouble, again!

Oddly enough, although we did travel on roads, none of those shown on our map seemed to be main trunk-type routes; perhaps that was a design error before it was printed, or maybe it had been deliberately simplified (remember, it was just the back page of a calendar), but it struck us as an odd way to display one's region on a map. Bigger towns like Châlons-sur-Marne, Verdun, and Chaumont seemed to be within easy reach, but they were off our desired track, so we needed to avoid them, anyway.

What we wanted was a quiet, hassle-free route, and luckily, that was how it turned out to be. As we were travelling at night in what proved to be a sparsely populated area, and the French seemed to be living under a curfew, we encountered no traffic at all, and so we made very good progress every night, still lying up during the day but getting ever-thinner as our accumulated pocketfuls of apples and carrots diminished.

It was Hanwell, his mind constantly on food, who suggested a change in 'begging' tactics; instead of looking for smallholdings to scrounge from, he suggested that we should look for big farms.

'Farmers never starve,' he argued, 'so it stands to reason that if we get on to a bigger farm, we might get better food – and more of it! Has to be worth a try – I'm starving!'

He got plenty of leg-pulling about that but, in principle, it sounded quite a good idea – providing that we took our time selecting a likely target. Obviously, we could never be sure that our would-be 'hosts' wouldn't just turn us in to the Germans, but we were becoming more desperate for help as each day passed, and I worried that we might fail in our trek due to a lack of nutrition. After a brief discussion, we decided to adopt Hanwell's plan and hope for the best.

Clefmont, our first target after Rimacourt, seemed to be much further away than our map suggested, and the coming of another day found us still on the road, but approaching what looked like a country inn. The people were evidently early risers, for as we got nearer a side door was flung open and a plump, red-faced man suddenly stepped out.

We halted immediately, nervously, and he looked quite astonished when he saw us standing there, but he recovered his composure very quickly and greeted us cheerily.

'Bonjour, Messieurs! C'est bon le matin!' he called, and we took cautious steps on to the narrow gravelled forecourt.

Taking his cue – and a deep breath – I replied in kind. 'Bonjour, Monsieur! Nous sommes aviateurs Anglais,' I told him, watching his eyebrows climb higher and higher as I completed my usual lines.

The man looked utterly astonished, then glanced around furtively and waved us inside, all a flutter. 'Entrez, Messieurs! Vite! Vite!' He stood aside as we quickly stepped through the doorway, and once we were inside, he rushed past us to lead us through another doorway into a back room. I was a trifle alarmed at his demeanour, as he seemed very agitated indeed – a far cry from the welcome we'd received from the Duchamps.

Our 'host' seemed to start relaxing, though, as I set to explain our story, and finally he was all smiles when I'd finished. He apologised for being so anxious, then called his wife. When she appeared – her shock at seeing us was obvious by the trembling of her hand over her mouth – he explained the presence of five rather scruffy-looking strangers, then he bade her prepare some 'déjeuner' for us. Her eyes flicked across our faces, then she gave her husband an odd look, nodded and departed for the kitchen; he lifted his chin in disdain at her expression, shrugged as only a true Frenchman can – and we all shared smiles again at the thought of decent food at last! True to form, Hanwell's stomach gave a low rumble, and our friendly 'landlord' laughed and waved us all to take seats around an ancient pine table.

Sure enough, our fare was really delicious; genuine coffee, fresh rolls, real butter but although we really enjoyed the 'déjeuner', his wife served the meal rather grim-faced. She didn't seem altogether happy with our presence, and she made no attempt at conversation, somewhat souring the previously jovial atmosphere. When we'd polished off all the food and coffee, she collected all the platters and items, then grunted at her

husband as she left the room. He shook his head at us as if to allay our
fears, then took us out of the back door and into what seemed like a combination of garden and farmyard, with a large barn at the far end. He
waved at a mass of hay inside the barn, then spoke fairly rapidly at me
– the gist of which sounded like, 'You stay here for now, until we decide
what is best to do.'

Needing no further bidding, we heaved some lumpy hay bales into a
corner, made ourselves comfortable, and tried to settle into our usual
shift-patterned sleeping routine, but we were all somewhat uneasy about
Madame's attitude toward us. Before long, we could hear them arguing
quite vociferously, although the only words that we could recognise amid
the rapid exchange were 'le RAF' and 'le Boches'.

Some time later, after things had quietened down, the man came out
to us and explained. After much arm-waving, and exhaustive calls upon
my straining French, also aided by much sign language between us all,
we got the whole story.

Translated, he said: 'Please do not think that my wife does not welcome
you. She adores the brave RAF fliers, but for us to have you here, you mean
danger. There are many Germans in this area – some of them even
come here for a drink in the evening! So, sadly, we cannot let you stay
here for very long – you must leave here as soon as it is dark, please? We
can hide you in this barn today – nobody ever comes in here – and we can
arrange for you to go this evening. That way, we shall all be safe, yes?'

It took some time to fully unravel his meaning, but once we all understood – after I'd interpreted as best as I was able – we could do nothing
else but agree with his plans, and hope for the best. We promised to
keep well out of sight, until he came back to tell us which way we should
go. I think we were also hoping that he might find a way to connect us
with the partisans or French Resistance movement for a more organised
departure; we would just have to wait and see.

The day passed very slowly, although there was one little interlude that
amused us at first, but then sobered us up very sharply. The daughter of
the house, a pretty young girl of about fourteen or fifteen, came to us
about noon with some bread, a little meat and some wine, all of which
was very welcome. As girls do, she stayed to chat, and we all got on quite

well in spite of the language barrier. Then she began to sing a song that we all knew – 'South of the Border' – and from old automatic habit, I joined in for the first verse, then I smiled at her and nodded.

'Vous connoissez les chanson?' I asked her, parading my 'superior' French to the lads.

'Mais oui,' she replied, 'le BBC!'

We sang on once more – quietly, of course – but suddenly the door was flung open and the girl's mother appeared, practically spitting blood. She harangued the poor girl with words like 'salles Boches!' very prominently, then grabbed her and hauled her back to the house.

She was back in a few minutes, still breathing fire. 'Vous êtes fous!' she cried ('You are mad!'), and she continued in that strain for a few minutes – far too fast and voluble for me to keep up, of course – until finally, the steam went out of her with a low growl, and she began to calm down.

'Pour vous,' she said, pointing an accusing finger at each of us in turn, 'c'est un gros aventure … mais, pour nous' she cocked a thumb at herself 'c'est la vie et la mort!' She followed that with a slashing motion of her hand across her throat; her meaning was very clear, indeed – we got the message: 'For you, it is a great adventure, but for us, it could mean life or death!'

Suitably humbled, we offered abject apologies, and at length – suitably mollified – she left us and went back to the house, occasionally shaking her head as she strutted across the yard. We didn't see the girl again, either.

As the evening drew in, we could hear voices rising – among them obvious German tones, first in chatter, then eventually in noisy songs. Our host had locked the barn door earlier, so we just had to sit and sweat it out as the noise grew louder and louder, but at long last the lights went out in the house, and silence descended once more.

After a while, the innkeeper opened the barn door and entered, then gave us a substantial cloth-wrapped parcel, which we later found to contain bread, meat and cheese portions for every man – a very generous gesture indeed.

'Et maintenant,' he indicated, 'il fout que vous portez' – time for us to go.

This had been obvious, of course, but he saw us on our way with instructions on how to reach Clefmont, about 10 kilometres away. He was directing us, using our meagre map, to avoid a German garrison by a slightly circuitous route, then he told us how lucky we had been to find 'room at the inn', here. All of this discussion took time, and I couldn't help thinking how much easier it might have been if only I'd really got stuck into my French lessons at school – but back then, I could not have foreseen such circumstances as these!

It was nearly midnight when we left the inn, with a hearty 'Bonne chances, mes amis!' from both the innkeeper and his wife, with her looking distinctly happier and much more friendly, now that we were moving on.

Feeling decidedly chastened, having been shown the difference between our (up to now) slightly slack attitude to the lighter dangers of our 'meanderings', compared with the risks that the French were taking for assisting us, we plodded on through the night, each of us deep in thought and humbled by gratitude for the help we'd received thus far; for the locals, assisting us could prove lethal, and we now appreciated their sacrifices all the more, resolving to be much more careful from now on. We bypassed the German garrison – as directed by the innkeeper – without problem, and paced out a good few more miles, up to and just beyond Clefmont. We even managed a quiet halt to devour our 'picnic' parcel, and very appetising it was, too!

We tramped on, and as dawn broke yet again we saw that a little distance to the right of our road was what appeared to be quite a large farm. Soon after spotting it, we came upon the modest side road leading down to it. A sign announced it to be the 'Ferme de Luzerain, Clefmont', and it seemed that Hanwell's earlier wishes had been granted.

Nevertheless, we approached the farmstead with greater caution than the other farms we'd previously visited, mindful of our lesson of the day before. Bigger farms usually meant more people – workers and the like – and obviously, the presence of more people wasn't necessarily a good thing for us; all it took was one wagging tongue.

The small road had hedges bordering both sides to keep us hidden from view until we were right up close; then we found a spot where we could lie down to spy on the activities, just out of sight of both the farm buildings and the road itself. Sure enough, as one might expect on a farm at six o'clock on a late spring morning, people materialised to begin a variety of chores. Firstly, two teenagers appeared, apparently cleaning out a stable block, and then byres, then an elderly man emerged with a collie dog at his heels. He disappeared into fields on the other side of the farmhouse, the dog seemingly attached to his left leg, such was its affinity with its master.

Hanwell carried on watching the people as he lay beside me under the hedge; the others were sprawled a little behind us, watching our backs in case anyone should approach and discover us loitering there, so I turned my attention to the house. It was a large, very solidly built two-storey affair – the home of a prosperous farmer in normal times, I thought – and the farm itself had that well-organised and well-maintained look about it, still. We were to learn later that the Germans kept a close eye on the premises, at the same time as taking more than their fair share of the produce.

The picture was completed by the appearance of the lady of the house. She was – to my mind, at least – everyone's idea of the typical farmer's wife; a buxom, rosy-cheeked lady in the prime of her life, who carried with her an unmistakable air of being the boss. She had only come out to feed the chickens (who seemed to be running around loose every-where), but she had a smile and an encouraging word for everyone she passed as she did her early rounds. Two more elderly men appeared from a barn, so it was obviously a busy, prosperous place. The lady finished feeding her chickens, then disappeared into the house. Shortly afterwards we heard a bell ringing out quite loudly, and the farmhands all stopped whatever they were doing and headed for the back door of the main house.

'Breakfast time,' said Hanwell. 'Now's your chance, Jack.'

'Right,' I replied. 'Just keep out of sight, everyone, and I'll see what I can do.'

With that, I eased myself upright (even though my body was crying out to just stay there and sleep!), before walking very cautiously to the back door, keeping a wary eye out for other strangers (or worse, Germans). I reached the door and waited again, carrying out my now-usual routine of listening before 'leaping'. I stood there for perhaps half a minute as I plucked up courage (there were a lot of people in there) – and then I knocked firmly, taking a deep breath.

The door opened, and one of the teenaged boys that we'd seen earlier hovered in the doorway, looking very surprised and more than a little apprehensive. He stood his ground, however, and said, 'Bonjour, monsieur. Que voulez-vous?'

'Bonjour,' I replied. 'je suis aviateur Anglais …' I began, going straight into my full routine of introduction. The lady of the house appeared by his side almost instantly.

'Anglais?' she quizzed me – then as I opened up my civvy overcoat to show her my uniform underneath, she beamed at me and unleashed a torrent of obviously delighted chatter, shook my hand, then kissed me soundly on both cheeks. 'Entrez, mon ami!' she bade me, practically pulling me through the doorway and into the house, calling to the others sitting around a huge breakfast table as she did so. They all smiled, then began nattering away, obviously also glad to see me, shooting quick-fire questions at me from all angles. I managed to work out some; 'Where do you come from?', 'How did you get here?', and 'Where is your aeroplane?' (this last one from a toddler whom I now saw for the first time). I began to answer them in my halting (but rapidly improving) French, but the lady jumped in quickly to ease the pressure.

'Fairez-vous! Fairez-vous!' she cried, silencing them all at a stroke, then to me she said, 'Asseyez-vous, monsieur!', forcefully shoving me down to a vacated chair. I found this enthusiastic welcome a little overwhelming, and I had to calm them down. I appealed to the lady, using my hands as though conducting an orchestra to slow the pace.

'Pardonez-moi, Madame, je ne sois parlez Francais que peu', my usual spiel ('I can only speak a little French'), then I added, 'Parlez plus lentiment, s'il vous plais?' ('Please speak a little more slowly?').

At this, the lady took total charge and told them to quieten down (I think!), then spoke to me, a big smile on her face and a twinkle in her eyes. 'Ils sont très excites!' she commented, then – speaking very carefully so that I managed to understand her almost perfectly – she said, 'I am Madame Eymann, and this is the Ferme de Luzerain. This is my father [the old chap we'd seen with the dog], my mother [an old lady, who'd been sitting very quietly to one side], my baby, Paulette [the toddler], and these two are my labourers [the teenage boys] – and they are all very happy to meet you!' She beamed again.

They all clapped excitedly at this; only the old lady kept calm, although she smiled cheerfully at me – then it was my turn, and my first words got them all really excited.

'I am not alone,' I told them. 'There are four more RAF friends outside' and that was as far as I got! They were all evidently startled by my 'news' and became very animated again, but Madame Eymann calmed them down and declared that they should be brought in immediately. 'And then,' she concluded, 'you can all tell us your story!' I was dispatched with the two boys to bring my crewmembers in forthwith.

I must admit that I had a reservation or two about the impending reaction from both the teenage boys and then the Eymann elders, for with several days' growth of beard each and coats that looked like they'd fallen off a rag-and-bone cart, they looked a right scruffy bunch – and I, of course appeared no better! Glancing slightly warily at my young companions as we stepped near, I hailed my colleagues and waited for the reaction as they stood up, seeming slightly nonplussed – but the boys just grinned and cheered, urging the lads back to the house.

'It's all right,' I assured them, 'the family are all happy we're here. Come on – breakfast's waiting!'

Hanwell needed no further invitation and turned with one of the boys, leading us all back to the house. I nodded at Beecroft, who flicked me a smile as we fell into step.

Madame Eymann took complete charge again as soon as we all stepped through the doorway. 'Maman,' she told her mother, 'these men need food!' With that, the two ladies set to and soon sat us down to an excellent solid meal of potatoes, meat and a veritable heap of vegetables. 'Mangé vous!' she urged us. 'Time for talk, later!'

We got stuck in straightaway, and Hanwell got his kick in with a quiet aside to me: 'Told you farmers never starve!' Madame Eymann heard him mutter, but whether she understood or not I'll never know, but she did smile back when Hanwell unloaded his best expression of appreciation of the meal – some facial expressions appeared to be universally understood, it seemed! The old lady wasn't so sure, though, so I hastily told her, 'He says that this is the best meal that we've had since landing in France, and I agree! Er – beau repas!' She positively beamed at that and dipped her chin slightly, accepting the compliment gracefully.

Finally, as we all finished our meal and sat back in our chairs, Madame

Eymann and Maman cleared the table except for the coffee cups, and it was time to talk. We felt absolutely stuffed to the brim and slightly sleepy now, but these were good French people and were curious (a traditional English understatement, if ever there was one!), and they wanted to know where we had come from and how we'd got here, so – by dint of much sign language and with my labouring French (kindly assisted by Madame Eymann's gentle prompts and infilling) – we gradually pieced together the story of our adventures so far, to the obvious delight of the two boys and the round-eyed toddler.

Madame Eymann was very understanding, for she seemed to know instinctively exactly what I meant whenever I became stuck for a word or expression. Her graphic gestures, helped by her mother and sons, enabled me to tell them much more clearly than I had managed back at the Duchamps' farm.

For her part, she told us that her husband had been killed in the early part of the war, and now that the Germans had occupied her country it was very difficult to run the farm properly. Two of her farmhands had been sent to work as labourers in Germany, and the local German force demanded a certain percentage of all that they produced. 'But they don't get all of that!' her father cut in with a chuckle.

'Fortunately,' Madame Eymann informed me, 'they don't bother us very much here – only a visit once a month.' She then added something that rather surprised me: 'We don't really hate the Germans, you know – we just seem to be natural enemies.' I couldn't help thinking that they must have been rather lucky with their local German commanders, given her comment, because the stories that we had read at home in both newspapers and in RAF intelligence reports were very different. She went on to say, though, 'It's the Italians that we really despise! They waited until the Germans had the war in France won, and then they came to stab us in the back!', and she rounded off with a swearword that I couldn't interpret, but understood the meaning of all too clearly as her father and mother both endorsed it with gruff sneers.

'Mais vous êtes très fatigue,' she declared at last. 'Vous dormirez dans la grange, et demain non parlons plus encore.' I took that to mean, 'We'll talk more tomorrow', and I made a feeble protest, mindful of being diplomatic with their generosity thus far.

'But, we would like to go on, tomorrow!' I asserted as gently as I could. 'We really want to get to Switzerland and home, vitement.'

'Non, non!' she talked me down, smiling. 'Le domain, vous restez et mangez!'

Rest and eat! It sounded too good to be true, but when I translated her meaning to the boys they all agreed instantly – there was no argument at all. I relayed this to Madame Eymann, although she could see from the lads' reactions that we were to follow her plan, and she smiled again.

All this must sound as though I was doing everything, but in fact my crewmates were involved all the time – particularly with the Eymann boys, who were interjecting with their own spare English words and plentiful hand gestures and arm-waving, occasionally letting loose with graphic noises (if that's how to describe some of the unintelligible sounds!). Madame Eymann had made a point of bringing each of the crew into the conversation, asking us what our roles were in the aircraft. When Beecroft told her that he was the pilot, our hosts showed their amazement (due to his height) with a 'Si grande!' exclamation, and the Eymann boys had immediately singled-out Crighton as a gunner due to his much shorter stature, but we took pains to assure them all that he was a very good gunner – 'Un tireur élite!', they told us, after working out what we were saying about him.

We retired to the barn soon after this long, but gradually more fluent, conversation, and mostly slept quite well – although, for our own security, we still maintained our rotation of watching duties.

The evening meal brought the old man more into the picture, for he had fought in the First World War, and he proudly showed us his medals and some sepia-coloured photographs of himself in uniform. The meal was noteworthy for its prized delicacy, a huge plate of cream cheese that turned out to be just as tasty as it looked. Madame Eymann produced some freshly baked bread, and indicated that we should help ourselves, so I took a slice and began to spread the cheese as if it were butter.

'Non, non!' cried the old man, with a smile. 'Comme ça!' He took the bread and knife from me, then plastered on the cheese about an inch thick! 'Comme ça!' he repeated, offering it back to me with a grin and a firm nod, and he was right – it was absolutely delicious, thus!

Eventually, the meal over, we repaired to the barn once more to our beds of (clean!) straw, well fed and drowsily happy, and so we all dropped into exhausted sleep, our watch rota ignored for the first time, and near panic ensued when we were all jarred wide awake when the barn door creaked open loudly, some time in the early hours.

It was Madame Eymann, in her nightdress and dressing gown, looking somewhat agitated, yet also embarrassed. 'C'est la jument!' she cried, 'elle est un poulain, et c'est très difficile! Pouvez-vous aidez, s'il vous plait?'

She wasn't panicking as though we were being raided by a German patrol, although we were all halfway to our feet in mild alarm. We all glanced at one another, mystified, then we scrambled from the hay and followed her into a stable – and there her words were explained, visually. Her mare (jument) was struggling to give birth to a foal (poulain), and she was having great trouble; the foal was already partway breach-born (hind quarters first), but the poor mare seemed absolutely exhausted, lying quite still except for her flank rising and falling from her exerted breathing.

All our eyes immediately fell upon Beecroft – the vet in our midst! However, he frowned deeply as he set about examining the mare in a very professional-looking fashion. I struggled to find the right French words to explain to Madame Eymann about Beecroft's previous profession as he checked the foal, and her eyes lit up with hope when she finally understood my poor translation, but sadly, it didn't look good.

'I don't think there's much chance here, Jack – can you tell her that, please? Gently, though,' he asked me. I nodded, and set to try to recall the right words. 'We'll give it a quick try, though,' he added, then asked the lads to try to find a stout rope as he crouched down again to examine the foal.

Brad, Henry and Alec stepped out of the stable, and very soon Alec returned with a length of rope, with Brad and Henry close behind him. John took the rope and set about tying it carefully around the foal's hind legs, but to me, they looked so very fragile. When he was ready, he motioned the lads to get a grip of the loose end of the rope like a tug-of-war team, and to get ready to pull. John gently slapped and rubbed the mare's flank to get her attention, and when it looked like she was beginning to 'push' almost by some instinct, John turned to the lads.

'Take the strain, then start pulling steadily when I say, but very slow and gentle,' he murmured, watching the mare's breathing and spasms.

'Now!'

They tried several times, but finally John had to call a halt, as the mare just seemed to flop, almost lifeless. Madame Eymann was gripping my arm tightly all this time, obviously upset and very anxious; I would have joined the 'team', but there just wasn't room for four men on the rope in that stall. Finally, John was shaking his head sadly as he stood up to face her with bad news.

'Madame,' he said, very solemnly, 'I am afraid that there is nothing that I – we – can do for her or the foal. It's stuck tight, and she is just too far gone. Had we been at home, with all my equipment at hand, we might have managed if I'd been called sooner. I'm very sorry.'

I translated again as softly as I could – which took quite some time – and although Madame Eymann took it very well, she was obviously somewhat tearful at the blow. One by one, we went back to the barn, leaving her alone to spend time with the mare.

In the morning, as we ate another hearty breakfast, Madame Eymann had regained her remarkable composure and gently told us that the mare and foal had died soon after we had gone. Beecroft seemed to take the news quite stoically, although I did see a brief flash of anguish in his eyes; however, there was no point in dwelling upon it for too long, as upsetting as the episode had been. We all murmured condolences, and although she quite probably didn't understand a single word, our tones and the meaning of our expressions were clear, and she flicked a sad smile and nodded to close the subject.

Very soon, we were helping the boys with their chores wherever we could, trying to 'earn our keep' and to repay some of our hosts' generosity – and for our efforts, the old man rewarded us with shaving and ablution facilities so that we could make ourselves look a little less like a bunch of roving tramps.

I'd had some trouble trying to recall the right word for 'lavatory' up until now; when I mentioned 'toilette', I was invariably shown the washbasin – but now, after the meal, the gourmet excesses of the past twenty-four hours drew forth a question from Crighton, who was apparently in some discomfort, holding his hand over his abdomen.

'See if you can find out where the toilet is, please, Jack?' he muttered. 'I need to go, badly!'

The two young Eymann boys were standing in the barn doorway, so I asked, 'Ou est la toilette?'

'La toilette?' asked Henri, and he made motions of washing his hands, but frowned when I shook my head, trying to remember the correct word – then Hanwell, ever the direct Norfolk man and always quick to put his foot in things, spoke up loudly.

'Oh, just tell him we all want a shit, Jack!' He wasn't being nasty at me, just frustrated – and evidently also in dire need!

'Ah! Shit!' said Henri, grinning as he realised their plight from Crighton's apparent 'sign language'. 'C'est la bas!' he urged, pointing to a shed at the bottom of the farmhouse garden. We all roared with laughter and the two boys joined in, although I doubt that they understood the underlining reason for our hilarity; we'd just had a first-class demonstration of a commonality of language between different-speaking countries!

Crighton was off to the outhouse like a hare chased by a hound, inviting more chuckles and banter as he fled, and I struggled once more to explain the sudden need to the Eymann boys. They eventually understood that we had eaten very little for several days, and that the sudden large intake of relatively rich food was taking its toll on our digestive systems – although I have to say that I seemed to be the least affected by this; perhaps I was just lucky.

With everyone cleaned, shaved and otherwise sorted, we settled down in the barn once more, passing the day on watch as usual until the evening meal – and after this, we made ready to leave; we simply had to get moving, and we felt that we had already outstayed our welcome. Madame Eymann understood, and gracefully accepted our profuse thanks for their hospitality. She and Maman packed us a good-sized parcel of food to take with us, and then Maman wished us 'bon voyage'.

'Le bon Dieu vous protégerez,' she said as we swung off down the track, with the two boys accompanying us to set us in the right direction.

Chapter 7

Bacon and eggs

We left the Ferme de Luzerain feeling much better and somewhat healthier for that dietary boost and good rest, and we now felt ready for anything. Our next aiming point, suggested by the old man after reference to our map, was the fairly large village of Traves, about 40 kilometres away. There were apparently no towns of any significant size along the way that he guided us, which was on mostly smaller country lanes, so all we had to do was travel carefully – and the first few nights were uneventful.

We made good progress, and the Eymanns had provided us with enough food to keep us going for two days – three, if we eked it out a little – so we had no need to seek further accommodation. We just plodded onward through each night until daylight came, then looked once more for a good hiding place for the day.

This area was much more heavily wooded than we'd covered previously, so finding a place of good concealment was no problem. While we walked at night, we talked very little for fear of stumbling into any German guards who would obviously hear us coming closer, but during the day, when we felt secure from prying eyes, we had some long chats between spells of sleep.

Our principal conversation now was fast becoming a general debate on what would happen when we reached Switzerland, for we were now certain in our minds that we would do so, and (we hoped) safely escape across the border. The general opinion, worked out from all the things we'd heard or read – both back at home on the squadron, and here at each stop-off point – was that when we managed to get across the border, we would probably be interned, then after a while the British authorities would find some way of getting us released and returned to England. The internment would be of a very loose character, so that would be very easy to endure – or so we dreamed! We really didn't know anything – we'd just 'heard' it, but we were ever-hopeful of a positive outcome, as anyone might be in our predicament. Note, also, that we didn't talk about 'if' we reached Switzerland, but 'when' we got there. Everything had been relatively easy up to now (except for that one 'hiccup' with the German bridge patrol) that there was just no room for doubt in our minds. Oh, the exuberance of youth!

During one of our resting chats, Beecroft brought up a subject that probably all of us had been thinking at least once, but had pushed to the back of our minds because it was in the past now.

'I've been wondering, you know,' he began, 'why you didn't bale out when you all had the chance?'

'Well,' said Hanwell, casting a glance around us for nods of agreement that he spoke for each one of us, 'we were confident that you'd get us down in one piece!'

'Baloney!' Beecroft retorted with a sly smile. 'You knew I couldn't land properly without the undercart down – that I'd have to belly-flop her!' He jerked his chin up, mocking us all. 'I reckon you were just too scared to jump!'

His comment brought a chorus of denials from the rest of us, although – as he saw that we were struggling not to laugh – he knew that he'd scored a point; of course we had been a little afraid!

'Well, perhaps what you said might be half-true, John,' I agreed, raising one eyebrow from Hanwell and grumbles from the others, 'but let's face it – how many of us have done even one parachute jump before?' I knew I had settled the issue with that as everyone nodded their heads besides which, I knew that we all thought, 'Who in their right mind would make his first parachute jump in the dark, over enemy-held territory?' Only those who knew that there was absolutely no other option, with their aircraft badly damaged and tumbling from the sky, as so many unfortunates had before us.

A general question and answer discussion then elicited the fact that not one of us had had even any basic training on the topic – even though the authorities must have known that some of us aircrew were almost certain to need the knowledge eventually. Further dialogue brought out the fact that even the idea of a basic demonstration hadn't been suggested on any of the courses that we'd attended.

'All we were told,' said Hanwell, 'was "Clip on your parachute, jump, count to three, then pull the ripcord"! They even said "It was as easy as falling off a log – don't forget to bend your knees when you land, and you'll be just fine, old boy!"'

'Well, that gives us something else to tell them when we get back,' I said. 'Mind you, I might be able to find an excuse for missing out on any training, anyway – at my last course at Pershore, we were supposed to be there for about three months, but I was sent to the squadron after exactly five weeks!'

'Ah!' Brad chipped in, 'that explains why you're such a duff navigator!'

I laughed along with them, but I retorted, 'Oh, I don't know – I've managed to get us there and back every time until now; this wasn't my fault – and we're still heading in the right direction out of here!'

Eventually, the banter dwindled into a meandering conversation, and one by one we dozed off (one still on watch, as usual!), and time passed.

The third night out from the Ferme de Luzerain ended with us seeking refuge at yet another small farm as dawn broke, although it must be said that the owners were nothing like as welcoming as our previous generous hosts had been. They allowed us to stay in the usual barn accommodation, and told us to keep well out of sight. They made no attempt to talk with us during the day, and although they brought us adequate supplies of food and drink, my efforts to engage any of them in conversation were met with indifference, or 'Je ne comprende pas.' Ah, well, I thought, shrugging it off, we couldn't expect everyone to be enthusiastic and go out of their way for us; at least they had offered us shelter and food – and for that, we were obviously extremely grateful.

When night came, we politely thanked our hosts for their assistance and set off once more; our objective was still Traves.

The next morning found us on the edge of a small wood with a tiny field in front, and on the other side of that field, an area of low, thin bushes were set in straight lines, which we took to be a vineyard. As the sun rose and the morning mist began to disappear, we saw that we were at the head of a valley, and down below smoke was rising from the chimneys of several houses – a village that we took to be Traves.

'I think we should give them a bit of time to wake up properly and get their breakfasts, then maybe we can go down and do a bit of "prospecting", I said, and everyone nodded as we settled under the treeline for a little while.

At about eight o'clock, I left the boys in the wood and headed slowly down to the settlement. The road down the valley was bordered on both sides by 'hedges' of quite high trees with fields behind them, so I was careful to stay off the road itself and follow along the edges of the fields on my right. My caution soon proved to be justified, for before I had got even halfway to the village, I heard the sound of several trucks coming along the road, overladen with the sound of men singing cheerfully: Germans!

I froze, then sank into the ditch behind the trees and watched, my heart pounding in my chest, as the trucks – packed with soldiers – crawled past me. I was fairly confident that they wouldn't see me beneath the undergrowth, but the trucks were grinding so gradually – because the lane was narrow but fairly steep as it climbed up from the village – that I was actually now quite terrified that one eagle-eyed trooper might just see me, and that would be that! All this way, easily – and now this!

As I peered through the leaves, the convoy rumbled past and, in spite of my fear, I was quite impressed with the turnout of the men. All looked young, fit and happy, and they were roaring out a marching song – I'd like to bet that their verses were probably a lusty version of any such song that soldiers of all nations corrupt for fun. Then the trucks were crawling out of sight, at last, and I heaved a great sigh of relief as the noise of the vehicles and accompanying singing died away beyond the woods.

Nevertheless, I waited a little while longer in case there might be any stragglers following along – such as a motorbike combination or perhaps a Kubelwagen, or similar – and, of course, to allow time for my thumping heart to calm itself!

Eventually, I continued along the edges of the fields, but no one else appeared to challenge me. I finally passed a road sign that confirmed that this really was Traves, then I saw that the village was entered by a bridge over a narrow river. Just over the river, on the right, was a large, quite opulent-looking house, and in its well-tended garden an elderly lady was manfully plying a quite enormous spade. As I approached, she looked up at me, dug her spade into the ground and rested on it as any gardener would do, and gave me a cheerful smile.

'Bonjour, Monsieur!' she greeted me, 'C'est un très jolie matin, n'est pas?'

It certainly was a lovely morning, and, encouraged by her bright expression, I plunged into my usual set piece. Her first look of astonishment was quickly replaced by another wide smile. Throwing down her spade, she cried, 'Mais, c'est marvellieux, Monsieur!' then flung open the garden gate and ushered me in. 'Dans la maison, vite!' she urged, and rushed me in through the open back door. Soon realising that my French language skills weren't very good, she spoke slowly and carefully, and between us we managed to have quite a conversation.

'Have you seen the German soldiers?' she asked (in French), and when I told her how I'd hidden in the ditch as they passed me by, she showed she was very pleased, and told me that they'd just left their barracks at Baume-les-Dames (the next place on our list), although she didn't know where they were heading.

While we were talking she led me into the kitchen, and then, rather fussily – as motherly old ladies will – she started laying the table for a meal, saying, 'You must be very hungry – what would you like to eat?' But before I could answer, she came out with, 'Mais bien sur! Les Anglais! Il fait que le bacon et des oeufs!'

Bacon and eggs! It sounded just too good to be true! But sure enough, out came a pair of large frying pans, some huge rashers of delicious-looking bacon and a bowl of eggs, and she placed a coffee pot on her cooking range to heat up. I soon caught a waft of rich coffee – real coffee, too! What a treat!

'Les déjeuner des Anglais, n'est ce pas?' she beamed, and set to with the English breakfast. I eyed the quantities of bacon and eggs going into the pans, and my mouth was watering even as my stomach rumbled.

'There's far too much there for me!' I protested, thinking that she might well be rationed in such delights, but she brushed aside my protestations with a typically Gallic hand-flap.

'Eat what you can!' I translated as she laughed. 'We have plenty more!'

Now, of course, it was my chance – and duty – to tell her about the rest of the crew, still hiding up in the woods. Far from being dismayed, she seemed delighted!

'You must bring them here!' she commanded, 'but first, you must eat', and with a flourish she slid an enormous plate into a place on the table, waving me into a chair – and I sat down to enjoy the best fry-up meal I'd had for weeks.

While I ate and savoured the blissful flavours that we used to take for granted in the sergeants' mess, she told me about herself. Her name was Madame Fouchon, and she was a widow whose husband had been a successful local businessman (I think!), and had left her this beautiful house and a sizeable sum – something I'd surmised from what little I'd already seen. Madame Fouchon also informed me that she had a daughter who lived with her but was out at work at that moment. We would meet her that evening, she said – then she paused for dramatic effect, and with a big smile added that her daughter spoke very good English. Better and better, I thought! It seemed to me that – at last – we might have landed on our feet; now, perhaps, we might make real progress.

After I'd finished my meal and made appropriate noises of thanks, she became all business-like.

'Tonight,' she began (as I mentally translated), 'as soon as it becomes dark, you must come here, all of you, and you shall have a meal and meet my daughter. Then we can talk some more, and perhaps see how we can help, yes?'

I had already told her of our plan to reach Switzerland, and of walking by night and resting by day, so it would be interesting to see how they may be able to assist us along our way.

'I'll go back and join them, now,' I said, standing up to take my leave.

'Mais non!' she exclaimed, horrified. 'You must take them some food, also! Asseyez-vous!'

With that, she turned back to the stove and set to frying a clutch of eggs and a fistful of bacon rashers, then hauled out a monster vacuum flask, which she filled with steaming coffee. I had no doubt that with her obvious wealth, they would have access to lots of little luxuries like that.

She carefully wrapped it all up, and lowered it into a shopping bag.

'We will see you after dark, mon ami!' she said, smiling warmly as she handed me the bag of goodies, then led me out of the house, pausing to check that the coast was clear before ushering me away. As I began to walk back across the bridge, I now saw that their house stood a little apart from the rest of the village, which indicated to me that the family were people of some consequence here, so perhaps things really were going to work out well, at last.

Little did I know then that this was just the beginning of what was to be an unforgettable day, easily the best so far of our long trek. Keeping to the edges of the fields once more, I trudged back up the hill. It finally dawned upon me what a dangerous 'game' we had been playing, trusting our freedom – and in fact our very lives – to perfect strangers in this random visiting fashion; it could all so easily have ended in disaster and capture – even death – had we fallen in with collaborators at any stage of our long march. And yet, here we were in occupied France, chancing fate with our various encounters, and having the luck of the very devil! I prayed that our good fortune would hold out, and that we would all eventually make it safely to Switzerland. Thus far, we had (mostly) fallen into sympathetic arms, but – although I've always prided myself on being a fairly quick and good judge of character – it would only take one deception from a good 'actor' of a Vichy-type collaborator, and that would be curtains for our freedom – perhaps our very lives!

I had just resolved to take extra care from now on as we were making such unbelievably good progress, when I reached the lads at the edge of the woods – and I had a bit of a shock! They were chatting quite amiably with a young lad of about fourteen or so, whose English was more intermittent than my French, but they were managing quite well without me.

It appeared that the lad had been working in the vineyard (we'd guessed correctly about that) and had wandered into the trees to relieve himself – whereupon he'd encountered the chaps and got the fright of his life! They'd calmed him down with passive gestures, it seemed, then managed to strike up a conversation with him – in fits and starts – and learned that the young lad lived in Ovanches, a village that we'd passed by in the night about 4 kilometres back. I took over the conversation at that point, and he told me that the village itself was just to the side of the main road that we'd been following, so that explained why we'd missed it in the dark.

Still highly excited, he said that he would now go home and give his parents the news of our presence. They were sure to help us, he told me – but something stirred in my mind about this turn of events; a nagging

fear that something might go very wrong, once the word got out that
we were in the area. I watched the youth almost run along the narrow road,
back to his home, and I worried.

By now, the lads had discovered what was in the shopping bag that
I'd passed to them before starting to chat with the youth, and they crept
a little further back into the wood to consume the contents; I could see
Hanwell almost salivating as he caught the delicious aroma of fried bacon,
once the wrappings began to come off, and I shrugged off my fears and
grinned at them as they systematically devoured every scrap of the meal,
then took turns at drinking a cup of coffee each. I had one, too, then I
told them my good news. For a while, we all sat back and made happy
guesses about how our luck seemed to have turned for the better now.

'The sun shines on the righteous,' chuckled Hanwell, as he basked in a
shaft of sunlight glancing down upon him through the trees. He was
evidently blissfully sated, and burped his delight to punctuate his statement.

'The only thing we need now,' Crighton chimed in, 'is a packet of fags
and a wee dram!' He was the only smoker of our group – but I think we
would all have welcomed a drop of something fiery and alcoholic right
then!

After a rest and a sleep, we had a look around and saw that we had picked
an ideal spot, for the little meadow in front of the wood was right at the
top of the hill, and we could see Traves quite clearly now, with a good
view all around. The vineyard in front of us seemed to be the only one
in sight, but the rest of the valley – as far as we could see – was a patch-
work of fields of corn, wheat, and grass meadows. On such a lovely day,
it looked so attractive and peaceful – 'Just like home,' Beecroft observed.

It was now nearly midday, for my excursion to and from the village had
taken longer than I'd thought. We settled down once more into our usual
system of sleep and guard, and I was just quietly dozing off after my
sentry stint when I heard the sound of French voices growing louder.
'We've got visitors, chaps,' Hanwell hissed. All of us jerked wide awake
in alarm, and he looked straight at me. 'Better talk to them, Jack?'

Toiling up the hill toward us came the youth who'd spoken to us earlier,
accompanied by two women and a younger girl. I stood up to greet them,

and Georges – our first acquaintance – introduced them as his mother, his aunt, and his younger sister Jeanette. We were introduced to them simply as 'Les RAF'!

After an initial shyness the women began to talk more freely, saying how delighted they were to meet us, then we had our usual question and answer session, with much amusement at our attempts to enhance our chat with sign language. I managed to convey to them how we'd managed to come so far without being captured, and they were quite impressed. Maybe I did a bit of 'line-shooting', but they seemed to accept all that I told them, and at length they got up to go. I must admit that I was rather relieved, for it was becoming quite a strain – and the lads didn't help much; in fact, they found my translations and sign-language efforts rather amusing!

As our visitors turned to go, they waved happily, and accepted my hand-signalled request for a promise of silence with sombre dignity and another smile, then they strolled off after another comment that took me a few moments to understand and then I was alarmed once more. 'The others will come soon.' Heavens! What next? The entire village, in shifts?

Sure enough, what followed was a succession of visitors throughout the afternoon at about half-hourly intervals, in threes and fours! They came to see and talk to us, some quietly, some too volubly, but all obviously delighted to meet us. I don't know whether they thought we were the forerunners of an invasion force, but they made it clear that they were happy to know that the British had not forgotten them.

The one good thing about all these visits, however, was that – by the end of the afternoon – my French language skills had improved quite considerably; I actually felt like I was talking quite fluently now, for by using signs and graphic illustrations, they taught me many 'new' words. I was becoming exhausted, but my vocabulary had improved vastly!

I soon noticed that they were all women and children, and when I asked them about this, they told us that some of the men were doing essential jobs such as building, farm work, and some administration, but more than half of the local male population had been transported to Germany to work as labourers.

'So, there are Germans around here?' I asked. It seemed odd that we seldom saw any, save for the bridge patrol that we'd encountered, and the convoy this morning (oh, how long ago that seemed now!).

'Ah, there are some,' said one of the ladies. 'They pay us a visit now and then, but we usually know when they are coming' – and with that, the subject was dropped.

By about four o'clock that afternoon, my head was in a whirl of fatigue and foreign language – although the lads did their best to chip in; they were learning, too! Many of the women brought us morsels to eat, and some dropped sly hints that there would be more to come.

Eventually, 'visitor hours' were over, and as the last group departed, we settled back with deep sighs of blessed relief. But not for long, however, as there came the rattle of a harness, and up the hill came a pair of huge, strong horses pulling a long flat trailer – upon which seemed to be the entire population of women from the village! Many of them were carrying baskets, and they were all very cheerful.

'Venez vous en!' they called. 'C'est le temps pour thé!' Tea time? Good grief! We were almost bursting, already.

They made room on the cart for us, and off we went back down the slope beyond the woods, to the village of Ovanches. They took us into what looked like the church hall, and there we saw the reason for all the excitement: there was a long table down the middle of the room, absolutely laden with food! I looked at Hanwell, and he was almost salivating once more at the glorious sight. I smiled at him and winked, then an old man rose from his seat at the head of the table. I took him to be a village elder – or perhaps the mayor – and he straightened to make a short speech as we respectfully stood in line, at ease, sensing that our actions were appropriate for the occasion.

I recognised that he was making a speech of welcome to us, and after the ladies applauded, I did my best to utter what I hoped would be a suitable reply. I told them how grateful we were to all the French people for all the help that they'd given us so far, and we trusted that we could repay them soon by driving the Boche from their beloved country. More applause greeted my words, and we were ushered to chairs, to sit and eat. The hall was almost full, mostly women with just a sprinkling of men, mainly elderly. Some of them sat down with us, and they brought – of all the unexpected things – a huge pot of steaming tea! We grinned and applauded vigorously at this gesture, then prepared to enjoy the meal. Even though we had been nibbling small treats most of the afternoon, we dug into this banquet like starving men. There were several kinds of cakes, all home made; pots of jam; plates of ham and other deliciously cooked meats – and knowing then how tightly rationed they were, we couldn't help wondering where it had all come from. 'C'est la guerre!' I thought, as we all tucked in; no doubt, they had their own black market, just as we had back home.

It was now that I committed my first language 'boob' – and what a chortler it was! I picked a delicious-looking scone, and began to spread a goodly portion of home-made jam from one of the jars before me. Purely to make polite conversation, I said in my 'best' French, 'This is the first jam we've seen in France', and for 'jam' I used the word 'preservatif', thinking of our English word 'preserves' … and there was instant silence at that, as I saw two women clap their hands to their mouths in apparent horror, while others appeared decidedly embarrassed. Realising that I'd obviously said something wrong, I pointed at the jam jar and asked 'Preservatif?'

Immediately, the frozen looks changed to smiles and even giggles, while the lady sitting next to me said, 'Non, non – c'est la confiture!' I felt my face getting warm as I blushed, but I nodded and thanked her for the correction, although it wasn't until the next day that I found out precisely what I'd said, that had caused all the embarrassment.

For now, we continued with the 'celebration', trying to eat and answer all the questions at the same time. I told Monsieur Delains – the old man who'd welcomed us – of our plan to reach Switzerland, and of our promised visit to Madame Fouchon at Traves that night.

'Bon!' he agreed. 'She and her daughter, Madame Haste, are very nice people. They will indeed look after you.'

So the meal continued, with everyone talking (even the lads could now manage a few basic words and phrases), although for my part I was trying not to eat too much, thinking ahead to our next stop at Traves, and the probability that there would be yet another 'feast' awaiting us there!

Eventually, it all wound down and came to an end, and I'm sure that if I hadn't told M. Delains of our promised visit to Madame Fouchon, they would have kept us much longer. It seemed that she and her daughter were held in high regard in this village and, with another short speech from M. Delains, then handshakes from the men and kisses from many of the women, we left the good people of Ovanches.

The horses and cart were produced yet again, and they took us back to the woods, there to wait the coming of darkness. Amid further 'Adieus' and 'Bonne chance!' calls, they clattered back from whence they came, leaving us to slowly ease our over-stuffed bodies down among the trees, there to doze off in short naps. What a day – and it wasn't over yet!

We waited until it was almost fully dark, then groaned as we stood to make our way down the road into Traves. We didn't hurry – we were too full to make any pace above a stroll, anyway – and Madame Fouchon was waiting for us as we reached her garden. She looked a little worried as she unlatched the gate for us to enter.

'I thought something had happened to you!' she exclaimed – but when I explained the cause of our delay, she smiled and simply said, 'Très gentiles, les Ovanches.'

Inside the house we met her daughter, Madame Haste, a tall, attractive woman, who greeted us in perfect English, much to our delight. Of course, I had to congratulate her on her excellent English skills, but she laughed and said, 'I see my mother didn't tell you – my husband is English, although he has worked in France for many years.'

When I rather tentatively asked her where he was, she said bitterly, 'He is in Germany, working as a labourer. He is an accountant, but I think the Germans deliberately humiliate such clever people by making them labourers.' He was only allowed to write to her once a month. 'Just like being a prisoner of war, he is in a labour camp. But enough of that,' she said abruptly, 'you must be ready for something to eat?' We explained why we were in no hurry, and she laughed and told us, 'We can wait, also – in fact, it is just as well.'

She told us of a tradition that I'd almost forgotten occurred in some cultures. Apparently one of the villagers had just died, and it was the local custom for everyone in the village to visit the house of the deceased to pay their respects on the day before the funeral. This could go on until quite late in the evening, and Madame Fouchon had already decided that we should not leave their house until about midnight to minimise the risk of contact or confrontation with anyone else.

'The less people who know about your presence here, the better,' she said – and we wholeheartedly agreed with her.

'I thought it was only the Irish who went visiting before funerals?' I commented.

'And I thought we were the only morbid ones!' she laughed again, adding 'Now, I'm sure that we have plenty to talk about before we eat', before leading us into a spacious and very well appointed lounge. We soon saw that my earlier guess about them being quite wealthy had been right, for everything about the room confirmed that first impression – and that was further confirmed when there came a subtle knock on the lounge door and we all turned as their maid, Marie, arrived to serve us drinks!

When Marie had left the room, Madame Fouchon bade us all to sit, and we soon found that we had plenty to talk about. What a pleasure I found it to speak in English once more, and the boys really opened up and enjoyed being able to join in the conversation for a change, and with Madame Haste acting as interpreter we all had a 'right good natter', as Bradley later called it.

We had to relate our story, of course, and they were both very interested – and congratulatory. When I told them about the Germans that we had encountered at the bridge at Rimacourt, they laughed loudly.

'You were very lucky there,' said Madame Haste. 'It's a wonder they didn't just shoot you!'

As if our comparatively opulent surroundings and the inhouse presence of their maid weren't enough to confirm their wealth, she told us that this was their country house; they had a larger house in Paris, which they were letting to friends, and visited it only occasionally.

'Paris is a terrible place right now,' said Madame Haste, shaking her head.

We talked on, changing subject smoothly from one thing to another, and Madame Haste and her mother were actually quite anxious to know how we were coping in Britain. Madame Haste's husband still had relations in England, and they were understandably having difficulties in keeping in touch with them. We were able to reassure them that, despite Hitler's early success at driving out the British Expeditionary Force and its Allies, we were nevertheless fighting hard and still very sure of eventual victory.

'And of course,' chimed in Madame Fouchon, 'we always have the brave RAF!'

We all raised our glasses to that, and Marie returned to tell us that dinner was ready. We trooped into the dining room, feeling sure that there would be something special – and true enough, we couldn't have wished for anything more appetising! Sparing all the details, the pièce de résistance was undoubtedly a separate course of what I believe was a lamb cutlet. It was absolutely delicious, and the rest of the meal was only scarcely less tasty. There were also a couple of bottles of excellent-quality wine. 'We managed to hide quite a bit of it,' said Madame Fouchon, with a sly wink and a smile.

Marie then joined in the 'fun'. She was a pert, pretty girl in her early twenties, I should say, and she was obviously enjoying the change of company. I assumed that she had done the cooking – at least, she accepted our congratulations with a very becoming modesty – and she did all the serving, but she flirted outrageously with the boys while Madame Fouchon smiled indulgently. I rather fancy that Marie was regarded as one of the family, rather than just a faithful employee.

At last, it was all done and cleared away – and I might say that I, at least, had just managed to struggle through the dessert – and then Madame Haste went to the sideboard and produced a bottle of dark red wine.

'Now, for something very special,' she announced. 'This is a blackberry wine that we made when France surrendered, and we swore that we would only open it when the first British soldiers came this way. We think that this is the right occasion for it!' She pulled the cork, glasses were filled, and we solemnly toasted France, England and victory – and then Madame Fouchon had the last word by adding, 'And for your safe return, my friends!'

A great day indeed!

Now, though – even though our sated stomachs were trying to drop us all into a deep sleep – we had to think of getting on. Before dinner, we'd told them of our adventures thus far and further plans, and now we were hoping for some additional help. I was rather surprised to find that they had no map of a scale large enough to assist us, so – using our little emergency map (which, by the way, had almost 'run out' on us) we plotted our way as far as we could, with Madame Fouchon offering snippets of information from what little she knew of our intended route.

'I see your next target point is Baume-les-Dames,' observed Madame Haste. 'It is a good-sized town with a population of about 5,000 people, and you will have to be extra careful there, as you will have to cross a bridge to get into it. There is a German barracks at the far end, and there is no way to get around the outskirts of the town so you will have to go right through. On the north side are the foothills of the Jura mountains, and on the south, there is no way across the river until you reach Besançon, and that is a larger town.'

So that was the bad news. …

'However, there is a curfew in force in all towns, so if you are very careful, I am sure that you will be all right.' She smiled her encouragement at that, then continued with one more warning. 'You will soon be getting near to the frontier,' she said, 'and so you can expect to see many more Germans.'

She and her mother had made a parcel of food, as had the good people of Ovanches, so we wouldn't starve for a day or two. More important still, she produced a French–English dictionary 'From my school days', she told us.

I immediately looked up the word that I had used for 'jam', as spread on that scone at Ovanches – and at once, to my immense mortification, I discovered the reason for the ladies' embarrassment: 'preservatif' in French meant 'contraceptive'! No wonder their faces had turned vivid shades of pink, and that they wondered what I was trying to say! A peculiar attempt at a compliment, indeed.

The lads, evidently puzzled by my huge grin and reddening face, just had to be told – and as I expected, they all roared with laughter, and so the ladies had to be told too; Marie, in particular, thought it a huge joke and absolutely squealed with laughter, triggering more from the rest of us. A good high note indeed, upon which to close the evening.

All too soon it was time to leave the big house amid happy tears, hugs and best wishes, and with Marie leading the way to keep us on the right track, we tiptoed through Traves as quiet as mice. When we emerged at the other end of the village, Marie pointed out which direction we should take, and she insisted on another kiss and a hug with each of us – and then, tearfully, she turned away, and we were on our own once again.

Chapter 8

No names

None of us was feeling very energetic; after all, we'd just eaten as much food in one day as we'd been used to having over three or four days. We plodded on, with frequent rests, and I reckon that that must have been the shortest distance that we had ever covered in one night. We'd gone almost a full day without any sleep, too, so maybe we had a genuine excuse for our sluggishness. By morning, we found another good spot – as usual, in a wood – and spent most of the next day sleeping quite heavily, each of us struggling to maintain the 'watch' stints with heavy eyelids. We were very mindful of Madame Haste's warning of the increase, now, in German personnel.

On the second night, fully refreshed and confident that we were on the right road for Baume-les-Dames, we kept up a steady and fairly brisk pace, eventually finding a signpost giving the distance to the town as 2 kilometres. It was still dark but not far from the break of dawn, so we left the road and prospected around until we found a clump of tress that seemed ideal for us, well covered but far enough from the road to be safe from prying eyes.

The day passed very slowly. We could hear a fair bit of traffic from the road, but careful sorties – first by Beecroft and myself, and then by Crighton and Hanwell – established that there was very little motorised traffic but, better than that, there had been no sign of Germans.

As dusk fell once more, we made our way cautiously to the bridge that we had been told was the only way into town, then found a 'hide' among some trees from where we could observe any comings and goings. But all traffic had ceased now, with only an occasional pedestrian crossing the bridge, and each one seemed to be hurrying – probably to beat the curfew, we guessed – although we still hadn't seen any sign of Germans to enforce it.

Eventually, we reached the point on our road watch where we hadn't seen a soul for nearly an hour, so we decided that it would most likely be safe enough for us to carry on.

It was quite uncanny seeing this sizeable town, yet there was no sound, no movement and not a single light to be seen anywhere. We decided to split up into groups of two and three, so if any alarm was raised, it would be each man for himself; five single men breaking off in several directions would stand a better chance of getting away than a group of five held by even a single armed German guard.

Crighton and I went first, stepping very carefully indeed as we found our footsteps across the bridge echoed alarmingly amid that eerie silence. As soon as we reached the shadows of the first two houses – a street of five two-storey residences – the others were set to follow on so that our two groups would be about 200yds apart as we walked on through the hushed town, stifling the urge to actually tiptoe through, almost holding our breaths as our eyes darted this way and that. My heart thumped in my chest with each yard that we paced.

Still nothing stirred, and we were beginning to think that this was going to be 'another piece of cake' when the silence was shattered by the roar of a motorbike starting up; it made us both nearly jump almost out of our skins! However, it was some way ahead of us, and we had no trouble in quickly finding hiding places. Crighton and I slid into a narrow alley between two houses, and when we peered around the corner of the wall and looked back, there was no sign of the others; they, too, had 'gone to earth', as the saying goes.

The sound increased as the motorbike grew nearer and I ducked back into the alley, my heart absolutely racing as I feared discovery; I could just about see the dread on Alec's face, too, even in this deep shadow – and then the roar of the engine rose sharply then fell as the machine passed the end of the alley, and we saw that it was a German motorcycle and sidecar combination, with both the rider and passenger calmly sitting there with their rifles slung casually across their backs, for all the world appearing to be on a night ride down to the local bar!

Were they just 'doing the rounds' to enforce the curfew, or perhaps going to check the bridge? There was no way that we could safely find out, so we gave them about five minutes (which seemed more like half an hour to us, in that alley!) before we dared to put our heads out to take a good look around. Peace had returned, and after a slow and careful look up and down the street, we emerged from the alley, looking back toward where we believed the others had hidden – and sure enough, they, too, stepped out of the darkness to follow us.

We carried on as before, keeping to the shadows and making as little noise as possible, but our nerves were as tight as harp strings even as we made steady progress. That was our only scare, however, and in less than an hour we realised that the number of houses were thinning out, and before much longer we had left behind the last one; we had thankfully passed through the town and were walking back as a group again, too uptight to chat but immensely relieved.

There was a new handicap now, though – our map had 'run out'! All we could do was to head as near to a south-easterly direction as we could manage, with roads that jinked in all the wrong-seeming directions. From this point we knew that we would have to become even more dependent upon the goodwill of the French people, and just hope that somebody might give us a map to see us safely to Switzerland.

We plodded onwards, keeping to the roads and seeking out signposts where possible and using our compasses at other times; our eyes and ears were always open for any signs of people. We knew we weren't far from the Swiss border now and, as Madame Haste had warned us, it was quite likely that anyone that we might encounter could be German rather than French.

However, all remained quiet, and eventually as dawn once more began to break the eastern skies, we carried out our habitual safe-haven search. Now our luck appeared to be running out; we were on what appeared to be a minor road with hedges on both sides, but behind those hedges was nothing but open fields! No woods, no sign of houses, barns or even people – so while it was still barely half-light, we decided to push on further, knowing that we just had to find a hiding place very soon.

In no time at all – so it seemed to us – it was broad daylight, and we finally saw what looked like a small village about half a mile ahead. It turned out to be more of a hamlet than a village, containing just a handful of scattered houses and other buildings. Almost miraculously, at the same time as we saw the hamlet, we came across a very narrow cart track running off to our left – leading to a farm perhaps? We decided to investigate, and trudged carefully along the ruts, wondering what we might find.

Just then we heard the sound of a rapidly approaching vehicle, but before we could do anything like dive through the hedges, a blue van appeared on the cart track, heading directly at us! With a squealing of brakes the lone occupant pulled up beside us – looking somewhat alarmed for a moment – and exited his van to challenge us; he was a red-faced, burly individual who squinted at us one by one, deep suspicion in his eyes – after all, he probably wouldn't often meet five scruffy looking strangers on such tracks as these!

'Que fait-vous ici?' he demanded quite sharply.

Now was the time to exercise my charm once more – and some newly learned French! I quickly explained who we were, and then I unbuttoned my civilian coat to show him my uniform beneath – then suddenly he grinned, and without further ado he led us to the rear of his van, opened the doors and ushered us inside, telling us not to talk. Naturally, we were very reluctant to trust this complete stranger at first contact, and we held back, glancing at one another as he frowned, perhaps realising our fears.

He smiled again, and held out his hands, palms facing us. 'Friend,' he said, evidently trying his hardest to reassure us.

We looked at each other, then Beecroft murmured 'Why not take the chance, lads?' With that, he gestured to the driver and stepped into the back of the van, sliding forward to allow the rest of us to join him. I glanced at the others, shrugged, and we clambered inside. The driver kept nodding and waving his hands in what he obviously felt was an encouraging manner, then slammed the doors shut, returned to his seat and drove along the track, taking us back to the road. It was a bumpy ride through those ruts, but we reached smoother tarmac very quickly and the ride became much calmer, although no slower.

'I hope he's friendlier than he looks!' Hanwell said into my ear, cupping his hands so that the driver wouldn't hear him – but whether our 'saviour' was a friend or not, there was nothing we could do about it now except pray that he wouldn't just drive into a checkpoint or guardhouse and hand us over.

We rattled and bounced down the road in the direction of the village, and after only five minutes or so, we felt the van slow slightly then run on to rough ground – and then it stopped. The engine died, there was the sound of the driver's door creaking open, and then the back doors opened and the driver stood there grinning in bright sunlight. We were fearful there might have been a German reception committee awaiting us, but there was just a large hut at the edge of a field, trees lining all around – and the hut door stood wide open, waiting for us.

'Vite! Vite!' he urged us, as we clambered out of the van and followed him into the hut – and then after closing the door, he turned and smiled again, exclaiming, 'RAF! Bon! Bon!' and vigorously shook hands with each of us in turn, more enthusiastically than anyone we had previously met.

Well, that settled any doubts that we had been harbouring, so all we had to do now was to introduce ourselves more formally – he told us that his name was Monsieur Joubert – and then we explained our position and intention, and hoped that he would be able to help us, somehow. I was able to put our request for assistance far easier than before, as by now my French language skills had progressed in quite a leap, following that 'banquet' and interaction with the good folks of Ovanches – and, of course, Madame Haste's very useful dictionary!

For his part, M. Joubert told us that he ran a light haulage business – much smaller, since those damned Germans had come along! – and that this hut was his storage warehouse. We looked about, then, and saw that the hut was quite a large one, and at the far end were quite a number of packages of various sizes.

'They have to be delivered this morning,' he said. 'I shall return at noon, then we can discuss what I can do to help you!' He produced some biscuits and milk, then packed the van and was ready to go. He refused our offers of help with this last task, saying (sensibly) that we must not be seen. He locked the door as he went out, assuring us that he would return with something more substantial to eat – and true to his promise, he returned just after midday, carrying a milk churn and a large parcel containing bread, meat and cheese. We tucked in hungrily. From a cupboard he produced a spotless white enamelled bucket that he filled with the milk from the churn. From the same cupboard came fine glasses, then a cardboard carton that contained jars of honey. We watched, fascinated, as he emptied several of the jars into the milk, gave it a good stir with a monster spoon, then sat down, beaming.

'Voila, mes braves!' he exclaimed, 'c'est très, très bon!' and he was absolutely right – it tasted delicious!

We chatted for a while until he had to go to work again, and we told him of our hopes of reaching Switzerland and safety.

'Not very far now,' he told us, 'about 40 kilometres from here – but much more dangerous now, as many Boche soldiers guard the frontiers.'

'Is there no resistance organisation around here?' I asked him, 'or the Underground?'

'I know of the Maquis,' he confirmed, 'but I have never heard of even a whisper of them in this area. The Underground, as you call it, belongs in the bigger towns and cities, I think. It is dangerous to ask about these things in this region, but I shall see if I can find out anything for you, today.'

That seemed to put paid to any hopes we may have had of finding any form of organised help. I must say that having travelled so far virtually on our own, and as not one person along the way had suggested even the possibility of such a body of people, it was at best a faint hope for us. France had been occupied for more than two years now, and the dangers of starting 'resistance' groups were only too obvious.

M. Joubert went off again in his van, and we were left to speculate on how we should proceed from now on. I must admit that our ideas of what we should meet as we neared the frontier itself were vague in the extreme. Would there be sentry posts on the roads? On the bridges? Guard dogs? Heavily armed patrols? We would have to wait and see.

It seemed that we must depend entirely on the continued goodwill of the local inhabitants. Up until now we had been extremely fortunate – but would the extra vigilance by the Germans upon the local populace affect and frighten the French into refusing us assistance? We hoped not, obviously, but everything would be heightened guesswork on our part, and we soon decided that all that we could do would be to sit tight where we were, and hope that M. Joubert might bring us a little more information and hope.

It was nearly seven o'clock in the evening when he returned, and we

were a little dismayed that he didn't have any such good news or information for us. He'd evidently had to be very careful and subtle with his
enquiries, of course, but whenever he'd steered any conversations around
to 'resistance' or 'Maquis', nobody would admit to knowing anything.
Although they hadn't any posters up as we had back home – like 'Careless
Talk Costs Lives' – this was obviously the local policy. All this 'news' we
received from M. Joubert was by dint of much questioning, delving
into the dictionary, and – on his part – considerable gesticulation.

We were beginning to feel almost depressed, when he produced
another of his beaming smiles.

'But,' he said, pausing dramatically, 'I think we can still help you!' He
glanced at each of us in turn to check that he had our full attention, then
he nodded and slapped his knees. 'I have a cousin who works at Belfort,
in a factory. He is on the night shift just now, and tonight he will call here
and collect you on his way there, to where a friend will meet you and
take you to a farm where the patron is eager to help. He will look after
you then!'

The crafty devil had fooled us – but we were delighted, and we congratulated him on the trouble he must have taken to make such
preparations.

'We French may be down,' he added, 'but we are not out!'

So, feeling much happier now from his news, we ate our last meal there,
and sat down to wait for cousin Georges.

He turned up on a bicycle at about 8.30, and introductions were
made with the now familiar mixture of French and English chat and sign
language. As soon as it was dark, we said a cheerful 'Thanks and good-
bye' to Monsieur Joubert, and set off with the usual calls of 'Bonne chance,
mes amis!'

Georges pushed his bike and walked along beside me, with the others
straggling along behind us. We didn't talk much for fear of being heard
by hidden Germans or others, but when things seemed clear enough, I
managed to convey to him a brief potted account of our adventures so
far. He was very keen to tell me about the factory at Belfort, where he worked;
they had built bicycles there before the war, but were now producing
motorbikes and small engineering parts.

'Why haven't the RAF bombed it?' he asked me. 'Not a single bomb has dropped here – you must tell them when you get home,' he urged.

I promised to do just that, and we fell quiet. After about two hours of walking, we parted company at a crossroads, Georges to go onto Belfort, while we were joined by our next contact – a furtive chap all dressed in black, who said almost nothing but managed to impress upon us that we should make as little noise as possible; he then set a brisk pace almost on tiptoe, and we glanced at one another, struggling not to chuckle at this sudden heightening of 'drama' as we clumped along behind him in our boots.

After another hour of steady walking, he turned off the road and led us down very narrow, rough country lanes for some time. Eventually he escorted us across two fields until we reached what appeared to be a very large farmhouse, where we were met by 'le patron' and his family. 'No names, no – how do you say – "introductions"?' Our black-dressed guide told us. 'It will be safer if they don't know your names – and that you do not know theirs, in case you are caught and questioned.' He was telling us something that we already knew only too well, but nevertheless, as he took his leave, the farmer gave a wry smile and shook his head, then he and his family made us welcome and gave us a good meal. After this, we were established in the usual barn for the rest of the night-time hours. After a restless night, as daylight came we could hear the now familiar sounds of a farm coming to life. Le patron came in to see us.

'You must stay in here for the day,' he told us. 'There should not be any Germans around, but be ready to hide if you hear or see any. There is plenty of straw in here. Tonight, we shall take you almost to the frontier,' he said, then off he went without further ado, and we settled down to another, occasionally tense, day.

A good deal of time was spent arranging the hay bales and piles into isolated 'cubby holes' with the intention of diving into them to hide, should the need arise; I doubt if they would have been very effective – especially if anyone searched with a pitchfork or a bayonet! – but it kept us busy for a while at least. The patron's wife and daughters appeared twice during the day to bring us food and drink, and were the cause of nervous moments when the barn doors rattled, and we all jumped like scared rabbits each time. Once our nerves had settled back down, we ate quietly, and they stayed for a little chat. There was something that felt quite odd in this farm – perhaps it was just that we now knew how close we were to our goal, and were each conscious of a greater perception of imminent failure. But all we could do was wait, hope, and pray that we would remain in safe hands.

The day passed slowly, but as soon as it was dark the patron returned and took us to their kitchen, where a good meal was prepared for us. While we ate, he told us all that he could about the dangers of trying to reach Switzerland. He notified us that the border was only about 10 kilometres from their farm, and that at that point the River Doubs formed the frontier. All bridges were, of course, heavily guarded, and the Germans maintained strong patrols along the riverbank.

He apologised for not being able to give us more information, but all he could reveal was that the river ran through a deep, heavily forested valley – and that anyone caught near the river itself would be running a very big risk of being shot on sight. This was something that we had all anticipated, of course, but hearing it from him sent a shiver down my spine, and we all exchanged brief, anxious looks before returning our attention to what he was saying.

'We're taking you to a farmer whose place is at the top of the valley. He may be able to help you more.'

With that, we all stood ready to go, thanking his wife and daughters for their meal – and then we set out on what I shall always remember as the most dramatic part of our long journey. The patron led the way, and as soon as we reached the road, he ordered us into single file with himself at the head, and his son bringing up the rear.

He impressed upon us the need for absolute silence where possible – no talking, and to tread carefully – and off we paced. We walked on the right-hand side of the road, along a broad grassed verge bordering a wide, deep ditch and a well-kept hedge on the other side of that. It was a cloudy night, so it was darker and therefore visibility was relatively poor, and our slow progress reminded me irresistibly of films I'd seen in which the 'heroes' had been either escaping or attacking something, always in great secrecy (yet with dramatically loud backing music!), and a brooding sense of danger everywhere.

In front of us, the patron strode confidently, wearing a long black cloak that reached his ankles; the cloak was topped by a pointed hood that made him seem as though he was about 7ft tall – and to complete the sinister picture he carried a long staff as though he was a monk on a pilgrimage, and his son – at the rear of our 'column' – was similarly garbed.

Striding along – with hardly a sound except that of our feet swish-swishing on the grass verge – to us the sense of imminent danger was very acute. We carried on for another hour or so – then, with only a quick 'Pssst!' over his shoulder to warn us, the patron dived sideways and rolled into the ditch! Automatically we all followed suit, our hearts in our mouths, and we all lay there scarcely daring to breath and wondering, What on earth?

Gradually we became aware of rattles and squeaks approaching, then German voices – and then two German soldiers clattered past us on rusty bicycles, their rifles slung across their backs, chatting away cheerfully as they passed us by. If only they had known! After a few moments, the patron got to his feet and signalled for us to continue.

So on we trudged again, ever more fearful in the deathly silence – and it struck me (a little late) just how lucky we had been that the ditch had been bone dry!

More than an hour passed again before we turned off the road on to a rutted cart track that eventually brought us to yet another farm. Our guide – the patron – introduced us to the owner, then told us that our latest host would show us a safe route down to the river the next day, and then, with the now-familiar good wishes, he and his son set off on their long trek back home.

Our latest host didn't impress me very much; in fact, I would go so far as to say that he made us all more than a little worried about him, as he talked very little and seemed far more anxious than the situation warranted. There was something about his demeanour that instilled an unsettling nervousness among us; however, we obviously had no choice but to trust this very twitchy chap.

I tried to find out from him how the border patrols were arranged, but he seemed to know almost nothing about it. He confirmed that the River Doubs formed the border between France and Switzerland with no 'overlap' areas either side that might catch us out, but when I asked how deep the river might be, and how we could expect to cross it, he simply shrugged and then mimed swimming motions.

'No boats,' he told us – only the Germans were allowed to have and use boats. And, suddenly, it dawned devastatingly upon me – neither Crighton nor I could swim! We'd discussed this point on one or two occasions, and the other three had dismissed the question with an airy 'No problem, we'll see you over all right' – but now that we were so very close to our goal, and although Alec and I exchanged nervous glances, there really was no point in worrying about it at that moment; we just had to get to the river and see what would happen – and pray we'd get across, somehow!

We were installed, as usual, in one of our host's barns. He told us that he'd call us at first light, and we settled down to try to sleep until then. Now that we were at last within sight of our goal, I had to admit to a certain tightness in my stomach, and it was obvious that the others felt the same – they, like me, found it almost impossible to sleep.

Time passed at an absolutely interminable crawl. At last, however, we heard a clunk, and we all stirred as the barn door began to creak open, then the farmer softly called, 'Messieurs! C'est le matin!', although it was still pitch dark outside.

We rose somewhat groggily, had a quick wash at a hand-pump, then joined the farmer in his kitchen for a breakfast of fried eggs and home-made bread. The farmer and his wife were evidently very much on edge, and there was little attempt at conversation as in our previous halts. I glanced out of the window, and the farmer took that as a cue to stand, looking obviously relieved.

'Vous êtes prêts, Messieurs?' ('Are you ready gentlemen?') – and with that, he led us outside as the first faint hint of dawn began to lighten the sky to the east. Each of us barely had time to express our thanks to his wife as we left the house – and then we were taking a very brisk march along a narrow path, struggling to keep up with the farmer for a short distance.

Almost immediately we turned off the path and began to thread our way across fields and along hedgerows until we could see, about half a mile ahead, a forest that seemed to spread right across the horizon. Our host was still looking very nervous and maintained a taciturn silence. Soon we reached the edge of the forest and followed a well-worn path, apparently leading right into the centre. After just a quarter of an hour, however, our guide stopped, then turned to us, a finger placed over his lips. Using his hands to express a 'slow down' motion, he carried on much more carefully, his head swinging left and right as the tension among us was reaching an almost unbearable level. He stopped again, signalled us to gather around, and pointed ahead. Through the gaps in the trees, we could then see that a road ran through the forest, right across our path. Our guide turned to me and leaned close to my ear, then spoke almost in a whisper.

'You must cross the road into the forest on the other side. The path through the trees is level for about half a kilometre, then goes down – très escarpé! [very steep!],' he voiced, indicating his meaning by tipping his hand downwards, 'until at the bottom, you will reach the river. Switzerland is on the other side of that – we must be very, very careful now!'

Moving on once more, he halted us just before we reached the road, indicating rather melodramatically that we should wait while he went forward to scout alone. We watched him creep to the edge of the tree-line, then make a great show of looking left and right along the road – and suddenly he turned back to us and flapped his hands in a frantic beckoning motion, urging us forward.

'Vite! Vite!' he hissed as we stepped past him, each of us scanning both ways as we stepped on to the rough tarmac and scudded across to the other side. I turned back, thinking that he would run across and join us, but I was dismayed to see him give us a thumbs-up gesture, then a brief wave 'Adieu!' – and he disappeared into the blackness, back the way we'd come. He was obviously very relieved to be rid of his 'burden', and who could blame him? By this time we could really appreciate the huge risks that our French helpers had been taking, made ever more acute as we neared the Swiss frontier. But now, we realised, we were very much on our own.

Silently, fumbling and stumbling a little in the almost total blackness in that forest, we pressed ever onwards, taking care to follow the path – luckily without losing our way even once – and sure enough, the path grew steeper and steeper until we were each grabbing trees, branches, shrubs and anything else that would keep us from slipping and falling down the rest of the slope, while at the same trying to keep our noise of

Jack Love.
(All photographs are from the author's collection.)

Bomber Command observer Jack Love.

Jack's first 101 Squadron crew, mainly Canadian: Pilot Al Moran, Front Gunner Bob Oxendale, Wireless Operator Jake Daniels, Rear Gunner Pat Wade, Second Pilot unknown trainee.

Unfortunately a rather degraded photograph of the D-Donald Crew. From left to right are Front Gunner Henry Hanwell, Rear Gunner Alec Crighton, Wireless Operator 'Brad' Bradley, Pilot 'Willie' Williams, Observer Jack Love.

Front Gunner Henry Hanwell

Pilot John Beecroft

(Above) Navigator's 'office' inside the 'Loch Ness' Wellington, N2980 'R-Robert' at Brooklands Museum. (Below) Astrodome/upper escape hatch, N2980 'R-Robert'.

(Above) Watch tower at Stalag Luft I (Below) Stalag Luft I

(Above) Sports field, Stalag Luft III. (Below) Sagan 1942 – Camp leaders Day, Massey, Deans.

Warrant Officer Bristow's steam boat, Stalag Luft III, 1942.

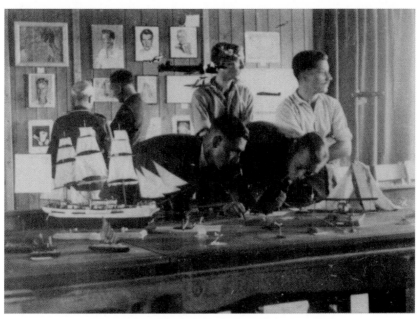

NCO's arts and crafts exhibition, Stalag Luft III, August 1942.

New theatre, Stalag Luft III, 1942.

'Bums on Broadway', Stalag Luft III, 1942.

Frank Hunt's Orchestra Concert, Stalag Luft III, February 1943.

Grand Christmas panto poster, Stalag Luft III, 1942.

NCO's Panto 'Aladdin', Stalag Luft III, January 1943.

'For the Love of Mike', Stalag Luft III, March 1943.

'Girls, Girls, Girls', Stalag Luft III, March 1943.

'Merchant of Venice', Stalag Luft III, April 1943.

'Girls, Girls, Girls', Stalag Luft III, March 1943.

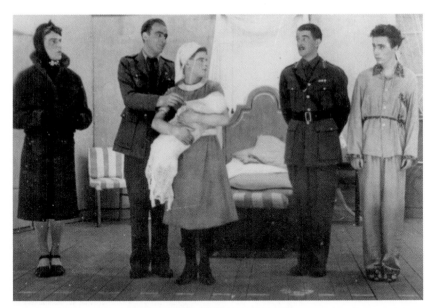

'Home and Beauty', Stalag Luft III, April 1943.

'Home and Beauty', Stalag Luft III, April 1943.

'Thru' the Music Sheet', Stalag Luft III, June 1943. Jack Love far right.

'Thru' the Music Sheet', Stalag Luft III, June 1943. Jack Love indicated by the arrow.

The Institute of Book-keepers
LIMITED (BY GUARANTEE)

INCORPORATED 20TH SEPTEMBER 1916

This is to Certify that

J. P. Love

of

Stalag 357

has been successful in passing the

ASSOCIATES' EXAMINATION

in

Commercial Arithmetic

Held on the **7th December, 1944**

Given, at London, on this **Sixteenth** day of **March, 1945.**

Members of
the Council

Secretary

This Certificate does NOT, in itself, entitle the candidate to membership of the Institute, or to use the Initials A.B.I.

Commercial Arithmetic certificate awarded to Jack Love at Stalag 357, Heydekrug.

Reunion in Cambridge, October 1990: Henry Hanwell, John Beecroft, and Jack Love being interviewed by Tony Scase of Anglia TV News.

Forty-eight years after they left on their fateful operation, the surviving crew members on a return visit to the now-derelict Sergeants' Mess at their old base at Bourn, Cambridgeshire, October 1990. (Left to right) Henry Hanwell, John Beecroft, and Jack Love.

passage as quiet as possible as we had no idea what we'd find (or meet) when we reached the bottom of the pathway. Eventually the ground levelled out – and, cheeringly, the heartening sound of gurgling water caught our ears, then at last we could see the river glittering between the trees ahead.

And what a river it was! This was no peaceful, quiet, fordable stream, but a raging torrent about 200yd wide at that point, racing by at great speed! More than a little shocked by this, we all decided to follow the riverbank northward in the hope of finding something that might increase our chances of safely crossing it. At this juncture, I had to ask Beecroft, Hanwell and Bradley if they truthfully fancied their chances of helping Crighton and me across between them, and they were quite emphatic that they would manage; I had my doubts, though – they could swim, certainly, but they were no cross-Channel heroes. Poor Brad had also been suffering from a stinking summer cold for the past few days and he was puffing and panting a little with exertion due to his breathing passages being blocked as a result, so he wasn't in the best of fitness to help Alec and myself.

We walked on slowly and very carefully, mindful of the possibility of German patrols. But quite soon it seemed that our crossing prayers were answered – as we rounded a bend in the river, to our great delight we saw what looked like a 'boom' of logs stretched right across from the French banks to the Swiss side of the river! It was bent in a huge curve, indicating the strength of the river current – but, hardly able to believe our eyes, we rushed right up to it. For once, I cast aside my reputation for being the cool man of the crew and plunged straight into the river in my sudden desire to break away to freedom, only to find that the riverbed shelved quite quickly away from the bank. I went in straight over my head, and came up spluttering and scrabbling for the chain between the logs! So much for cool, calm and collected. I managed to scramble back to the shallows, then grinned stupidly at the others as they rolled their eyes at me Then I started out again, this time much more carefully.

My idea had been to simply straddle the first log I could reach, and to see if we could cross the river using this method from log to log. I reached out, grasped the first roll of wood and tried to haul myself up and over – but the next thing I knew was that I was once more splashing wildly in the water, inverted as the wood had rotated, and I was fighting desperately to regain a footing on the riverbed as the current pulled hard at me. I managed to grip the linking chain again, and with a last supreme effort I heaved myself over one of the logs. Even so, as soon as I tried to sit upright, 'splash!' – I went back in again! Somehow, gasping for breath and almost pulling my shoulders out of their sockets, I contrived to haul myself upright on the riverbed once more and staggered back to the shallows as the others stood open-mouthed, at first too shocked to haul me out.

Beecroft was the first to move and grab my arm, but as he steadied me, I said to him, 'It's OK now, Skip – just hang on until I see what's what, here.'

I soon found two reasons for my near-catastrophe; first of all, the logs were so slimy that it was impossible to grasp them – rather like the old 'greasy pole' pillow-fight game – and therefore just as impossible to sit still on them, let alone try to move forward. To make things even more difficult, the chains between the logs were about 2ft long and secured each end by swivelling eyes that would allow the logs the ability to roll fully without ever binding the chains. To complete that little picture, the chains were also so slimy that it was very tough to keep even a temporary grip, even if anyone could traverse the gaps between the logs; a dastardly design, indeed!

I struggled back to the riverbank, squelching and dripping water everywhere as I slopped to a halt beside the lads. We conferred, rather unhappily, over the next step to take; for once, no bright ideas were offered and I felt thoroughly miserable as I carried on dripping water, soaked to the skin and beginning to shiver …until I had another bright idea!

'I wonder' I said aloud to the others, waiting as they turned to look at me, 'if we can secure ourselves to these last couple of logs, then perhaps we can somehow disconnect the chain from this end, then the current should swing us all across to the other side?'

They became rather excited by the idea, and we all set about inspecting the anchor point in earnest, seeking out a weakness in the chain links or the huge ring-bolt set in a concrete block. But we were soon dismayed by the discovery that it would take either explosives, a flame-cutter or a huge effort and many hours with a good hacksaw to cut through either the chain or that anchoring ring. I could see the disappointment on the others' faces, and felt their pain quite deeply. This was beginning to look very grim indeed.

The log chain seemed out of the question now as a means to cross; the only other possible way that we might stand even a faint chance of using them might be if we'd had lumberjack spikes or something like them – but of course, we couldn't even improvise one set here, never mind five.

Once again I asked the others if they really felt that they were strong enough swimmers to be able to help Alec and myself over, and they finally admitted – rather shamefacedly – that they had little hope of towing us two between them across such a wide, fast-flowing obstacle as this river was. It was obvious to me that whatever pride and confidence they'd had in their swimming prowess had evaporated at the sight of me floundering in the water. Even being able to swim, none of them suggested they might be able to use the logs in some way to help, and Brad was showing signs of fear at the prospect of swimming that torrent in his current physical state, snuffling as he was.

Alec and I looked at each other speculatively.

'Well,' I said, 'short of taking time to try to find a long rope somewhere, then stealing it and asking you three to swim over and then pull us across – and that's hardly likely – there seems to be only one realistic choice: you three can swim across without us, no problem, and Alec and I are not going to stand in your way or hamper you. All right, Alec?' He agreed at once.

'Aye – you lads get along,' he confirmed. 'We've come this far without much trouble, and I'm quite sure we two will think of some way to solve this problem. Go on – get going, lads,' he urged them.

There was only a nominal demur from the three of them – in fact, I couldn't help feeling that they were glad to be relieved of the responsibility of helping us across. Brad protested a little, but in his condition I don't think I would have asked him to help personally anyway; I rather had the impression that the prospect of swimming 200yds in that racing water – even without two non-swimmers in tow – was really beginning to frighten him.

'Right,' I said, taking the lead once more, 'we'll wander up the bank a bit further and see what we can find; you never know – it might be just shallow enough somewhere that we can manage to cross.' I patted Beecroft and Hanwell on their shoulders, then Bradley, and as Alec followed suit, I said, 'Go on, lads – good luck, and we'll see you in Switzerland later!'

The trio swapped glances, then we all shook hands firmly with good grace, and we agreed that it would be a good idea to draw slightly back from the riverbank and start walking in the upstream direction. Alec and I exchanged rueful glances of regret as we turned away, but, as we had already seen, it was simply impossible to try crossing here with the others. We were obviously disappointed at having to split our group up, but remained hopeful that we'd get across to freedom somehow and meet up with them in a warm, friendly Swiss bar for a celebration drink (or more!).

Alec and I set off, and when I cast a last glance back over my shoulder, the other crewmembers had started taking off their outer clothes and stuffing them into the sacks that we'd been carrying for the past few days just for this purpose. They were soon lost to view in the darkness as we carefully picked our way into the trees, trying to be extra vigilant against snapping twigs and general noise.

Climbing a little way up the bank, we turned upstream and moved on, already looking down toward the waters' edge for a hopeful sign of safer crossing – but we were far too casual about it.

Chapter 9

Hande hoch!

Despite being well into the trees, there was just enough light reflecting in from the river to allow us mostly to see where we were carefully placing our feet, although I have to admit that we weren't doing particularly well at quiet progress. Twigs cracked and branches popped dully underfoot as we made very slow progress; we had hardly gone any distance at all from the others – then Crighton ducked slightly as he squinted down at the river and pointed excitedly.

'There, Jack! Maybe a shallow stretch?' he breathed, beginning to move down between two large trees. I followed, trying to watch my footing at the same time as looking where he was headed.

'Halte!' came a sharp cry to our left, and a dog barked so loudly that we instantly dropped to our haunches and froze, terrified. There, emerging from the trees only about 50yds away, were three German soldiers, rifles levelled at us – but as scary as they looked, they weren't as fearsome as the dog that the fourth soldier was barely managing to hold in check on its leash – a huge, snapping, snarling Alsatian!

'Ooh, looks like we've had it now, Jack,' Alec muttered, his eyes like saucers.

'Oh, hell, no!' I replied, my heart sinking like a cold stone in my chest. For just a fleeting instant of desperation, I pondered about taking a sprint and a dive right into the river – but I couldn't even manage a basic dog-paddle, nor could I desert my friend, and the sound of breech bolts being engaged put paid to all such thoughts of 'flight' as one of the Germans yelled again.

'Halte!' he repeated. 'Hande hoch!' The lead soldier whipped out a torch and flicked it on, and we screwed our eyes shut against the glare in our faces as he jabbed it in our direction. Absolutely terrified and thoroughly deflated, we raised our hands and slowly stood upright to face them as they approached us cautiously, the dog growling fit to burst. The soldier snapped, 'Was machst du hier?' – which I guessed meant something like 'What are you doing here?' – then I saw his eyes drop to my opened, still-soggy coat.

He squinted in the poor light, lowered the torch beam – and it took the soldiers just seconds to see our RAF uniforms; they were obviously highly delighted to catch us! They motioned us to move into a wider, lighter space where they began to search us.

'RAF!' they confirmed, one of them pointing at our half-wing badges, and started a rapid dialogue that neither Alec nor I could possibly have any chance of understanding – not even random words – but we did gather that they were very pleased, and we were duly marched off, with the dog still tugging and snarling right behind us, itching to sink its teeth into a piece of prime British 'steak', by the look of it.

We were guided at gunpoint in the direction that Alec and I had been heading – and it struck me then, a line from the old-time melodrama, 'The girl who took the wrong turning'; why, oh why, hadn't we gone the other way?

But we marched on, and after about ten minutes, we came to the very thing that we had been hoping for – a bridge! It simply emphasised still further our plight, however, for it was very heavily guarded, and we could see Swiss soldiers at the other side. I know I felt utterly despondent at that moment as the German bridge guards whistled and catcalled to our captors, who replied in kind, happily, while the Swiss guards watched with interest as we were pushed away from the bridge; I wanted so much just to nudge Alec and run for it – but I knew we wouldn't stand a chance against all those guns, not to mention that damned dog's vicious-looking bared teeth.

At length, we reached the German barracks and were marched into the Kommandant's office. He too, was very cheerful – and no wonder, as we were later told that he and his soldiers had probably earned themselves a two-week bonus of leave for capturing us!

'Aha, my friends,' the Kommandant told us, 'for you, the war is over!' And how right he was! It was a bitterly disappointing end to our great adventure for Alec and myself; a very long march, indeed – almost five weeks to travel nearly 300 miles on foot only to walk straight into the arms of a border patrol at the 'finishing post'.

The Kommandant rattled away in his native language – not one more word of English passed his lips, so we assumed that he'd already exhausted his linguistic maximum with that statement (we were later informed that every British serviceman was greeted with the same phrase upon capture); however, he bade his attending guards to strip us completely for a search, and while we reluctantly complied, he picked up the telephone and seemed to be reporting to his senior officer. After a string of brusque-sounding sentences, he listened for a minute or so, his only barked comments were occasional bursts of just three words – 'Jawohl, Herr Kommandant!'

This went on for a few minutes more while his guards were picking very thoroughly at our clothes, and each time I heard the officer bark his answer, I thought 'Crawler!' and half expected to hear his heels clicking together and for him to snap a salute, such was the edge in his voice!

By this time, Alec and I stood there stark naked – but evidently desperately dangerous-looking characters, because our four guards were still with us, rifles held half-ready across their chests; one at each door, another at the window, the other standing close behind us with that damned dog still grumbling and snarling away (no doubt still sizing up our 'rump steaks' for his tea!).

Finally – to complete the almost farcical scene – the officer snapped 'Heil Hitler!', he and the guards snapped to attention, and he even flicked a salute before hanging up the telephone! How Alec and I managed to keep our faces straight – even though we were at a distinct disadvantage – I will never know. To round things off, he grinned at us, reached into a basin of eggs at the edge of his desk, selected one, cracked it in his teeth and downed the contents in one swallow; I almost choked with mirth.

The officer's English being extremely minimal, he tried us with French, and I soon discovered that his level of fluency in that language was far below even my own modest level. He tried to question us in this halting fashion – and, of course, as trained, I made no attempt to help him along – so he gave up very quickly and sat down with a shrug. After a while of near silence – we two standing there still shivering, as he scratched away with his pen on some very rough-looking paper – we were given back our uniforms, told to get dressed (which we did, very sharply indeed!), and escorted outside as the officer repeated the standard 'For you, ze var iz over!' statement just to hammer the message home.

We were pushed into the back of a truck with two rifle-toting soldiers to guard us – no dog, we were very happy to see – and driven off along a bumpy lane that passed through what appeared to be almost a tunnel of trees, our guards seeming very casual in their attitude to us.

It seemed a perfect moment to flit. 'Best tackled as soon after capture as possible, to cause maximum confusion', our evasion instructor had said. I cast a glance at Alec, then out at the trees, my normal self-caution briefly overridden by a crazy contemplation of overpowering the guards momentarily, then making a dive for it and to just run (if we survived the fall) – but one of the guards was more alert than I'd credited, seemed to pick up my thoughts and swung his rifle around at the ready. Alec's eyes widened as we swapped quick looks, and we both subsided, our hands now raised to placate the guards.

After about half an hour, we droned into what appeared to be quite a large town (we were to discover that this was Besançon) and eventually arrived at a German barracks that had been the local police head-quarters, where we were searched yet again (but only lightly), then briefly questioned to establish our identities. We gave only names, ranks and numbers as per the Geneva Convention, and we were lodged in separate cells and that was when it really hit me, as the door clanged shut and the key was turned, crunching the lock home.

My first time ever in a prison cell, and it was a German one; now I really had time to contemplate what the future might have in store for us, and I began to worry. I found that I had no idea about how prisoners should be treated; would it be hard? Would we be tortured? Would we even be fed? Might we end up as slave labour – or worse, before a firing squad, just to get rid of us? All sorts of ideas and fears buzzed around in my head for too long, and I realised that it was all guesswork – that I knew sweet Fanny Adams about it – and so, as I finally came to that conclusion, I stopped guessing. Being a fairly philosophical type of chap, I came to the inevitable assumption that I'd just have to sit tight and see what happened next – and try to get some sleep, now that the fear was finally subsiding enough and exhaustion was beginning to take hold of me.

As I lay on a very hard so-called 'mattress' (a thin palliasse of stained fabric filled with straw), I couldn't help wondering what had happened to our three crewmates; in the little questioning to which we had been submitted, we had made no mention of the others, so it gave me a slight sense of dubious satisfaction to think that our own capture had almost certainly distracted our captors from hunting further for anyone else. Given the lack of increased excitement since our seizure, I felt certain that Beecroft, Hanwell and Bradley had in fact escaped – small consolation for me, but it helped to keep my spirits buoyed at that moment.

Time passed so very slowly, but eventually came the clatter of a key in the lock, then the crunch of the lock being released, and the door squealed open – just as in a stage or film drama – and a soldier brought in a tray with two slices of bread, spread with what looked like butter (but definitely wasn't, as I was to discover!), accompanied by a cup of what proved to be a form of coffee. The whole lot was just about the most unpalatable meal I'd ever tasted, but I forced it down, not knowing when my next 'meal' might arrive. I found out later that the bread was known as 'black bread', although it was a sludgy-coloured shade of brown, and the liquid 'refreshment' was 'ersatz coffee', made from acorns, of all things. At least it was wet and warm, and the 'bread' eased the gap in my stomach.

After about half an hour, the same soldier returned for the empty tray, and even by then, my clothes were still very wet and I was shivering quite badly – the cell was made of stone blocks, and there was no heating at all; the 'mattress' didn't reflect what little body heat I generated as I lay on it; instead it seemed to suck the warmth right out of me. I indicated this dampness to the guard, making signs to ask if they could be dried, and he nodded and left me.

A few minutes later he returned, this time carrying a coarse blanket and accompanied by another (armed) guard, and I took off my outer clothes and wrapped myself in the blanket. I spent a very miserable night chilled to the bone, occasionally drifting into a fitful sleep, once dreaming of what we should have done, what we could have done. And finally, the coming of the morning was a great relief as meagre daylight crept through the cell window, its simple promise of warmth seeming to begin to thaw me out as I watched the light getting slowly stronger.

I must have drifted off to sleep again, but all too soon I was abruptly awakened by commands being barked at full volume right outside my cell window, accompanied by stomping, militarily timed boots. It was all in harsh-sounding German, of course, but it had an all too familiar sound, taking me right back to our square-bashing days in England, not so very long ago, it seemed now.

Once more, as the truth sank in, I felt my heart plummet. Eventually, however, the cell door rattled and opened once more, and a guard entered with a second helping of the previous night's 'delightful' cuisine – but far better than that, he also had my full RAF uniform, all dried, still warm, and beautifully pressed! Maybe these Germans weren't such bad chaps, after all!

A while later, the lock clunked yet again and the door squealed open once more, and this time both guards reappeared, accompanied by Alec; it was apparent by their gestures that we were on the move again, this time perhaps to a German POW camp. But there was no truck this time; we were simply marched through what appeared to be Besançon's main shopping centre, on our way to who knew where.

It was a fine day in June, and most of the citizens seemed to be sitting at tables on the pavements outside numerous cafés, drinking whatever was available off-ration, gazing at us apparently disinterestedly as we passed with our guards. Everything here appeared perfectly normal, and the only sign of war was that there were more soldiers about – German, of course – than usual. Otherwise, people shopped, drank and gossiped as sparse traffic drifted on through with Gendarmes controlling it where necessary. An ordinary, warm, lazy summer's day – and I felt like shouting at them: 'Don't you know there's a war on?' But of course, to them, the war was 'over', as much as it now was, I reflected ruefully, for Alec and myself.

We hadn't trudged very far when we came to the railway station and, once through the ticket office and on to the platform, the guards commandeered a bench seat, then sat one either side of us as travellers cast curious glances in our direction.

The platform was quite crowded, but when, after about half an hour, a train came rumbling, thumping and screeching to a halt, a way was made for us through the crowd by another pair of soldiers, then three civilians were ordered out of the carriage compartment so that our group could travel alone.

The transport was still in first-class condition at that time, and so we rolled on through the countryside with very few stops. Most of the stations through which we passed (without stopping) seemed very busy, with a large number of soldiers on every platform, but most of the civilians seemed quite cheerful in spite of the German occupation, and were mostly quite well dressed.

I fell asleep after a couple of hours of rocking and rattling along, lulled by the monotonous movement and somewhat exhausted from the lack of chilled sleep that previous night, and when I awoke once more, Alec was snoring gently opposite me, with his own guard stifling a yawn.

At some point we must have crossed the border into Germany, as the next few railway station signs flashed by in standard German gothic lettering, illegible due to the speed at which we passed them. However, we slowed to a crawl through another station, and the balance of the type of waiting passengers was definitely far more biased toward civilians rather than military uniforms; I knew then that we were now fairly deep into Germany, and I sighed deeply to myself as I crossed my arms across my chest and tried to move slightly into a more comfortable 'slouch'. One of the guards – the one on watch duty, I presumed – looked me in the eye, and I merely lifted my eyebrows and chin slightly to show my misery. He gave me a rueful half-smile – I suppose he was trying to express sympathy for our capture – and I nodded and twisted a little more to get as comfortable as I could, then settled back and eventually sank into a fitful doze; I was just too tired to fret further.

At Kassel we stayed overnight, where Alec and I were put into a small waiting room with only a large table for furniture – which we had to put to use as a bed; very uncomfortable, indeed. The only door was, naturally, securely locked and two of our guards took their places in front of it, and a quick glance through the only window showed us that even if we could have got out and slipped away from the guards, we wouldn't have got very far, for the platforms were crowded with German military of all types – and we, of course, were still wearing our distinctively different RAF uniforms.

Our guards woke us early the next morning and took us to a German equivalent of our NAAFI canteen, where we were given slightly better coffee, and a few slices of a higher-grade of bread (though still smeared with that awful 'butter' they used). Not long after 'breakfast' – following the same procedure as the previous day – a carriage compartment was once more commandeered. Two of our guards left us, we two and our remaining pair of guards settled down once more, and we were off again.

By mixed and mangled French and sign language, we'd managed to discover from our warders that we were bound for Dulag Luft, the Germans' initial interrogation centre, near Frankfurt, and so, after another long, weary day's journey, we pulled up at that city's station and the guards hustled us out.

They took us to an office away to one side to meet a German officer who simply glanced at each of us in turn, signed and stamped some papers, and we were promptly marched back out again, then away from the station and into the street. Rather to our surprise, we boarded a fairly crowded tramcar, and off we moved once more.

The passengers barely bothered to look at us as we travelled through the city, apparently unsurprised by our presence and not in the least bit curious; we learned later that the reason for their lack of interest was probably due to the fact that Dulag Luft was the reception centre for all captured RAF personnel, and the place from which they were sent on to the various prison camps – and many of the prisoners, of course, would have travelled on this same tram, and so the civilians were very accustomed to the sight of our uniforms.

After about twenty minutes' travel, we alighted, and then came about ten minutes of trudging until we reached Dulag Luft, and what a depressing sight, it was!

As we expected, there were rows of wooden shed-like barrack blocks, surrounded by high wire fences, topped and interspersed with rolls and rolls of barbed wire. Two guards stood at the outer main gate, and they opened one gate to let us in, where we were diverted to a small hut (presumably a guardroom-cum-reception office). Here we were met by a different set of soldiers – this time in Luftwaffe uniforms – while our two escorting Wehrmacht guards went off to report our arrival, and presumably sign us into Luftwaffe custody. They returned with a Feldwebel (sergeant), who glanced at Alec and me, then handed the Wehrmacht guards a form to sign (rather like taking delivery of a parcel, it felt to me!) – and then, to our astonishment, the Feldwebel said in clear English (even if with an American accent), 'Follow me, lads – it's nearly bedtime!' – and with that, he led us into a long, low building which, once inside it, we realised was the prison itself.

Several doors were set on each side of a long corridor, and above each door a small plaque bore a number. About halfway along the corridor sat an elderly man, looking uncomfortable on a small wooden stool.

'Looks more like a lavatory attendant than a gaoler,' I thought, but gaoler he was, for he stood slowly and produced a large bunch of keys, then led us a few yards further and opened two opposing cell doors, directing Alec into one, and myself into the other. The doors remained open for a minute or so as the Feldwebel and the gaoler stood talking, then another guard joined them.

'Get stripped,' the Feldwebel told me.

'Why?' I asked him. 'Are we getting a shower?'

'Wise guy,' he said, grinning at me. 'Not yet – I gotta search you, to make sure you ain't hiding arms or escape material' – and this he proceeded to do, and when he was finished, the old gaoler entered with a pile of khaki uniform items and took mine away. I looked askance at the Feldwebel.

'For X-ray,' he explained. 'Some desperate characters among you guys – and anyway, you won't get far without your boots, will you?'

A right cheerful character, I thought, glumly.

I spent four days in my cell, only allowed out to visit the latrines, but we weren't short of visitors. At least once – sometimes twice or three times – each day, I was visited by a young, very smartly dressed Luftwaffe lieutenant; a very friendly chap, who started out by commiserating with me on my bad luck at being captured, and then started with the 'softening-up' questions about my family, home life, etc – and then he got down to asking about my squadron and almost everything that concerned the conduct of the war.

He spoke perfect English, and tried to persuade me that the war would soon be over – with Germany victorious, of course – but to every question that he aimed at me, I gave him only my name, rank and serial number, as directed and trained by our squadron intelligence officer at home. The 'softening up' and questioning routine soon became very boring, but the

lieutenant remained polite during each of his visits – as did another officer who visited me twice – and I suppose they must have eventually realised
that they were to gain nothing from us, for on the fifth day, Alec, myself
and another ten chaps were moved out into the main camp, where we
were met by the permanent staff – the camp adjutant, the doctor and the
padre – and were issued with better clothes before being placed in a six-
man barrack room.

We spent the next few days comparing notes with our new companions
on how we'd become prisoners, hard luck stories galore, escape chances,
etc. – in fact, the usual first-time prisoners' behaviour, so Alec and I discovered, which we found was repeated over and over as time went on.

One thing that surprised us was the number of 'permanent staff'; apart
from the three already mentioned, there were kitchen staff and waiters,
and a very good jazz band who provided an excellent concert one evening
for all of us newcomers. These 'staff' and band members lived in a
segregated section of the camp, and all looked well fed and usually
smartly turned out. The adjutant told us that he, the doctor and the padre
had all been there for about eighteen months or so, and as the first officers
in Dulag Luft, they had been given these jobs – apparently (and evidently)
in return for which they were granted special privileges. Needless to
say, we were mighty suspicious of them all; dark mutterings of traitors,
Nazi supporters, quislings were rife, as were the wishes of what would
happen to them after the war, should those rumours be proven true.

However, we learned much later that the adjutant – at least – was not
all he seemed to be. The man so despised by the prisoners who passed
through his hands and (surprisingly to us) also disliked by the Germans,
was apparently 'acting' that way deliberately, and at one point found a way
of passing information back to the Allies. I never found out how long
he stayed there, but I believe he was decorated for his bravery after the war.

One or two of the prisoners seemed to have gone a bit 'strange', too,
such were the different effects and strains of captivity on various 'inmates'.
A few kept themselves to themselves, obviously very depressed, while
some mooched around the camp, snapping and snarling at anyone who
tried to get friendly with mere polite attempts at conversation. There
was one poor chap – a Czech pilot – who definitely seemed a bit 'gaga';
his moods swung up and down unpredictably, sometimes hilariously,

at other times violent. One day, he asked me, 'Do you know why your neck is shaped the way it is?'

'No,' I replied, trying to humour him.

'Well,' he said, very sombrely, 'it's so that when you go to the toilet, you can hang your belt around it ' – I almost chuckled, but he continued – 'and if you get the chance, German necks are perfectly shaped to get your hands around and squeeze the life out of them!'

I held back the laughter as he began to rage when he reached that latter part about throttling Germans. I shook my head slowly and sadly as he stomped away from me; he was really angry, shaking his clenched fists above his shoulders. Something had obviously caused him serious distress at some time – and not necessarily the bitterness of capture, but perhaps some wicked incident during the German invasion of Czechoslovakia, if one of a few later rumours were true.

It wasn't all doom and gloom at Dulag Luft, however. We had been impressed back home by the intelligence officers that we had to be extremely careful of our conversations with fellow prisoners and country-men if we were captured, and also to be very wary of the possibility (or more likely, the probability) of hidden microphones that the Germans could use to eavesdrop and therefore garner information during off-guard moments in our barrack rooms.

Another issue was the temptation for passing 'disinformation' (or false intelligence) to our captors, in the hope that they might instigate a huge time- and labour-wasting search looking for something that didn't exist – but the desire to get them digging for such intelligence might actually set them accidentally 'tripping over' something really secret.

We heard of one 'wag' who succeeded in generating keen interest from the Germans, apparently almost triggering a serious follow-up investi-gation until a knowledgeable German spotted the lie. The story was that one recent captive told his interrogator about a huge new bomber air-craft called a Huntley-Palmer, powered by secret Crosse & Blackwell engines, and equipped with wingtip turrets! I also heard that the 'wag' had even said that these super-turrets also had new 'McVitie' 20mm cannons fitted, although I can't be sure that the latter embellishment was true (or even if the whole account was right, for that matter, as the names included seemed to change from one story-teller to the next). The tale gave us all a good opportunity to snigger behind our captors' backs, at least, although we had to explain to other nationalities that these names were British food and drink manufacturers, not engineering companies!

Chapter 10

Stalag Luft III

Only two weeks were spent at Dulag Luft, then a 'purge' saw about twenty of us passed on to a permanent POW. camp.

We were roused early one morning, told to gather any possessions that we had, and were jostled into a group just outside the camp gates, where a large team of guards were awaiting us (more guards than prisoners!) with a smartly turned-out officer in charge. He proved to be quite fluent in English as we were lined up in rank and file, and once he had our collective attention, he issued us with a stark warning.

Remember, the guards have orders to shoot at anyone who causes trouble or tries to escape!' he barked, then told us that we were going to Stalag Luft III, at Sagan; this statement caused a good deal of murmured excitement, as we had been told by the adjutant of Dulag Luft that Sagan was the best-organised POW camp of them all, so – far from feeling trepidation over our shared fate at the departure from Dulag Luft – we were actually somewhat relieved and, oddly, a little excited!

We had to march to the railway station – a distance of about 4 miles – but because of that 'promise' of supposedly better treatment at Sagan very soon, we did so in style, each of us striding with 'shoulders back, chests out, arms swinging' and doing our very best to keep time and rhythm, to demonstrate a little pride in ourselves in spite of our captive predicament, and to show those Germans 'what for'. Our guards smiled in appreciation and marched likewise, their officer somewhat surprised at the transformation, but evidently pleased!

When we reached the station, we found that one section of the train had been allocated to us. Each short carriage had hard wooden seats (evidently third-class citizens, us!), and with ten prisoners in each carriage plus one guard to each carriage, and all the other guards crammed into the corridors, I don't think anyone had serious thoughts about escaping; far too risky, and probably impossible!

Those wooden bench seats were mighty hard and uncomfortable for long periods of time, and so the guard in each section allowed one man at a time to stand and stretch his legs for a few minutes – but little did we know that even those benches were luxury, compared to transport that we would have to use, later.

There were several stops, some of which were about two hours long, during which time our guards all got out and surrounded the carriages in our section of the train. When they did this at a station, we all felt like exhibits at a zoo, so curious were the civilians on the platforms.

Two days of this brought us to a small station, in the middle of nowhere it seemed. There we alighted and were lined up in two ranks, counted – an inevitable accompaniment of all such journeys – then marched off across what seemed like a very flat plain – no roads!

We marched for almost two hours, and toward the end of that trek we were flagging badly from poor diet and very little sleep in those carriages. Eventually, just as the evening was drifting from dusk to almost dark, we saw the camp ahead – a great circle of arc lights, with searchlights sweeping back and forth across what seemed to be empty compounds, but we soon realised, of course, that all the prisoners would be confined to the barrack huts by now.

As we approached a massive pair of entrance gates they swung open by some sort of signal from our German officer, and as we came to a halt one of the searchlights swept across and homed in on our sorry group, dazzling us all with its incredible brightness at close range. As the outer gates groaned shut behind us, I couldn't help thinking, 'Abandon hope, all ye who enter here' – then I thrust the thought away, and instead turned to Alec, standing beside me.

'Not much of an advert for that famous German efficiency, landing us here in the dark,' I murmured to him. He gave me a wry smile by way of reply, then jerked his chin at our escorting officer, who barked orders to our guards as the inner gates in turn creaked open.

We were led inside at a gentler pace than on the march, then directed into an empty barrack hut, there to be greeted by our camp leader. To our surprise, he was only a sergeant like us, and so, too, was his adjutant, or secretary. 'Dixie' Deans (as he was known) was that camp leader, and Ron Mogg his assistant – both to become renowned for various acts of bravery during their entire spell of captivity.

Later we learned that most RAF prison camps paid little lip service to rank, but more to common sense and natural leadership abilities. The first requirements, ideally, were that the selected camp leaders and their assistants should be able to speak German well, and both Deans and Mogg could easily hold serious conversations in excellent German – and more than that, Dixie Deans was very highly respected by our adversaries, for he really did look after the prisoners' welfare, even though that level of dedicated care often got him into trouble with the authorities for his stubborn stance on many issues of basic human rights under the Geneva Convention.

At that first meeting in the empty hut, he greatly impressed us all. Of medium height and stocky build, he welcomed us to Stalag Luft III as warmly as circumstances permitted.

'No prison camp can be a bed of roses,' he began, 'but here, we like to think that we're well enough organised to make our lives as tolerable as possible, although that will largely depend on each individual. Without sticking your necks out, you can – at the same time – also make life as difficult as possible for the Germans. If we all behaved ourselves, they could probably get away with stationing just one-tenth of the guards that they have here now – think of what that would mean for their ability to wage war everywhere against the Allies, if every POW camp was to do likewise, and all be good boys!'

He gave us a wicked grin and a wink and, having dropped his huge hint, he clapped his hands together and changed tack.

'Now, I know you're all very tired, dirty and hungry, so there are men waiting to take you to your various barracks – I'll let you all go now, and we'll go into further detail tomorrow, ok, gentlemen?'

And with that we set off in pairs, guided by a camp inmate to the barrack blocks to which we'd been allocated. Alec and I stayed together, of course (not realising that we would do so throughout the next three years!), and we were taken to Block 40, whose leader was a chap named 'Plum' Warner, a regular RAF man.

'The whole barracks is arranged in "combines", as you can see,' he told us. 'Some are in fours, some in sixes, some even more. They've sorted themselves out into friendly groups as time has gone by – now here are your lot, for the present, at least', and he introduced us in turn to Jimmy Ferguson, Jack Knight and 'Bull' Shannon.

'I'll see you again tomorrow morning,' he finished, then with a wry smile, he added, 'and don't believe all the bull-shitting that these characters might tell you!'

Amid rude noises and catcalls from our new mates, off he went, and as always happened on such occasions at all prison camps, a cup of tea or coffee was offered along with a biscuit. With such luxury in hand (Alec and I were bone dry and gasping for a hot drink, after that journey), we settled down to an exhausting barrage of questions.

Where, and how, had we been shot down?

How were things back home?

What squadron were we from?

What did we fly?

What had happened to the rest of the crew?

And so on, seemingly for hours.

We answered as well and as honestly as we could, and although our new mates were actually very friendly and natural, Alec and I both suspected that some of the questions were pointedly thrown in to try to catch us out. In time, I learned that this was standard procedure at every POW camp, a session designed not only to make genuine new friends, but also to try to weed out German (or other 'Axis'-supporting) infiltrators – something of a necessity that neither Alec nor I resented in any way, as it was the best means to safeguard the inmates' security and safety interests, long term.

Finally, it was our turn to fire questions back, to find out what kind of a life we could expect, and to get to know our new 'combine'.

Jimmy Ferguson was a Glaswegian, slow speaking and witty in a rather cynical way. He had been a prisoner for more than a year, and was a fount of information; he and Alec hit it off almost immediately, as Alec was also from Glasgow.

Jock Turner was an ex-school teacher from Redcar – a PT teacher who certainly looked the part (he and I got on very well, too, as our hometowns were quite close and we shared the same accent!).

'Bull' Shannon was an Australian, big and jovial – typical of the 'breed' – and one of several 'cobbers' in Sagan; it was they who had coined his 'Bull' nickname, and it had stuck (not that he seemed to mind). He was still receiving treatment for a hand injury, incurred when he had been shot down; he had been at the camp only a few weeks.

The barracks at that time housed about 100 men in each hut; there was a clear passage from end to end, and on both sides of that aisle, the 'combines' had arranged their two-tier bunks around a table, so that each combine more or less had a 'room' to itself. We were much better off here than in our later camps (we were eventually to find), with a big pot-bellied stove at each end of the hut, and a kitchen stove with hot plate and oven provided for each set of about thirty men. Rotas for cooking were arranged for each set, and we were particularly fortunate here, for the camp Kommandant was a Major Von Lindeiner, who (we were told) was a local coal trader, and such was his generosity that we were rarely short of the coal briquettes used around here; he was a pretty decent chap – for a German, anyway.

The next morning was reserved – as promised – for our final briefing by Dixie Deans and his staff. The new 'Kriegies' (the natural abbreviation for 'Kriegsgefangener' – prisoners of war) met him in the camp theatre block – an unexpected facility itself, and a very pleasant surprise for us new boys! I have to admit that I was truly astonished to find such an unexpected 'treasure' as a fully equipped theatre deep inside a prison camp – it seemed almost incongruous that such a facility should exist – yet I should not have been so surprised, given the accumulation of so many multi-talented and skilled men all concentrated in one place with so much spare time on their hands.

As Dixie convened the 'welcome' lecture, I was still casting discreet glances around me, taking in my new surroundings and determining to seek out whoever was in charge of the theatre; I was very keen to ask if I could join up, for back home – before joining the RAF – I had been an enthusiastic participant in the Ashington Amateur Dramatic and Operatic Society, and at that moment I could think of no better way to while away captivity than to pursue that interest further … unless, of course, I managed to find a way to escape and return home! Ever the optimist, I settled down to focus my attention on Dixie's briefing.

As I suspected, he began by saying he hoped that we'd gained the basic grounding that we needed from our 'combine' colleagues, and that we would quickly settle down to our new way of life.

He then set his staff to hand out Red Cross forms to fill in. As we passed the forms from man to man, Dixie told us that we were receiving one Red Cross parcel per man per week, and this, with the addition of bread, soup and occasional gifts from our captors, meant that we didn't starve. It was up to each of us to find the best way to use these things. We were allowed one letter per month, and we could receive parcels (not food) from home, too. Letters in both directions were strictly censored, as we had to be very careful what we wrote – as, too, had our families by return.

He gave us some time for a questions and answers session, and then back to the huts we went, a little bemused, but determined to make the most of things, and of course, like all Kriegies, to escape as soon as possible! We knew, certainly, that doing so wouldn't be easy, and Dixie had made it very clear just how difficult (and potentially lethal) it could be. Briefly, he'd said that the relatively easy part was breaking out of the camp; the hard part was finding a way out of Germany and then getting home! With the camp being built on a kind of shale-like sandy soil, tunnelling seemed the easiest way – 'But don't forget,' Dixie had cautioned, 'the Germans know that too, and they have planted all sorts of devices and microphones, et cetera, to try to prevent just that.'

As in all POW camps, there was an escape committee, to which all escape plans had to be submitted, lest one plan overlap and possibly interfere with another already planned, or in progress.

'All escape plans will be carefully vetted and assessed for their chances of success,' Dixie had also told us. 'Each committee is made up of very experienced men, and anyone with a scheme that has even the smallest chance of working, will be considered. However,' he warned us, solemnly, 'in the words of the Bible: "Many are called, but few are chosen"!'

From this, and from our own individual dreams of freedom, we newer Kriegies had the early impression of a camp full of would-be absconders, although Dixie had made it brutally clear that escaping was very difficult. It soon dawned upon me that there had developed almost two distinct sections of prisoners. Those who were really devoted to attempting to escape, however successful, or short-lived, or even dismally ineffective, and the greater majority, who had neither the ambition nor drive (and dare I say, the sheer bravery to plan and plot such escapades that could ultimately prove lethal to those caught in the attempt). Both sections played vital balancing parts in maintaining the general morale of the entire camp, as the escape fanatics could always rely on the assistance of the others for any help they might require in order to make their attempts to break for freedom.

For those brave souls who were prepared to take the huge gamble in their 'home-run' aims, I developed the deepest respect and admiration. They caused the Germans endless hours of trouble and the subsequent diversion of manpower, and, in that way, they played a very important part in the war by keeping our captors' forces occupied with constant searches for escapees.

For my own part – at least to begin with – I decided to simply settle down and observe life in my new environment, and to learn how to survive in what were evidently tight circumstances – something that was to prove surprisingly easy for me, as I had been relatively accustomed to thrift in my earlier years having grown up in the deep recessional times before the war. Aside from losing too much weight too quickly owing to poor rations from our captors, though, it took me only a few weeks to get into the swing of things at Sagan.

Once I had settled into POW life and had soon heard the depressing result of a failed escape attempt from an adjacent compound by way of gunfire and later verbal confirmation, my own initial desire to break free became more and more muted until I felt that I could not afford to take such a massive gamble. As much as I yearned to be back home with my wife and son, I had to consider what might become of them should I never return home due to my demise from taking that chance and getting caught in the act. And, anyway, we 'knew' that we were winning the war, and that it shouldn't be very long before we were all safely back home with our loved ones, so why take the risk? To many readers, that choice might seem to be a slightly cowardly outlook, but that was the decision of the vast majority of prisoners of war, primarily for personal safety; only a tiny percentage of hard-core bravehearts actually took up the challenges of escaping.

As it happened, I soon discovered that there was just so much to do to occupy one's time at Sagan, so well organised and remarkably inventive were the inmates. There were a great many 'clubs' and schools that developed within various huts, and so our lives were not quite so dull and empty as one might otherwise surmise. I also saw that while everyone seemed to be busy getting as fit as they could (within reason, bearing in mind the food rationing) and becoming very much occupied with hobbies, education, theatre roles and other activities, there was also a great deal of monkey business going on behind the scenes; they certainly weren't just sitting back and do nothing – far from it! Not only were they helping to support or kit-out escapers (either directly or indirectly, from just small acts of generosity by donation of Red Cross rations, to assistance with creating contraband escape items and clothing), they were always hatching other dastardly schemes, every one seemingly designed to make life as awkward as possible for our gaolers. Mischief was always present, in one form or another.

This manifested itself in many ways – sometimes from sabotage, other times from running diversionary tactics to avert interest from the 'goons' (as the Germans were affectionately known) – and occasionally, way beyond the safe call of duty, direct physical intervention if diversions failed. Just about everyone in the camp had a role to play – minor or major – in both escape assistance and causing a nuisance in one form or another, and many were highly enthusiastic with their varied efforts, to the point where some frequently landed up in the 'cooler' (solitary confinement) for doing so.

Once I'd seen the 'the lie of the land', it didn't take me long to decide that it would best suit me to become one of the 'backroom boys' and support the escape fanatics and 'saboteurs', while endeavouring to survive my incarceration and to try to help improve not only my own lot, but also to help better the daily lives of my fellow POWs by whatever means and methods that I could, depending on what facilities were available. In my own aims, that would include becoming involved with the theatre and entertainment productions, and also to use whatever sports facilities there were to attempt to keep fit and encourage my fellow inmates to do likewise, with the resolve to emerge from our predicament more prepared for whatever future awaited us when the war was finally over.

Chapter 11

'Legitimate' activities

The sheer multitude of personalities thrown together in Stalag Luft III soon revealed astounding levels of imagination and ingenuity for the creation of all manner of items from objects that would normally be considered as throwaway rubbish back home. For instance, food tins were taken apart by de-soldering the seams, and while the metal skins themselves were put to a wide variety of uses for matters both licit and otherwise, the jointing solder was reformed into blobs and tiny ingots for reuse in all kinds of creations; the Poles among us were particularly skilled at the de-soldering work and always keen to dig in when asked for such assistance – especially when any hints were dropped in connection with 'underhand' mischief, such as the repair and duplication of a secret radio, to give just one example.

A wide variety of hobby clubs were also formed to suit many interests. There were art, crafts and even model making, all of which were creations of incredible genius when our conditions and lack of such working goods and facilities were taken into consideration. Given that their only tools were pocket knives and home-made nail files for carving and shaping wood, and pencils for sketching and colouring, the 'crafty' ones in our midst created excellent models of ships, aeroplanes, cars and motorcycles, miniature carved busts and all manner of animals and other objects, while artists produced landscapes and portraits in varying shades of pencil lead or home-made charcoal sticks; all in all, they were a highly creative and admirable crowd, who never failed to amaze us all with their talents. Regular exhibitions were organised in the camp, and as our captors took great interest and even a little pride in the skilled handicrafts, they once set up an outside exhibition for the local townsfolk to visit.

There were also reading groups, born out of our somewhat limited library, where participants would read passages or chapters to a cluster of inmates, each taking turns, thus allowing others to enjoy the stories rather than just one reader at a time. The good old Red Cross provided such books, but with well over a thousand men in our compound at that stage to cater for, the 'library service' was sketchy at the best of times. A bonus for me were some of the studying and education classes; these were instigated for those wishing to learn a wide variety of subjects (even down to earning diplomas that were promised to be validated as qualifications in 'Civvy Street' after the war), and I brushed up on my French language skills and learned a little German in this way – useful for even basic communication with our captors, despite our very mixed and broad regional accents!

For the more physically demanding among us, another set of activities that was very popular was sport – mainly football and rugby, although we also played cricket for a little while, and sometimes tennis and other games to fill in the gaps when the weather turned adverse or equipment supplies stopped for various reasons.

Ground-wise, the 'appell' area (where we were herded together for roll calls, daily) became a football pitch, for which the Germans supplied the goal posts, and the Red Cross provided the footballs; the latter had to be looked after extremely carefully, as they were in very short supply. Each hut had its own team, every one of which was given the name of an English First Division club; we ran a league, but the number of games played were determined very much by that limited ball availability. I was in Hut 40, and we played as Derby County. We had quite a useful team, as it proved, and I was delighted to be selected as a member.

There were some very good players in the camp, although only two professionals. One was Johnny Breck, who (at eighteen years old) had kept goal for Portsmouth in the Cup Final of 1939, the youngest 'goalie' to have played in such a final at that time. He also kept wicket for the Hampshire Cricket Club. The other professional football player was Duggie Gardner, a Scot who competed for Luton Town. There were others not so well known who played for lower-league amateur-level teams, but were equally good on the pitch.

For me, though, the 'Daddy' of them all was Johnny Dance; he was over thirty years old then, and anyone less like the popular image of a foot-baller would be hard to imagine, let alone find! He was tall and strongly built, but he had lost most of his hair, had big buck teeth, was knock-kneed and splay-footed; he played most of his games with an amiable grin on his face, and at centre-half was the mainstay of any team in which he participated. His biggest rival at centre-half was Jerry Ratcliffe, himself over 6ft tall and very strong, but strangely not so nimble and mobile as Johnny. There was also young Blackburn ('Blackie' to everybody) who played at left-half and was probably the most promising player in the camp; but for the intervention of the war, I'm sure he would have become a talented professional.

There were many others who developed excellent football skills, of course, and our matches usually gathered the entire compound as an audience (and also many of the Germans, too), such was the popularity of the sport … but woe betide any players falling victim to overenthusiastic tackles! Anyone dropping to the dusty pitch from injury would usually earn collective derisory cries of 'Hang him on the wire! Let's have the substi-tute on!' or 'Dead man on the pitch – bury him and carry on!' – all in good -natured jest, of course!

There was one little snag about all our ball-based pastimes, though, and that was the pitch itself, which was a mixture of shale and sand. We used to sprinkle water across the ground before the start of a game, espe-cially in hot weather, but it still churned up. The result was usually a heavy pall of dust hanging over the pitch when a match was in progress, and at the end of the competition the players came off looking like they'd been working down a coal mine!

I really enjoyed my football there, but it was to generate one of my greatest disappointments. A match was arranged between our compound and the officers next door, which was to be played in their compound, which meant (we were told) that all the players would get a slap-up meal afterwards. To my immense delight and pride, I was selected to play at right-half for the NCO's team – and what a line up: Love, Dance and Blackburn! To add to the pleasure, I learned that the officers' goalkeep-er was to be 'Ossy' Osbourn, who had been my navigation officer with 101 Squadron when we had been briefly stationed at Oakington along with 7 Squadron (he was lost on an op while flying from there).

The match was to be played at 2pm, and a limited number of NCO spectators were to be allowed to accompany us into the officers' compound. But at eleven o'clock a squad of guards marched into our area, and we were all called out to a special 'appell', where camp Kommandant Major Von Lindeiner told us that the match was off as some of the officers had been 'misbehaving', so in future, no more privileges of this nature would be permitted. We later learned that the 'misbehaviour' was an escape attempt, and with the usual confusion and German ire that always followed such episodes, it had been mid-morning before they had it all sorted out. It was very disappointing indeed, but we soon got over it; after all, escaping was far more important than a mere football match!

Rugby wasn't as popular as football, but a contest between officers and NCOs was arranged, and played in our compound. I'd never been very interested in the game until then, but I saw enough action in that match to realise just how exciting Rugby could be – especially to the players. My one outstanding memory of that particular game was to see one of the officers' forwards score the winning 'try' by running the last 20yds to the line with four opponents clinging to him, but all unable to bring him down!

I was never going to be that kind of player, although I could run a bit, but I allowed myself to be persuaded to give it a try. After a bit of coaching and instruction, I played three games and actually quite enjoyed them – except perhaps the last one. As you'll recall, I mentioned that the pitch was fashioned over shale and sand, and that last game was played on a very hot, dry day, and I came off the pitch at the end of the match with my knees very badly scraped and grazed; I must have been 'grounded' a bit more than usual, that day! Anyway, it took nearly three weeks to heal, during which time I couldn't play any soccer, nor could I walk or 'drill' very well on the 'appells', so that was my last ever game of rugby.

The Red Cross also provided us with cricket kit, but we soon discovered that our sports 'field' was useless for that as the bowlers could not exert any directional control of the ball, and so it proved very frustrating for both sides. Few runs were made as it was so difficult to hit the dulled or deflected ball with the bat, and so matches were usually abandoned from sheer frustration. That isn't to say that cricket was never played at Sagan, but was very limited because of those poor ground conditions. A great pity, as I usually really enjoyed playing that particular sport.

We tried one more outdoor activity. Winter in Sagan was bitterly cold, as low as minus 23 degrees on one occasion, with harsh frosts and deep snow. With the Red Cross promising to send us some ice skates, we set about creating an ice rink. How? It was simple: we chose the flattest area on the edge of the parade ground, built up small sand bank ridges to contain the ice, then had squads of men marching up and down to compact the surface as hard and as level as possible. When the skates finally arrived it was in the middle of our coldest spell, and we organised a few bucket chains from the washroom to the site of the 'ice rink', the buckets were filled and rapidly passed along the human chains. When each bucket reached the last man, he simply turned and threw it across the hardened area, which was so cold that the water froze as soon as it splashed down; ergo, we had our skating rink (even though it was a little bumpy, here and there)!

A timetable was made and a day also allocated for every hut so that everyone could have a go on the skates and, even with the limited number of skates that we had available, we reckoned that we'd all get the chance to learn to skate.

The first two days went well, but on the third day, horror of horrors! A thaw set in, and by the end of that day our 'rink' was just a soggy mess of sandy, sludgy shale. A very sad end to what had proven to be a great new experience for all those who had managed to get some time on the skates – and the Canadians (apparently all brought up on blades from infancy!) were bitterly disappointed that their turn never materialised.

If I've given the impression thus far that life in Sagan was mainly leisure and pleasure, then that's simply because I'm concentrating particularly on that side of our sojourn in the camp. However, there were only so many ways to pass those long, boring hours and days in a compound, albeit largely restricted – as I have already mentioned – by whatever we were given by that marvellous Red Cross organisation, and also by whatever our captors could supplement or would permit as 'legitimate' activities. The majority of us kept busy to stave off boredom and depression and to keep reasonably fit, but for all this fruitful effort and enjoyment, there was still a void to be filled in the minutes and hours between various activities.

Many of the chaps were married or had been courting back home, or simply wanted to keep in touch with their parents and siblings, but letters to home were strictly rationed to just one each month; we really had to make the most of the luxury so we learned to write very small to fill our cards! The letters that we received from home were similarly rationed and, of course, were heavily censored – even to the point of obscuring any neighbours' names, for fear of fuelling German intelligence! It wasn't at all unusual to receive letters from home that were almost entirely blacked out by British censors – very frustrating indeed, when yearning for even the most mundane home 'news' and family gossip.

I was, however, quite pleasantly surprised at the speed of delivery of the first letter that I received from my wife Evelyn – a mere two months or so after our capture and arrival at Sagan – so it was evident that either Beecroft, Hanwell and Brad had made it home quickly, or perhaps officialdom had proved usefully efficient somewhere along the way, for once!

Not all letters received were good, though; all too often, an unlucky chap would collect a letter from a wife or girlfriend, with devastating news that his sweetheart had 'strayed' with another man and was writing to say it was all over for them. We British used to call them 'Mespots' – a term that once signified a posting to an RAF base in what was Mesopotamia, almost always resulting in the same ruination of relationships due to its remoteness, so the term became synonymous with jinxing marriages and courtships. It was to prove the same for too many POWs, unfortunately. We later adopted the American term for such communications – the 'Dear John' letters – and many chaps would pin their letters to the compound notice board as a form of consolation or therapy for themselves – a form of burden-sharing – and as a 'lesson' to everyone else. Not all such missives were sad, however; many were downright hilarious! Examples were:

'I heard nothing from you for two months, so I married your father.'

'I'm sorry, dear – I've fallen in love with a soldier; he's not as likely to get captured.'

And from a lady who posted a parcel containing socks and a scarf, and had been sent a letter of thanks from the grateful (allotted) POW who'd received the package: 'I'm sorry you got the parcel – I had intended it for someone on active service.'

Chapter 12

A highly treasured facility

While the arts, crafts, classes and sport were a great boon in keeping boredom at bay for many, not everyone took interest in such creative or sweat-inducing activities. Those chaps who preferred not to get involved in more physical, organised sports and games, often settled instead to partake in the less strenuous 'walking the circuit', as our parade ground perambulations were called. This simply entailed pacing around the 'appell' ground several times as a very mild form of exercise, although, inevitably, it became very tedious after just a few laps; it was, however, a very good opportunity to chat with others and expand our social circles a little more. On days following matches and games in which we had expended too much energy, or when the weather didn't lend itself to such exertions, I merged with the throng and shuffled around, usually joining in with ribald banter as we trudged along.

However, as much as I greatly enjoyed those available activities, classes and sports, they were still only of secondary significance to me. For my prime interest, I was drawn to the camp theatre like a moth to a flame!

As previously mentioned, I had been stunned by the unexpected existence of that theatre and its humble magnificence; to my mind, at least, this was quite probably the greatest triumph of all POW-instigated (peaceful) creativity, utilising reconstitution and ingenuity on a grand scale. The simple fact that prisoners of war had even managed to create such a marvellous theatre and so many of its component parts from almost nothing (at first) was awe-inspiring, and one could not help but be hugely impressed by the simple grandeur of its design and construction.

The whole theatre project was achieved thanks largely to the enthusiastic agreement and cooperation of the surprisingly generous camp

Kommandant Von Lindeiner, although it was evident that despite having said that his motive was simply to keep his inmates happy, in truth his 'charitable' concession was more to keep the prisoners busy and therefore out of trouble (or so he hoped!).

With the supply of thin plywood tea-chests that our Red Cross parcels were packed into, along with some substantial building timbers, materials and loans of tools – which had to be signed in and back out each day – the prisoners converted one of the huts and thus created a stage worthy of many a theatre in any town. To round off the production side of the stage, the Germans also provided decent lighting equipment (although they controlled the electricity supply, naturally) and tins of paint and such-like to enable the creation of scenery and backdrops.

Finally, to complete the theatre, seating was obviously a requirement. To that end, even more of those Red Cross tea-chests were refashioned into several rows of 'stall' seats for the audiences to enjoy some comfort while watching the numerous shows that were produced, and the whole facility became the envy of many other camps when word was spread by transferred prisoners; several camps tried to follow suit with their own theatres, but none equalled the splendour of Sagan!

By the time that I arrived at Stalag Luft III, the theatre was already in full swing, with regular shows being staged, so I 'enlisted' into the throng as soon as I could in order to take part in something worthwhile (and in which I was quite familiar) and, in my conscience, to try to help alleviate my fellow prisoners' misery by working to entertain them and thus – at least temporarily – provide a little light relief from the boredom of our otherwise dull and depressing lives.

I ought, also, to mention that we always regarded the theatre and its related activities as a very real privilege, and something that was usually paid for – at least in part – by the kindness of our officers in the adjacent compound. According to the terms of the Geneva Convention, officers were entitled to be paid by the holding power, and the Germans' method of payment was by 'lagergeld' – a currency specifically created for POW camps and utterly worthless outside them, so it could only be spent within. As there was precious little worth buying within the wire fences compounds, instead they saved it all and used it to exchange for special items under arrangement with our captors – particularly stage costumes hired from agencies in Hanover and Berlin, to be used both in the officers' and NCOs' compounds; we NCOs were extremely grateful for their generosity, and the costumes really made a huge difference to our varied productions, adding that vital dimension away from retailored uniforms and other rag-like clothing.

This huge 'perk' made a big impact on the otherwise mundane Kriegie 'stay', so while we genuinely enjoyed working in the theatre, we were aware that its privilege could be removed at any time for misbehaviour; therefore we always did our utmost to (outwardly) show good gentlemanly conduct – while more often than not, there was skulduggery afoot behind the choreography and rehearsal scenes.

The theatre was very well used. With the help of those various costumes provided by the good graces of our officers 'next door', and the remarkably good-quality musical instruments provided by the Red Cross, coupled with the production, acting and musical skills of many of my fellow 'Kriegies', we put on all sorts of entertainment, often running repeat shows on 'runs' of several nights long in order to allow as many audiences as possible to enjoy the performances, although it was inevitable that some would still miss out for one reason or another.

There were plays ranging from *The Merchant of Venice* to one or two shows from the London stages, such as *Home and Beauty*, and another written by our own 'in-house' experts titled *Meet Mrs Mondon*; this last play was written by Alan Dixon, a BBC producer, and the leading part was played by Trevor Alderwick, a professional actor until his call-up to the RAF.

In Christmas 1942 we staged a pantomime, *Aladdin* – but this would be no ordinary panto! We saw that the chaps really needed a morale-booster, knowing that we would all be pining for our homes during what would normally be a close, family-based time of year, and recognised that a really strong but entertaining effort would have to serve as a useful distraction from such understandably morose thoughts – so we contrived to add a line-up of high-kicking chorus 'girls' into the storyline! This addition really 'hit the target' and created absolute uproar every night with all manner of ribald, amorous comments being yelled from the highly appreciative female-starved audiences – including the German hierarchy, who attended by special invitation … and even Von Lindeiner himself greatly enjoyed the show!

Little did he (or I) know, though, that right at that moment – as we were roaring with enthusiastic laughter (the Germans from the 'stalls', and I from backstage) – an escape was taking place at the compound gates (more of which, later).

On another occasion soon after Christmas, our choir performed selected portions from *The Messiah* – but by far the most popular productions were the variety shows and several concerts arranged by the various musical experts within our ranks.

The talented musicians and leaders among us included Stan Parris, a bandleader at Eastbourne before the war; Stan Hunt, an orchestra leader in Civvy Street; and Jack Murray, a New Zealander who organised and conducted our choir and most other choruses and singers who became involved in such productions.

There were a good number of quality singers, too, along with some very gifted instrumentalists, the most notable (during my time at Sagan) being Frank Bergmann. Frank was an American-Jewish concert pianist who had flown to England and volunteered for the RAF as soon as the war started, but unfortunately was shot down and ended up in Stalag Luft III. He had managed to keep his bloodline secret for quite some time, but eventually the Germans discovered his true identity and whisked him away one night; very sadly, we never heard of him again – his musical talents were very much missed on that stage.

Another prominent figure in our musical shows was Larry Slattery. He was an excellent violinist, but his greatest 'claim to fame' was that he was Kriegie Number One! He and his gunner, George Barth (RAF lightweight boxing champion) were shot down on the second day of the war, flying a Bristol Blenheim – and Alec and I thought we were unlucky with D-Donald!

At the time that I entered Sagan, the best-known singers were Frank Greaves and Hugh Brown, although there were many others who could croon a good tune.

And last – but by no means least – on the roll call of theatre casting were, of course, those 'girls'! Wearing dresses, costumes and even bikinis made both in-house and hired from outside, the 'girls' were a vital ingredient of all the variety shows that were staged in the camp. As chorus 'girls', high-kicking their way through routines like the cancan, their dancing was usually quite energetic, if not always 'uplifting', and on more than one occasion, I teamed up with one of the longest-serving POWs, Alfie Fripp (an elfin-like, often mischievous co-producer of great repute in the POW camps) to create and choreograph some very vigorous routines full of bouncing kicks – particularly during rehearsals – to create a storm of noise on the stage in order to mask periods of highly nefarious activity beneath those boards.

I was never sure just what went on beneath that stage and didn't dare ask (for obvious security reasons – if we didn't know, we couldn't tell), but I learned months later that we had been covering for various 'contraband' manufacturing and concealment sessions in aid of escape activities – some of it apparently connected with foundation work for the later 'Great Escape' from the officers' compound in the following year (although I couldn't fathom out quite how any such contraband might be smuggled from our compound to theirs – but that was someone else's problem, not mine, and I didn't need to know!).

I had seen, however, that our bed-boards were being appropriated regularly now, and a few old hands had told us of previous goings-on in other Stalags; thus, we learned that the boards were suitably sized for use as props for tunnelling purposes (each board measuring about 6in wide and 2ft 6in long), so it was evident to us that there was something afoot, somewhere underfoot in the compound!

Naturally, with that form of intrigue developing, it was sometimes a struggle to contain our excitement at being involved with such secretive activities (something that obviously had to be very restrained, for fear of alerting the goons) – but when we were asked to make as much noise as possible to blanket any such industrious din below decks, we obliged very enthusiastically by whipping the 'girls' into a high-kicking frenzy of thunderous rhythmic accompaniment, almost to the brink of exhaustion – and when the 'stars' of the chorus line flopped down to rest, our back-up 'heavies' high-stepped in to create comedic pandemonium! Always good for a laugh, there were many such animated souls who would take part in almost anything to help with the cause and to lighten otherwise gloomy days.

One or two of those chorus 'girls' also made splendid 'leading ladies' in the plays. The star of them all was 'Junior' Booth, a diminutive young chap who – when wearing his stage make-up, plus a dress or costume – could easily be mistaken for a real girl. He developed into quite a good 'actress', but I hasten to add that he was no 'cissy' in normality; thanks to the Red Cross supplying us with some sports equipment, we played a great deal of football and rugby when not in the theatre, and 'Junior' was right there in the depths of the rugby scrums, kicking and gouging and hooking at shins for all he was worth, leaving a trail of bruises behind him!

Of the inmates who gave their 'all' in the theatre, however, possibly the greatest name of all to emerge – certainly from my own time at Sagan, anyway – has to be Roy Dotrice, although not in any masculine roles! It might surprise readers to know that Roy played mostly female parts in the camp theatre, yet after the war he went on to become world famous in a wide variety of roles as he took to acting male parts with gusto in films and, much later, in television. His equally famous daughter, Michele, emerged later still in the *Some Mothers Do 'Ave 'Em* series as the long-suffering wife to Michael Crawford's character, Frank Spencer.

My own personal acquaintance with Roy concerned only one variety show, our last – and best – at Sagan. The programme was called *Through the Music Sheet* and was written and produced by our own team of experts, using well-known songs and also some parodies of others. My part was paired with Roy, and also some of the other 'ladies'; they appeared at a door through the scenery at the back of the stage, then first Dave Fraser would enter 'stage left', then myself 'stage right'. We strolled to the door, kissed the ladies' hands then escorted them to the front of the stage, all the time with Dave and me singing 'A pretty girl is like a melody' – how very romantic!

In our last week at Sagan in 1943, we had been rehearsing what should have been our best ever show, an adaptation of Gilbert and Sullivan's *The Mikado*. We'd solved the problem of having no sopranos by using three men who were quite small in stature, but all good tenors who could stretch their vocal chords when required, and who surpassed themselves in a dress rehearsal when made up as the 'three little girls from school'. They would undoubtedly have been the big hit of the performance – but just as we were almost ready to stage it, we were given our marching orders (literally!) for movement to another camp, so, to our bitter disappointment, it was never staged.

There were many others who participated in several plays, although I have mentioned only the names of those with whom I became well acquainted. Many more were to tread the boards after my departure from Sagan, all of them worthy performers, and some of whom went on to become household entertainment names in peacetime; I hereby salute them all for their collective and successive efforts at uplifting Kriegie spirits during their stays.

A number of chaps played varying parts in several productions – some important roles, others small – but all were enthusiastically rehearsed. Alfie got in on many acts in frequently comedic characters, and even my own wee crew-mate Alec was cajoled into playing the 'wife' of one of the leading players in *Home and Beauty* – and to his own surprise and pride, he performed his part very well indeed!

The 'handsome hero' in many of our productions was often Peter Thomas, tall and good-looking (as befits a leading actor, naturally!), and prominent in almost every activity that went on in our compound. He was also a regular in the occasional debates that we staged, and a real asset in almost anything that needed proper organisation. So it was no surprise to me to learn (in confidence, of course) that he was also a stalwart on the escape committee, and after the war, he went on to become a Member of Parliament, eventually serving the Conservatives as Minister for Wales.

Then there was Ken Bowden, a comic 'turn' in whatever part he had to play, no matter how serious the production was supposed to be. His friend Jack Lipton usually aided and abetted him; Jack was the brother of Sid Lipton, the leader of one of our best-known bands in England, so 'stagemanship' seemed to run in his family. Jack was also a very good, keen footballer, along with many others; good entertainers seemed almost always to fare well in sports, for some reason. The backstage crews shall also be crowned with a good portion of glory. Miracles were undertaken in the costume 'department'. In the face of such hard times, its members carefully converted our old uniforms and spare clothes from home into passable costumes either to supplement those others that were hired in for occasions, or when that wasn't possible they'd be found working feverishly against the clock to prepare a whole set of character clothing from what were almost scraps and tatters that had been donated or scrounged from all over the compound (some even light-heartedly filched as we slept!). Luckily, there were a good few tailors and the like in our midst, but what the Germans didn't know was that quite a few of those costumes were actually being produced or converted for escape use. The scenery was created and painted by our art section, often again from scraps and materials scrounged from those ubiquitous Red Cross tea-chests and some from the Germans themselves (especially the paint, although the artists were wizards at concocting all kinds of colour shades from the most unlikely sources, it seemed). One chap that I must mention here is Geoff Roper; he was a real 'jack-of-all-trades' who could literally turn his hands to any task and do it really well, often making a 'silk purse out of a sow's ear', as the old saying goes – and it wasn't just stage production scenery that passed out of his skilled hands. The theatre was also used for purposes other than entertainment. Every Sunday it became an ad-hoc 'church', ministered by the deeply religious New Zealander, Jack Murray, who became a firm friend indeed. His story was another tale of bad luck – he had left his home in the Antipodes to come to England for his aircrew training, but on the latter stages of that incredibly long voyage, the ship in which he was sailing was attacked and torpedoed by a U-boat. Jack was one of the survivors who took to the life-boats and rafts, was picked up by the German Navy and eventually reached us at Sagan, still only a 'lowly' leading aircraftman (LAC) – but he soon made his presence felt. Along with his carefully thought-out sermons, his other abilities as a musician and a choirmaster were great assets, and his fervour was well respected by all. He continued this great work in all our camps as we were moved on, in spite of poorer and poorer conditions and facilities as the war progressed and Germany began to suffer. He was also – as we would expect from a New Zealander – a very keen and a powerful rugby player, as many of his opposition found to their cost, suffering 'dead-legs' from his hard shoulder tackles to their thighs!

All in all, the theatre did a sterling job of keeping up the spirits of the entire compound. We always seemed to be very busy in there, yet I was surprised to realise that in the thirteen months that I was involved, we had put on just nine plays and variety shows, each running for a week to give everyone a chance to see them. It seemed like many more in that time due to the amount of preparation work and rehearsals, but we had great fun in presenting and performing them all – and the German staff soon found out which productions were worth seeing; it paid us, of course, to invite them, as this would usually curry favour by return, eventually.

That theatre was a highly treasured facility that was immensely enjoyed by just about everyone in the camp and proved to be a massive morale booster throughout its existence. I was very proud to be a participant in the team, and thoroughly enjoyed every minute of the hours of effort that I put into the productions. And I always enjoyed a secret smile at the amount of 'masking' that we carried out to cover those illicit activities.

Chapter 13

Christmas 1942

One of the longer-standing facilities at Stalag Luft III was the POWs' 'swap shop', devised from the early days to allow a system of bartering among prisoners, but at a committee-set 'price' to prevent black-market-style inflation.

Thanks largely to the regularity of the Red Cross parcels, supplemented by packages from families and well-wishers, and, later, the influx of bigger American and even larger Canadian deliveries, the supply of some basic and occasional luxury items (and sporadically a surplus) meant that the recipients were willing to trade unwanted goods with their fellow inmates via the swap shop, allowing the shop itself to make a small 'charge' for enabling the transaction, with the profits thus generated going into a central camp 'pool' for either assisting those who received nothing or simply diverted into the escape 'bank', where not claimed or required.

Generally speaking, things like clothes, food and cigarettes became a form of currency, with a 'points' system developed on the agreed (tabled) value of each type or grade of item. In this way, if an inmate had – say – twenty cigarettes that he didn't want, and another inmate had a spare shirt but wanted the cigarettes more, then the cigarettes and shirt would change hands via the swap shop, but a 'fee' of perhaps two or three cigarettes might be charged as commission, and placed in the 'bank'.

An additional way of trading was that if another inmate had a tin of corned beef surplus to his requirements, but didn't need anything in exchange at that time, then his corned beef would go into shop stock for an allocation of points that would then be accrued against a future personal need – and the shop would then trade that tin for something else to match the value (minus a few points to generate that important profit, of course), and so a healthy stock had slowly developed over the months and years, resulting in a reserve that could be dipped into, both for the prisoners' welfare, and also to provide the escapers' evasion rations.

I didn't smoke, but I still received a ration of cigarettes, so I naturally traded them in (both with the shop and sometimes directly with hut-mates if time was pressing) to gain a few extras to make life a little more bearable for Alec and myself.

Among the various parcels arriving at Sagan, we found such delights as powdered dried egg (which made excellent omelettes, when milk was available!), tins of Spam or corned beef, and another favourite, the 'Klim' biscuits; these were large, thick, plain biscuits that provided a very welcome change from the black 'bread' issued by the Germans.

On that latter point, if we'd had to depend solely on the rations provided by our 'hosts', I think we'd have starved; that black 'bread' was rationed to one-quarter of a 'loaf' per day, and as a foodstuff, it took some getting used to – although we found it a little more palatable when lightly toasted, and coated with a rare smear of thin margarine. The rest of the German ration was made up of potatoes (often going bad), various watery soups, a little cheese (from which the consumer often scraped a sheen of mould), a little portion of sauerkraut, and sometimes fish; not exactly a mouth-watering menu, but still better than absolutely nothing, we mused.

On occasions we would also trade rations (some things were more acceptable to other nationalities, it seemed!); the cheese was known as 'stinkfinger', and the only men who would eat it were the Poles among us, and they also swapped the evil-smelling 'klipp fish' (we never knew – or even asked – what that 'delicacy' was!) for the equally foul-tasting sauerkraut, the latter only marginally more appetising in flavour but at least had some calorific value for rumbling stomachs to digest very slowly. The 'abort' (toilet) blocks were always something of a major endurance, following such delightful meals.

As Christmas approached in 1942, food occupied our thoughts even more than usual. Small Christmas puddings began to arrive in those vital Red Cross packages, and, of course, were hidden away for that day.

Alec, Bull and I were even more ambitious – we decided that we would have a Christmas cake, too! As some of the other chaps had similar ideas, we had to create a hut timetable for 'oven time', and this had to be meticulously allocated and disciplined. As anyone who's handy in the kitchen will know, Christmas cakes take a long time to create and cook, so we had to extend oven time allotments well into each night in the weeks preceding the festive season so that 'combines' could take turns outside of normal hut cooking times, and the resulting aromas really made our tummies rumble with acute anticipation of gourmet delights!

Taking advice from longer-resident Kriegies, we saved up our Klim biscuits until we had enough for our cake, then we crushed and rolled them all into a fine powder that we were to use as flour. Packets of currants (a regular 'ingredient' in Canadian parcels) were saved, and on mixing day were added into the 'flour' along with powdered dried egg, the mixture of which was leavened by as much of our meagre ration of margarine that we felt we should spare, along with some of our modest (luxury) sugar store. We added the necessary water, then the stodgy mixture was given its official 'ceremonial' mixing (each of us taking turns until our arms ached), and we were ready to bake it! Allowed as much time as we needed after official 'lights out' at 11pm, we duly scraped, smeared, prodded and pushed our precious mixture into a borrowed bread tin, and into the oven it went.

The Germans had given us extra coal for the Christmas period, but even so – on Alec's advice – the cooking had to be as slow and gentle as could be, so he, Bull and I took an hour each to watch over it, using small Kriegie-pattern night lights by which to see. When we finally removed our concoction from the oven, to our immense relief it both looked and smelled absolutely delicious! The 'proof of the pudding', to adopt the typical pun, would follow on Christmas Day.

When that day finally dawned, cold and bright, we arose from our bunks in a collectively peaceful and jolly mood, every one of us doing our best not to become morose for the company of our families back home.

The padre came over from the officers' compound to conduct Morning Service, and we sang carols quite lustily, covering that yearning for home in a manner that really impressed our 'hosts'.

Midday arrived, and along with it our modest Christmas dinner; no turkey – obviously, not to be expected in a prison camp – but our 'best cuts' of Spam or corned beef, saved for that day. No feast by any stretch of the imagination, but our chefs produced some very good meals by adding a little extra flavouring from experimental concoctions (again, we didn't ask!) and we enjoyed what little we had, which was the most important point.

In spite of all the hardship, we did our best to foster the true spirit of Christmas, with friendly visits to other huts, spreading bonhomie and goodwill beyond our own barracks to as many as we had time to share such moments with. Normally, the huts were all locked as soon as it was dark, but tonight we were allowed to move around freely until nine o'clock – with all the searchlights switched on in the guard towers, of course – and we had to move between the huts only along set lines, so that the Germans could at least keep some semblance of order with their charges.

After lock-up came teatime, and our big cake tasting! We were rather guiltily aware that our own cake had felt pretty heavy when we'd taken it out of the oven, but slices were carved (not simply cut, as it proved to be a little more stodgy than we'd hoped for), and we all took a big bite each from our portions. As we half expected, it was pretty solid and took some chewing – but it was incredibly tasty all the same! We couldn't eat much of it at a time, but that was all to the better as it lasted us for a few days, so we considered it a 'modified success', all things considered.

Boxing Day was quiet, but in the theatre that evening, the choir gave powerful renditions selected from *The Messiah*, specially arranged by Jack Murray and our leading pianist Walter Bradley. We couldn't manage the soprano parts, of course, but our tenors – of whom, I was one – coped quite well; although I shouldn't say it, our performance was great! Of course, we'd had lots of time to practise, and Jack Murray was rightfully showered with praise for his arrangement and adaptation work to the various arias, as were we who had worked our larynxes to our limits; a great night, indeed, that was also enjoyed by a few invited German officers.

Chapter 14

All manner of escape plans

And so we entered another year, and the nostalgia brought on by the Christmas festivities soon disappeared under the daily need to keep occupied. Even with all those activities to keep us relatively fit and busy, morale was always a fragile thread to foster and maintain.

There was a weekly newspaper, *The Camp*, issued by the Germans, and as you would expect at that time, there was little good news in it for us Kriegies. What information there was printed was inevitably biased toward the Germans; their army 'never lost a battle', nor even had they needed to carry out a 'tactical withdrawal', they wrote. It was, however, a sad fact that our adversaries really were very much on top of the ground fighting in the western and eastern European theatre of war, but we stubbornly refused to believe all their propaganda (or 'bullshit', as we preferred to call it). You see, we knew better, because – as in just about every POW camp that was ever written about – we had a secret radio hidden away!

The story of how it was created is quite an interesting tale. Several of the present Sagan inmates had previously spent many months in Barth, another Stalag near the Baltic coast. In the early days of the war, many aircrew were just below the rank of sergeant, and were sent out of the camp to work. It transpired that the security officer at Barth had been a POW in Britain in the First World War, and had a certain amount of sympathy for the Allied prisoners, based upon his own humane treatment in British captivity. He arranged for a party of them to work at a local electronics factory and, needless to say, enough small parts disappeared from that factory to help John Bristow, a Blenheim wireless operator and brilliant engineer, to build a radio from these and several other handmade parts.

I didn't actually see it, but I was told that it was made in such a way that it could be stripped down into chunks of innocuous-looking items to be secreted in hiding places in huts, and also to enable it to be transported in kitbags, yet be quickly reassembled and operated when opportunities arose. Thus, it arrived at Sagan, and provided BBC news stories just about every night for a long time, so we got the real news – both good and bad.

The process was all highly organised; while others guarded doors and windows, ex-Daily Express reporters Ron Mogg and Cyril Aynsley would listen to the BBC World News broadcasts at nine o'clock each evening, transcribing the reports verbatim before making several copies; these were then shared among a team of 'newsreaders', who in turn were organised to take the bulletin sheets into the huts and to read them as a BBC newscaster would – all at varying times of each day to avert German suspicions of regular service – and so we were all kept up to date with worldly goings-on almost as soon as they occurred and were broadcast.

No chances were taken; as soon as a reader appeared in a hut, all doors and windows were closed and guarded by our own 'sentries' and, at the approach of any 'goon' or other German official, reading was stopped and everyone hastily (but calmly and innocently) returned to whatever they were doing before the newsreader appeared in their midst.

That particular radio travelled from its 'birthplace' in Barth to Sagan, then followed us further on to our next camp at Heydekrug and finally Fallingbostel. It was occasionally repaired from a 'spares kit' or from home-made new components like tuning condensers made from tins, and capacitors from rolled foil (very clever, were our engineers!) when the relevant parts weren't available from the spares, but it was rarely out of service for more than a day, to my recollection.

We had no doubt that the Germans knew of the existence of our radio, but they never found it, nor any trace of the spare parts due to the cunning concealment plan. Come what may, that radio was sparked-up as often as it was safe to do so, for the benefit of our collective comfort, sanity and general morale, and, ultimately, it was to prove to be a real life-saver, right at the end of the war.

The radio service had quite a profound effect on morale in more

ways than one. Not only did it provide news from home on many fronts
and topics and therefore raise our collective spirits, but such stories
and accounts also served to galvanise and embolden those brave souls
in our escapers' fraternity into dreaming up ever more daring schemes
and making determined attempts to break free and get home – some
hoping to return and continue the fight, others just happy to get back
to their families. And, of course, for every escaper who managed to
accomplish the 'home run' (as it was dubbed) and get word back to their
Kriegie pals, morale was always subsequently given another welcome
boost, even if it could only be acknowledged in a subdued and discreet
fashion lest our captors wonder how we'd learned of each victory
(often by coded message via the BBC radio service).

To succeed in that monumental challenge of escape and evasion,
fraught with acute danger at every moment and turn, was obviously a huge
achievement indeed and worthy of all our congratulations and praise –
even if (in the case of a radio message) the feat could only be honoured
discreetly by the simple raising of humble toasts of tea brewed in our
home-made tin mugs, and a mumbled 'Well done!' The more brazen
postcard messages that got to us past the camp censors were usually
celebrated quite loudly, to take a poke at the Germans' 'missed catch'!

As already mentioned, for my own part I had decided to settle into
camp life and do my best to support our braveheart escapers wherever
I could, and I believe that that was the right decision for my own personal
circumstances. The news bulletins from the radio service (when read
between the lines) gave me the feeling that we (the Allies) were turning
the tide of the war, and I had begun to hope that it wouldn't be very
long before it was all over – so why take unnecessary risks? I reasoned,
comfortably, that if I could do my best in support of those who wished
to both cause trouble for our captors, and also to escape and hopefully
get home, then I believed that I would have made a good contribution
to the war effort in another way. As, I should add, did the majority of
my Kriegie compatriots; even if only a few were actively involved with
the background creativity and organisation of every escape, the vast
majority were always game for an impromptu 'riot' to completely muddle
the German attempts to keep order when escapes were detected or

other events took a turn for the worse – or simply if a diversion of attention was required while someone made a break for freedom.

So, most Kriegies were moderately happy to sit back and make the best of what we had, some to learn and improve their futures with facilities such as the so-called 'Barbed Wire University' (a subject I'll return to later), and others to support their fellow inmates in many different ways – not only in escape activities, but also in welfare and suchlike.

As you would expect of such a prison camp, though, among all those highly skilled and resentfully contained young men, there was a select few determined individuals with 'itchy feet' whose only waking thoughts were to escape at all costs, who found captivity impossible to bear for too long, and who just had to take every single opportunity to try to beat the Germans' security, then give them a bloody nose by getting all the way home.

All manner of escape plans were dreamed up, often from the talents and ingenuity of the individual escaper, but each scheme had to be presented to the escape committee for approval, to be checked, scrutinised, questioned and hopefully passed as favourable, primarily – in principle at least – to protect both the escaper from his own desperation (if it was a really hare-brained method), and to coordinate attempts to avert clashes with other plans already being put in place. Obviously, nobody wanted to have two tunnels crossing each other, or two 'German' officers trying to pass out of the main gates at the same moment.

A few attempts actually succeeded, but unfortunately it seemed that nobody managed to evade recapture for more than a few days. Several tunnels were dug from our compound – certainly no easy task, given the nature of the shifting sandy soil – but by now the Germans had developed the most sophisticated means of combating this method of escape by installing underground microphones and primitive seismometers (so we'd heard). After they'd discovered one tunnel, they instigated snap inspections of the 'no-man's-land' between the low warning trip-wire and the compound fences, with one or more of their 'ferrets' (as their technical investigators became dubbed by us) pacing around, hammering a long spike into the soft soil as a means of detecting sub-surface tunnels.

Nevertheless, two of the most famous and successful breakouts of the whole war took place here: the 'Wooden Horse' shallow tunnel in

1943; and also – after the NCO prisoners' departure and the subsequent conversion of Sagan into an 'officers only' camp – the major one that became known as the 'Great Escape' in 1944. With the subsequent murder of fifty of the escapers in reprisal, the latter was a sad and costly event.

Whenever anyone (or any group of prisoners) managed to escape – and particularly if it was more than one – we used the ensuing confusion to cause total mayhem and chaos at 'appell' parades. We had two such roll calls daily – morning and evening – and we paraded in ranks of five (easy for the Germans to total up), and the goons counted us and reported back to their Feldwebels (sergeants), who in turn tallied each numbered rank and reported onward to Major Von Lindeiner. We soon learned that the Germans were hopeless at counting, and so we played all sorts of tricks to confuse them when we needed to cover for absences – much to their intense annoyance! Appells would carry on until the numbers added up correctly, though, so we had some very long parades.

Guards stood behind as well as in front of us, but we still managed to duck and dodge among the ranks to swell or reduce numbers to suit and complicate, with each recount generating more anger and even more confusion. This would result in some hilarious situations involving 'sheep-counts' (being 'funnelled' between ladders, yet being unwittingly allowed to run back around to rejoin the throng), or being counted singly into huts, only to leap out of windows to rejoin the queue, and several other systems of (mis)calculation that almost always ended in chaos. Eventually, with Teutonic tempers frayed and rifle bolts clicked, we'd calm down and settle into ranks for a final tally – but even then the Germans sometimes found that no one was missing (bad counting again!), and so wondered why we'd played them for fools.

The funniest episode that I can remember from such an extended parade was when two bored Kriegies decided to mime a game of imaginary darts. After watching them for a minute or two, one of the Feldwebels hauled the miscreants out to stand in front of Major Von Lindeiner. The Feldwebel then had the job of trying to explain their behaviour to the Kommandant, but as they'd only been miming, and the Feldwebel obviously didn't have a clue what they were supposed to have been doing, he could only imitate their acting (badly); it didn't go down too well with Von Lindeiner, who evidently also knew nothing about playing darts.

Herr Kommandant insisted that the Feldwebel repeat his actions – much to the hysterical delight of the assembled POW ranks – and, finally, the hapless pair of Kriegies were marched off for a seven-day spell in the cooler on a German equivalent charge of 'dumb insolence' with Von Lindeiner being jeered, booed and whistled for the sentence. To be fair, though, he was quite a tolerant chap (for a German) and had the good grace to return a wry smile, and the pair served only two days instead.

During my year at Sagan, there were a few who escaped, but were soon recaptured; they would automatically earn a spell in 'the cooler' (the solitary confinement cells), usually for up to a month on a diet of just bread and water (and whatever the miscreant might have managed to hang on to, in the body searches). A canny Kriegie, however, could usually supplement that stark diet by bribery – Canadian or British cigarettes were powerful 'currency' among the German guards.

Still, the determined few kept trying to get away – and nobody could have been more motivated to escape than a man I met toward the end of our stay in Stalag Luft III; a chap who could well have been crowned the 'King of All Escapers' – the highly determined and very resourceful Sergeant George Grimson.

He had arrived at Sagan from Barth, and men who knew him from that camp (and others) told us that he'd spent every waking hour plotting ever-more detailed escape methods and learning to speak German like a native following his first few escape failures. He was resolute that these skills were the real key to staying away once out – along with decent intelligence information – but like a bad penny, he kept returning; something was obviously amiss with his methods. It might have been just plain bad luck, but after each recapture and subsequent spell in the cooler, he would give a wry grin and shrug it off, reckoning that it was well worth the effort; every escape attempt was a trial run that might fully succeed, he would say – and every recapture just a lesson that he'd missed out on detail, somewhere.

Once he'd landed in our midst at Stalag Luft III, he then set about testing revised escape plans and new ideas. I never found out about the methods that he had previously tried, but he, it was, who made a break for freedom while we were roaring with laughter during that high-kicking chorus-'girl' routine in our adapted pantomime, *Aladdin*.

Together with fellow Kriegie Alan Morris, they had been kitted out with copied German uniforms, impersonating two guards who most resembled them. Apparently, Grimson and Morris had had to wait for two or three nights in full regalia as they waited for the 'Tally Ho' watchers to tip them that these two particular guards were in the panto's audience and, soon after, the intrepid duo marched out of the gate to freedom – although, unfortunately, it was just another temporary departure from captivity; they were recaptured in just a few days, and were ensconced in the cooler once more at the Kommandant's 'leisure'.

True to his form and spirit, though, Grimson just kept on trying to get away – and I witnessed the climax of his cheekiest effort to date in what proved to be the very last week that we were at Sagan, and I marvelled at his courage and imagination.

In June 1943, the shock news that we were to relocate at such short notice had a jolting effect across the camp as the transportation plan was revealed and detailed by the Kommandant. The entire Stalag Luft III was to be converted to an officers' only camp, while all NCOs were to be moved; a relative few were to return to Barth (mainly those who'd been there before and knew it well), but the majority of us were being transferred to another camp at Heydekrug, in old East Prussia. This mostly unwelcome news had a galvanising effect on Grimson, and he set to with his most audacious scheme yet, hoping that the frenzy of activity and confusion surrounding the preparations for the mass move would help to cloak his breakout.

Naturally, most escape attempts only happened on the old 'need to know' basis, with 'stooges' (our watchmen) keeping track of the comings and goings of Germans in and around the camp, so – as one would expect – most of us hadn't a clue what George was going to do, or when.

The first that I knew of it was when I was busy in our hut, morosely packing the meagre contents of my bedside 'locker' and modest laundry pile in readiness for the move that day. Alec popped his head around the door, a huge grin on his face as he saw me and stepped in and advanced to the window between us.

'Jack! Here – look!' he hissed, pointing at the wire fence. I stepped up to the window, but he held up a hand to stop me getting too close to it.

'What's up?' I asked, puzzled, as I peered around the window frame.

'Over there!' he urged, nodding at a figure pacing purposefully along the outside of the fence, some distance away; all I could see, however, was a German 'ferret', with a toolbag slung over his shoulder. Baffled, I looked askance at Alec.

'It's George, ye dafty! He's away again!'

I squinted harder, trying to see his face … and then the 'ferret' glanced once sideways into the compound before pacing onward in a determined strut; it was George, all right!

'Never in the world.' I breathed, swapping smiles with Alec, dropping into my native Geordie accent, normally very controlled so that others would understand me better. 'Get away, man! How the hell?'

My camp-mate nodded to the left, and I followed his prompt to see – of all things – a ladder propped against one of the fence posts, snugly jammed beneath one of the perimeter lights. By the time I'd seen the ladder and then looked back again, George had vanished from my line of sight, obscured by another hut.

I must have looked very perplexed indeed, so Alec obliged with the story of what he'd seen taking place; his excited account, mixed with the rest of the story shared later around the camp, was remarkable.

Somehow, George had procured the standard uniform of a camp 'ferret' (a technician) – blue dungarees and a forage cap – then borrowed a ladder from the theatre. Over one shoulder he toted a toolbag, inside which (beside a collection of hand tools and his escape kit) was an extra master-piece – a dummy electrical test meter fabricated by two of our skilled resident 'tinsmiths' from a couple of food containers, complete with a glued-on dial face made from paper, and resplendent with a pair of test wires to complete the instrument! He'd really looked the part of a German electrician as he stepped across the trip-wire, ladder over one shoulder and toolbag over the other, then headed toward one of the watch towers set into the huge perimeter fence.

Propping his ladder against the nearest fence support post to the tower, George shouted up to the puzzled guards and explained that there had been a report of an intermittent fault with those particular floodlights and, without further ado, he climbed the ladder as boldly as can be – as though it was a completely natural routine – then eased a board across the fences, balanced between the ladder and the top coil of barbed wire and began to dismantle the first of the lights while still casually chatting with the nonplussed guards.

He'd 'tested' the bulb with his 'meter', scratched his head a little, then reassembled it and moved across the plank to the next one. The guards seemed to have lost interest as he'd checked the second lamp, and they'd moved to the other side of the tower 'nest' to allow him to finish his work uninterrupted.

After 'testing' three lights without finding faults, he'd shrugged and begun to pack up his toolkit, and when he'd felt the moment was right, he'd 'accidentally' dropped a pair of pliers – as planned – and, as he'd hoped, they landed just inside the outer fence. Cursing loudly (yes, he'd learned that in the German language, too!), he'd stepped up and balanced himself atop the barbed wire, calling to the tower guards to tell them that he'd climb down the wire and walk back around to save himself a double journey there and back from our compound. They'd merely nodded and turned away again (probably to light cigarettes) so without further ado, he'd climbed slowly and carefully down the other side. Then casually, yet confidently, he'd walked briskly away, passing stationed sentries without even a hint of a challenge from them, for all the world a daily occurrence that the guards wouldn't think to question.

Some time later, another Kriegie (who was in on the scheme) stepped up to the trip-wire and called to the watchtower guards that he wanted the ladder and board back as their lazy so-and-so electrician hadn't bothered to return them, and without thought or care the guard organised for one of their own chaps to take them down and handed them over. The Kriegie marched back to the theatre with the ladder on his shoulder and the board snuggled under the other arm, acting completely naturally, thus covering George's escape tracks very efficiently.

All this had happened in broad daylight. I was astonished, and Alec and I muttered our best wishes after him. Unfortunately, Grimson was recaptured only a few days later, but by then over half of our NCO contingent had already vacated Sagan, and so – after his customary 'stay' in the cooler – he was escorted more carefully with the second 'batch' to join us in Heydekrug.

Chapter 15

The 'getaway'

Even though the journey to Heydekrug was unwanted and promised to be incredibly depressing, it had been decided that we'd exit Stalag Luft III in good style to show our hosts that we still had our pride, with everyone pressed and polished in our smartest possible appearance.

Once assembled in marching order, carrying our very meagre possessions and just a few tidbits from our Red Cross parcels in a variety of home-made backpacks over our shoulders, we proudly marched to the railway station, escorted by a suitably impressed German guard troop – but we were greeted with a very glum scene when we reached the railway sidings: our transport consisted of a cattle train, dozens of wagons long, labelled on the outside as '40 hommes, 8 cheveaux' ('40 men, 8 horses'!).

Each wagon was divided into two sections by a yard-wide passage down the middle, and each 'half' was barricaded by barbed wire. We were crammed into each end of the wagons, 'scientifically' calculated so that half of those in each section could stand, and the other half sit – swapping during the journey – and to make sure that we caused no trouble for the duration. There were as many guards on the train as prisoners (or so it seemed), with several 'camped' in the divide between each half of every truck; presumably, the rest of the guards were given 'luxury' cattle wagons all to themselves, interspersed throughout the train. Until then, I had had no idea that we were deemed so 'dangerous'!

It was a very long, grindingly slow and agonising trip, similar in kind to that from Dulag Luft to Sagan, although this time there were many more prisoners involved – around 1,500 or more – so the Germans were much more strict with us. There were several stops along the way, and at every halt, the guards piled out. However, we were only allowed out a few times, and even then we found that our wagon guards were joining up as a huge cordon as we clambered on to the trackside to stretch our legs and to answer calls of nature – with guards aiming their rifles at us throughout! No privacy for us.

Occasionally, the train came to a rest at stations – usually in sidings – often for feeding with watery soup or stale bread, by what I suppose was the German equivalent of our NAAFI, or perhaps WRVS. With so many mouths to feed, these stops were by necessity very long indeed, and as they didn't happen as often as they probably should have (by Geneva Convention standards), we arrived at Heydekrug dirty, unshaven, smelly and for all the world an 'army' of tramps.

We almost fell out of those cattle wagons, so very weary were we, only to find that we still had another 4-mile 'march' (a misnomer in our condition) to complete to reach the camp. Eventually, we made it to the gates and through into the main compound, whereupon we were subjected to a (thankfully brief) roll call to be allocated huts, before being given some more soup and issued with bedding (such as it was – one blanket and a thin straw palliasse each). Finally, we were only too glad to be able to collapse into our 'pits' and settle down for the night.

Appell the next morning was a very long, protracted affair and, after the usual head count had been completed (we were all still too exhausted to muck about with it this time), we were given the run-down of the general layout and methods of working at this camp. Dixie Deans and Ron Mogg were thankfully still with us, and they were a great help in settling things quickly.

The huts at Heydekrug were of a terraced format, unlike the separated huts we'd left behind in Sagan; there were four such terraces, each divided into nine rooms with about fifty men to a room. Three smaller huts were used for the camp office, stores and ultimately a theatre. There was a sports 'playing field' – the usual sandy shale surface mixture – at the north end of the compound, with the latrines and wash-houses beyond that, and at the south end stood the cookhouse.

The main sustenance difference between Sagan and Heydekrug, we found, was that the Red Cross parcels went straight to the cookhouse where our meals were made, then shared between the kitchens to provide our basic dietary needs. Items provided by the Germans – such as potatoes, bread and soup – were obviously held and dealt with in the cookhouse, but compared to Sagan we were to find that we would be on very meagre fare here, as we had no individual parcels delivered; evidently, we wouldn't be getting fat at Heydekrug!

The few luxuries within the parcels were now 'pooled' in what was still a moderate swap-shop system – oddly nicknamed 'Foodacco' – although it was very restricted indeed due to that trickle of supply. This bartering system had been set up by the 'Tally Ho' organisation (our 'stooges', who kept the 'duty pilot' goon watch scheme on a constant boil), and was run very tightly by Ron West and Gerry Tipping, initially to combat 'privateer' exchanging within the camp by individuals who sought to profit for their own selfish benefit by plying guards with bribes. Once more, the profits of 'Foodacco's' points system went to the Tally Ho committee for escape 'funds' or for bribery, and so – although there were a few grumbles initially due to the scarcity of extras – everyone soon accepted the system as a boost for the common good.

One rather important change was the availability of water; it had to be pumped – by hand! In the wash-houses were two manual pumps, each fitted with 2ft-long handles; the pipes from each pump fed the rows of taps for our ablutions and, as one can imagine, at very busy peak times there was a shift-rota system in place for teams of men to pump those handles like mad, just to provide even the merest trickle from the numerous taps. The pumping shifts were arranged by room leaders and, of course – for fairness – every man in turn had to flex his muscles for the greater cause of the many, with numerous grumbles from those who caught the responsibility of supplying the earliest shifts of weary washers! Someone had a sense of humour, though – a wag had printed the obvious motto on the wall above the point where the pumps were installed (an adaptation of the RAF's own motto): 'Per Ardua Ad Aqua'!

The other difference here was that our previous hut group 'combines' became room combines by necessity, as we were packed in like sardines with little elbow room between us. Alec and I were still together, thankfully, but 'Bull' Shannon had joined with his Australian 'cobbers' in another room, whereas Jimmy Ferguson and Jack Knight had been sent to Barth.

Once we'd all settled down, however, life resumed pretty much as before; the same appells, the same old boring 'circuits' around the compound perimeter, the same conversations and much the same letters from home.

Nevertheless, the organisers soon got busy arranging activities and, fairly soon, we had several football and rugby teams, and even a couple of cricket sides, as the ground was marginally better for ball control. Classes began again for all sorts of subjects, artists and craftsmen set to with their creative hobbies, and, of course, escapes were plotted and prepared for.

The escape committee was better administered now, with so much experience behind them, and they soon managed to acquire German uniforms, civilian clothing, maps, passes and money. A system of escape-method examination and approval was set up once more; they were back in business!

The theatre wasn't established in Heydekrug for some time, so the 'costume department' were able to devote all their attention to helping would-be absconders. A fair bit of bribery went on in the new camp, as it seemed that the German guards were either more susceptible or just greedier (or more likely, both!), and so it was relatively easy to acquire a great deal of contraband material from them, even though we had fewer Red Cross parcels at our disposal.

The Germans, however, had their usual means of escape detection – but, here, they soon displayed their hand with a cunning 'secret weapon': an ancient, wheezing old steamroller to break down tunnels in the sandy soil. While it caused one or two heart-in-mouth episodes on occasion when it was trundled out, there was great merriment in the camp one day when it 'discovered' such a shallowly dug 'mole'-type tunnel, and fell in so deep that they had to augment their digging with a tractor to extract the steam roller, and even the tractor became well and truly dug in, too! There were some very red faces among the soldiers by the time they'd cleared the two machines out of the way (ruddy-faced both with embarrassment and from huge effort, I'd say!), and the whole incident was the subject of jokes and jibes for some days after.

Because the craftsmen among us were only just beginning the conversion of one hut into a theatre, there was little that I could do to assist with such practical work (I had never been too handy with toolkits), and so I became involved on the fringes of the Tally Ho, taking turns to assist with watching out for goon activity around the camp when asked to do so, covering for all manner of skulduggery taking place within the huts and compound.

At first, I simply helped out on odd occasions as watchman, not knowing what activities were being guarded – but fairly soon, when we had proved trustworthy enough, I was astonished to learn that our erstwhile diggers and ex-miners had 'pushed' a tunnel nearly 150ft from the wash-house block – the nearest building to the wire fence – to a spot in the 30yd-wide grass 'belt' beyond the wire, in just under two months! Until that moment of revelation, I'd believed that we were keeping guard over background activities, because although we'd heard whispers that a tunnel was being dug out, we'd discounted it to be only a rumour; we had had no real idea that it was actually being excavated. In fact, three had been started, and one discovered – the shallow one 'detected' by the steam roller – so it came as something of a pleasant shock to us to learn not only of its actual existence, but also that it was almost ready for use!

When the time came for the breakout, a Tally Ho roster call was made and a full briefing followed for all watchmen to prepare to take up stations on a particular night at a specified time. As you can imagine, come the time, the excitement was palpable, and we all had to be very careful not to 'transmit' this anticipation to the goons.

The 'getaway' took place in autumn 1943. The exact location of the 'outlet' end of the tunnel had been checked by way of a stick prodded carefully up through the turf and plotted by sharp-eyed observers, so the planners knew that they were sufficiently beyond the wire; however, the greensward was patrolled by guards, and so they had be extremely careful when breaking up to the surface to avoid a catastrophic clash. Once through, they would then have to try to work out the patrol and searchlight swing timing to allow every one of the escapers to exit safely.

The full story of this tunnel has been published several times over in other books, but the following account is a mixture of my experience, and the narratives of the participants when we discussed the event, some time later.

Zero hour came, and as we watchmen strained our eyes in all directions

through the cracks and tiny gaps of the boards covering the hut windows, the man at the head of the tunnel cautiously cut upwards through
the turf with his home-made spade. Success! It went clean through, and
he very carefully enlarged the hole until he could raise his head and shoulders. The next man under him helped to push him up enough to take a
good look all around – and once he was sure that he had a clear exit, he
climbed out and ran at a crouch for the woods; that was the first one away!

One out, forty-nine to go – and after a thirty-second countdown, the
next chap checked for a clear departure, then sprinted after the first.
The process was repeated until eight had gained the cover of the trees
and dispersed.

As this was happening, the atmosphere in our hut was electrifying;
Alec and I had no way of seeing or knowing what was going on as we
were stationed on the opposite side of the hut, keeping watch for stray
goons, so all we could do was pray that things were going well.

There was obviously a relayed signalling system in place by way of wall-
tapping to warn of any imminent danger from goons or 'ferrets', but
I so wished that there might have been some form of returned tapping
to keep us up to speed on progress; the escapers' 'launch pad' – in the
wash-house several yards away – was thus impossible to communicate
directly with. Something must have been established, though, just in case
– I had wondered if they might have improvised with the old schoolboy
science of the tins and string method of 'telephony' between the huts,
but that would obviously have been somewhat risky for fear of a trip-over
discovery by a possible, unseen, guard or 'ferret'. Nevertheless, something along those lines could have been useful in such an instance!

Then, suddenly, there came a shot – and we all jumped in shock, groan-
ing in dismay when we heard Germans shouting hoarsely. More rifle
shots followed that first one; evidently, judging by the increasing din outside, the balloon was well and truly up.

With our hearts thumping in our chests, we scrambled across the hut
to join the others, all trying to force open the shutters outside the
windows in an attempt to try to see what was happening, but without
success. One group managed to get a squint through a gap in the boards,
and confirmed that two searchlights were focused on one spot – the
tunnel exit – and that they could see our chaps emerging one after

another under the guns of several guards. We groaned again and shook our heads before squeezing past each other, returning to our bunks as quietly as we could manage, hoping not to draw attention to our hut as we could hear the guards running around in the compound now, obviously seeking the tunnel entrance.

We quickly snuffed out our home-made lamps, trying to put on a show of innocence for the inevitable hut raids, and we kept our fingers crossed that nobody had been injured or perhaps killed. And then the hut doors crashed open, and guards stormed into our rooms yelling unintelligibly as they fanned out either side of the doors, rifles levelled in nervous fashion. Not one of us moved a muscle; everyone was well and truly frozen in fear.

While we were being shaken to life with all this feverish activity, those in the tunnel must have been terrified for their very lives; some of the would-be absconders told us later that the guard who had discovered that ninth escaper had actually fired a shot directly down into the tunnel exit hole, although somehow didn't hit the next man due out. They gave us their side of the story.

The men in the tunnel were completely helpless; those in the wash-house end, after the obvious delay from lack of information coming back along the tunnel, tried to reverse out – an almost impossible task in such extremely cramped conditions – but when they finally did emerge, it was to be confronted by a German 'welcoming committee' of armed guards, awaiting them with rifles aimed.

At the exit end of the tunnel, the potential escapers were in an even more perilous situation as more guards arrived on the spot, some threatening to shoot down the hole again if the men didn't make an effort to exit faster – and with three or four snarling guard dogs straining to enter the tunnel after them, they were petrified of 'summary dispatch' and therefore somewhat reluctant to emerge.

Eventually, German officers arrived to take full control, and the Kriegies fearfully appeared one by one. It was well over an hour before the last man clambered out and then the dogs were sent down to make sure that nobody was still hiding underground; finally, when the goons were satisfied that it was clear, everyone was marched off to the cooler.

Soon after, a series of guttural commands from within our compound reached the ears of our twitchy guards, and they backed out of our hut, their eyes flicking from side to side as if they expected us to pounce on them; nothing could have been further from our minds, though – they had the guns, not us!

We heard the locks being turned and more orders issued, and one of our chaps quietly sneaked to the door, peeked through a gap and used hand-signals to confirm that they'd left a guard outside; presumably it would be the same with every hut, and so the majority of us tried to settle back down, wondering what the morning might bring. For some, how-ever, it was a busy night as they did their best to fully conceal items of 'contraband', in expectation of a very intense hut search the next day. It was a long, fearful night.

Chapter 16

Shocking news

We were turned out of our huts and bullied on parade at first light, many of us wrapped in our blankets against the morning's chill, an atmosphere of trepidation in the air as we didn't know what to expect. Would the Germans be trigger-happy or just plain brutal with rifle butts, fists and boots? However, what followed was to prove to be one of the most farcical episodes of entertainment that I'd ever experienced in captivity.

Our bleary eyes were greeted with the sight of hundreds of guards – evidently they had more than doubled their number for this occasion, perhaps anticipating trouble from our unarmed ranks; nothing could have been further from the truth, though, as we grumbled and shivered, wondering how the day would proceed.

As soon as we were all lined up, the fun began! During the initial melee of the first totting up of prisoners, some of the braver Kriegies were up to their usual tricks of dodging about, changing places, jumping rows – in fact, anything they could manage to confuse those counting. Even the threats of being sent directly to the cooler – or even of being shot – didn't deter these hardy inmates, until, after two totals over which the 'tally-men' failed to agree, two particularly disruptive prisoners were grabbed and hustled off at gunpoint to the cooler.

After the third abortive attempt, the Germans held a very bad-tempered consultation (entertaining in itself, with officers glove-slapping their minions in front of the parade!) and we were all sent back to our huts and locked in; we were then told there would be another appell that afternoon, and we settled back down to wait.

At two o'clock the hut doors were unlocked once again and we were told to take some food with us, for it was likely to be a long parade, but what an amusing sight awaited us!

We were housed in four long barrack huts, between each of which was a wide space – and in the centre of the first 'divide' the Germans had set down two converging rows of forms (long benches), lined all the way along on the outer sides by guards, their lines extending in front of the huts and cutting off all access around the furthest end of the barracks. At one side of the 'neck' of this erstwhile 'funnel' was a table, behind which sat the Kommandant and his second in command, his security officer, who had a number of boxes before them, each one containing identity cards, complete with names, photographs and fingerprints of every prisoner. Evidently – with what we termed 'typical German thorough-ness' – they were going to check every single man through the 'funnel' until they knew who was missing.

Bemused, we stood in our ranks, waiting for the Kommandant's address; this had all the hallmarks of a 'good day out', we thought – and we weren't disappointed!

'Now, as you all refuse to cooperate vis us, ve vill haf a sheep count,' he commanded – and naturally, we all let loose with loud choruses of 'Baaaa!' by way of reply as many dissolved into fits of laughter.

To their credit, several of the guards struggled to stifle their own merri-ment (many could speak English well enough to understand what was going on) – until the Kommandant screamed at them to get us all moving, at which they became stony-faced and began herding us into the 'funnel'. Many of our numbers were still muttering the odd sheep noise, but soon desisted when certain guards and an officer or two glared at them.

The inmates of each hut were escorted between the forms toward the table, checked against the identity cards, and then channelled away. We were not allowed back into our huts, but had to go around the bottom end of the barrack and into the other two gaps between the second, third and fourth huts. These spaces were, of course, heavily guarded and cut off from the appell group still on the parade ground; completely fool-proof, thought the Germans, but how little they knew their Kriegies!

First of all, what the Jerries hadn't yet discovered was that many of the inmates had swapped barracks since arrival in camp to join with friends and such, neglecting to inform the Kommandant's clerk, and therefore were no longer on the correct barrack registers.

This immediately caused much confusion, not helped, of course, by Kriegies feigning misunderstanding, playing dumb, and doing anything else that could cause further delay and add to the developing chaos. Obviously, the longer this could be carried on, then (it was hoped) the further away our escapers might get – but we knew that we would have to be careful not to push the Germans too far.

This counting and checking process – already painstakingly slow by its concept – was steadily grinding down to a near halt; the guards were getting more and more fed up, and several became quite inattentive as a result of their boredom, and so several Kriegies – perhaps braver or just more ingenious than most – managed to slip past these guards to rejoin the group not yet counted, and were checked again!

Dusk was creeping in by now, and 'Teutonic' tempers were beginning to fray. By the time they thought that they had finally accounted for every prisoner, we learned that they had totalled twenty-five more inmates than they were supposed to have!

The final straw came when they discovered that two whole boxes of identity cards had been pinched from the counting table – from beneath the Kommandant's nose, it would appear – causing another furious bout of bad-tempered glove-slapping, then the screaming of orders and stamping of boots as a frantic search was organised.

Word passed that they eventually found the cards dumped into the effluent beneath the latrines, and in no fit state to be used for identifying anyone, as one can imagine. We later heard that before this somewhat nauseating method of disposal had taken place, the photographs had apparently been steamed off the cards and had been squirrelled away for escape use (although quite how they achieved this in such a short space of time, I do not know – but Kriegie ingenuity should never be underestimated!); the Kommandant was not best pleased.

By this time it had become too dark to see properly, and rather than have more Kriegies slipping unseen past the guards, they gave up; the Kommandant stormed off, ranting and fuming while his hapless garrison hustled us all back into our huts for the night.

Sharp repercussions were expected the next day, but it was something of an anticlimax. We were hauled out on appell as usual in the morning, but were simply returned to barracks and thus confined thereafter, except for our orderlies whose task it was to collect our midday meal from the cookhouse. Slightly mystified by this apparent 'shrug off' by the Germans, we remained suspicious as we settled down to sleep that next night.

Our mistrust was justified, for around 2.30 in the morning, the hut doors crashed open as half a dozen guards stormed each room, yelling their usual 'Raus! Raus! Schnell!' Those who were slow to stir from their bunks were prodded wide awake by the guards' bayonets, and we were ordered to stand still by our bunks while Feldwebels and 'ferrets' carried out an intense search, looking for anything that they could loosely describe as 'illegal' or incriminating – which didn't take very long, as we had so little in our possession – but as soon as they had finished, the door crashed open again, and in walked two tall figures wearing their fabled long black leather overcoats and black trilby hats: the dreaded Gestapo had arrived!

The Jerries had evidently decided to take their 'Teutonic thorough-ness' one step further; every room was to be intimately searched, every prisoner was to be checked against his (new!) identity card and compared with his POW neck-tag – only this time, the Gestapo would do it all, not our common goons.

Confined in this manner within our rooms, there was no chance (or the will) for any horseplay or obstruction in which we had indulged in those first tally attempts, and even the slightest hint of intent or any attempt at causing trouble was promptly stamped upon by these evil-looking agents, and the 'offending' Kriegie was immediately marched off to the cooler while his living space and meagre belongings were given an even more thorough going-over, the agents' suspicions further heightened by such distraction behaviour.

No one was shot, fortunately, but the threat was ever present from those Gestapo men, one of whom carried out the searching while the other – with his revolver unholstered and laid within quick reach – examined the findings at a table in the middle of the room; the pistol was obviously intended as a direct intimidation to us all, so there were only token protests.

By late morning, the search and check procedure had been completed, and we later learned that the Gestapo were satisfied with the results. All eight of the escapers had now been identified, and they had netted a sizeable pile of 'contraband' items that would take some time to replace, but even the Gestapo didn't get away lightly! When they prepared to leave us, they were short of a few items of their own – such as a trilby, one leather overcoat, a briefcase full of papers, and – most amazing of all – one of their pistols had also gone missing!

The hapless agent who'd 'lost' his revolver had a screaming fit, all manner of threats were levelled at us collectively as several of their number retraced their search pattern, steaming through all the rooms in that hut – until, finally, the culprit gave up the gun in order to avoid the inevitable repercussions that would surely have followed, had it not come to light. Naturally, he was wheeled off to the cooler, and the rest of us breathed huge sighs of relief as we watched those black coats eventually march out of the camp gates.

And so, the first major escape episode at Heydekrug ended. Unfortunately, all eight of the absconders were recaptured within a few days, but it remained a talking point for quite some time – and, importantly, several valuable lessons had been learned.

It wasn't long after this massed escape attempt that George Grimson got 'itchy feet' once more – but not for him the claustrophobic confines of the tunnel; as always, he preferred to go 'through the wire', not under it, or better still, out through the main gate – and so it was again with his final 'sortie'. This time, however, he was extremely determined to get out and stay out, to contact the Polish partisans, and to set up a line of 'safe houses' to enable the passage to freedom for other escapers!

From the moment that he caught up with us in Heydekrug and, driven by his own sense of failure in evading recapture so many times, he had really become a steely eyed devout advocate of the RAF's 'duty to escape' mindset. Hence, he had been a prime motivator with the tunnelling group and in jollying along other getaway ideas, as well as directing and assisting the administration of the escape committee and many of the associated shenanigans that took place to disguise related 'projects' – but all the while, he was planning and setting up his own next breakout.

Working with Alfie Fripp and his mailroom cohorts and other Tally Ho operatives once more, George managed to acquire most of a German guard's uniform by a combination of their collective bartering, bribery and blackmail on a few of the more vulnerable (and apparently sympathetic) guards. What they couldn't obtain by these methods, our erstwhile tailors created by converting other items of clothing to suit, and rumour had it that one of our highly skilled craftsmen even manufactured a highly detailed replica rifle – something that could have resulted in serious (possibly lethal) repercussions to the harbourer, had it been discovered in a hut search.

I did not witness George's eventual escape in this disguise – for obvious security reasons, only a trusted handful of watchers knew exactly when his impersonation attempt would take place, to avoid potential giveaways from less-than-careful spectators – but it happened during one of our more riotous appells, when there were distractions galore.

On such rebellious occasions, and with the usual levels of increasingly high-spirited 'organised chaos', the number of guards surrounding the ground swelled gradually as extras were drafted in; with such numbers present, and given the Germans' very evident lack of head-counting skills, George would have been banking on the gate guard's boredom from witnessing such a long and drawn-out parade. And so it was to be; one moment it seemed that George was among us, and the next, he had vanished!

In the following months, Paddy Flockhart followed George out and managed to get back to England (oh, how we rejoiced a few weeks later when we heard this news!), and then Jock Callender escaped by deception to follow their footsteps, but was never heard from again; it was believed that he had been caught somewhere on the rail journey and shot by the Gestapo, but that was never proven conclusively.

After them went R.B.H. Townsend-Coles and Jack Gilbert, who left together. Unfortunately, T-C was caught as the two were attempting to board a Swedish ship; Gilbert, however, managed to get on board and stowed away, becoming our second 'home run' escaper from Heydekrug – even more rejoicing ensued!

Soon after their departure, Nat Leaman tried to escape under great pressure, following a German attempt to segregate him from us (he was a Jew, serving in the RAF). Sadly, he was caught at the gate and taken off to the cooler, but the story followed that he had been badly burned while trying to destroy his false papers in their office stove – bad news indeed, as it was feared that the German security police would use that injury to torture him for information. I can remember a tense atmosphere in the camp for a time after as all manner of intense searches were anticipated – yet none came for a while, which led some to believe that Nat had managed to hold out and keep the origin of his documentation secret.

There was something of a fuss, though, over the Germans standing firm against returning his uniform to him – a rumour circulated that he might be shot as a spy, as he had been caught wearing a full civilian outfit – but somehow his uniform was smuggled into him, and Nat eventually returned to our ranks a good deal thinner and quieter, and still nursing that bad burn.

An edgy atmosphere settled over Heydekrug for a very short while – then after the lull inside the compound, tragedy was to follow from without.

One morning in April 1944, we were ordered out on to the parade ground for what began as a normal morning appell, but we were soon told the very grim news from the Kommandant himself that following a mass breakout from our last camp at Sagan, a number of our officers had been shot 'whilst attempting to escape'.

This shocking and tragic news almost caused a riot as anger flowed rapidly through our ranks. There were many low growls across the parade ground and the guards looked very nervous as they began to fumble with their guns, but Dixie Deans kept the lid on our feelings with a few sharp orders to keep quiet – and then an extraordinary thing happened as a few chaps began cheering; they had realised that 'a number of officers' meant that some might still be at large and could get home, and so they felt compelled to cheer them on. And at the same time, as we all joined in with loud voices, we were vocally applauding the brave souls of those who had lost their lives in what had sounded like a vile, wholesale slaughter. The Germans were astonished and looked very confused by this unexpected turn of events before them, and the Kommandant stamped out, angrily flapping his arms at us; evidently, this was not the shocked, dumbstruck and cowed reaction that he might have been hoping for – but what else could we do, rather than mope and mourn?

It seemed only right, then, that we should wish their spirits Godspeed, and so we raised our voices to them all, culminating in three cheers – much to the Jerries' consternation.

We didn't know at that moment just how many had been shot, of course – that information did not come out for some time, although the massacre was reported with great anger by the BBC at the time – but we learned later that fifty out of seventy-six had been gunned down in cold blood, while three managed the 'home run', with the rest recaptured and returned to camps.

It was, indeed, a very grim atmosphere for some time, and somewhat discouraging to others contemplating escapes here at Heydekrug – yet a few more managed to slip away in the coming months all the same.

Things settled down quietly again in the compound, and life carried on as frugally as before.In May, however, my heart lurched when I received a letter from my wife Evelyn, which included a comment that had been missed by the censors back home; 'look out for 'J'", she had written, meaning James, my younger brother, as referred in previous letters.

At the outbreak of the war James had joined the RAF, and served as an Ambulance Driver at RAF Uxbridge. When we had last spoken during a uniformed family group portrait photograph session in 1941, along with our other younger brother William (then an Air Training Corps cadet), James had only recently volunteered for aircrew duty with Bomber Command and had told me that he was to be trained as an air gunner. From Evelyn's comment, I guessed, therefore, that some aerial mishap had befallen him, and that he may be on the ground and hopefully uninjured. Of course nobody would know for some time if he was either on the run or in captivity, but his wife Vera would have received that dreaded telegram or letter listing him as 'Missing In Action' – the same notification that Evelyn would have received after my own bumpy landing in that field, two years previously (was it really that long ago?!). I hoped fervently that they would not have added the frightening line, '…Believed Killed.'

I kept my fingers crossed that he had survived intact, and if captured that he would indeed join me in the ranks here fairly soon, safe and reasonably sound. I also prayed that Vera would be able to cope at home with their toddler son, Alan. I wondered – even hoped – that Evelyn might find some way to help support her, somehow, from her own experience of the same existence. Perhaps she would find a kindly way, such was her softer side – although the main difficulty lay in the fact that they lived over 200 miles apart; such were the challenges during wartime.

Chapter 17

Keystone Kops

In between those spells of high excitement or extreme anxiety in this 'new' camp, life carried on much the same as it had back in Sagan,

Soon after our arrival at Heydekrug, we had set about re-forming sporting activities and teams once more, although we were restricted to being able to play certain sports only as our Red Cross supplies of sports equipment allowed them. Unfortunately, those deliveries were becoming fewer and further apart as the tide of the war had begun to turn against the Germans, but until such time as we might be overrun and hopefully liberated, we had a few games and matches to play – or we would simply suffer from interminable boredom, physically.

We had quickly created new football and rugby teams, but, just as we had found at Stalag Luft III, the rugby was very limited due to the similar risks of serious injury and skin infections from the unforgiving surface. As a result, football became the larger game of choice once more, although come the summer, we were able to field cricket sides, at last!

The ground at Heydekrug was a slight improvement over Sagan, in that we could bowl a proper cricket ball and actually manage some good spin and bounce from the harder-packed surface; therefore, wickets fell to he who could spin, a happy turn for me, at least, for I was one of those bowlers!

In our barracks, we discovered that we had a goodly collection of fair cricketers and one 'secret weapon' in the person of 'Smudger' Smith, an excellent wicket keeper (as well as a very good goalkeeper) who – when at home in England – played as 'opening bat' for Suffolk's county cricket club.

Each of the four barracks created a team, and we organised a 'test tournament' between the huts. We played really well, and ended up in the final. Our opponents batted first – and I am pleased to state that when it was my turn to step up to the crease and do my bit, I managed to bowl out eight of their players for twenty-eight runs between them; it could so easily have been nine out, but I missed an easy catch at the end of my 'over'. Nevertheless, I was chuffed to bits!

They were all out for just over 100 runs, and then it was our turn to bat, our first wicket going down with only a few runs on the board. 'Smudger' was the next man in.

'Take it easy,' we implored him, as he was renowned as a 'big hitter'.

'OK,' he said, smiling, and strolled to the crease as we fretted at the prospect of our valuable ball getting hit for six over the barbed wire and into the trees!

He was as good as his word, though, and kept his strokes fairly tame – yet he still scored a massive seventy-three runs in less than twenty minutes, including forty-three in two overs! Mind you, the boundaries were compelled to be a little short due to the constrictions of the compound, and neither the bat nor ball were of very good quality – but Smithy didn't bother with trying to beat the 'outfield' – he simply 'lifted' the ball over the boundary ropes each time.

I was a little peeved the next day, however, when our daily 'newspaper' – posted on our noticeboard – was full of Smithy's performance at bat, yet hardly mentioned my bowling! Oh well, I thought with a shrug, it's always the showy ones who get the glory!

When winter duly arrived that year, we developed a new 'craze' – the card game, bridge. We all had to be back in the huts as soon as it was dark, although we were allowed to visit the other huts until about nine o'clock – but we could only move thus as long as we stuck to certain set lines, marked upon a large camp plan in red, obviously known thenceforth as 'red lines'.

Bridge became so popular that we organised a league in three divisions, and sometimes we played practically all day, only stopping for meals, calls of nature or circuits (the latter for the exercise and to clear foggy heads!). I usually partnered Ted Lacey when playing; he was a cockney youngster about twenty years old who had only recently joined us in this camp. He was quite naive and hadn't had the advantage of a grammar school education, and because of that his general standard of English was poor, yet he was a very good mathematician (I was quite good at the figures, too, but he was just a little better). We played in the Third Division in the bridge league – and climbed steadily up the table from our combined efforts!

Ted was determined to learn many subjects, however, and so he entered a few of the GCE exams being organised and invigilated by the Red Cross. I, too, entered into exams – in my case, they were Commercial Mathematics and Economics, thinking ahead to our eventual return home – and so we spent some time learning together, sharing a couple of subjects. I was able to help him with his elementary English and grammar, and his previously poor spelling and written work improved considerably in a short time. To illustrate Ted's keenness and dedication to his efforts – even in spite of the disruption to our studies caused that year by moving (twice!) to other camps – I learned after the war that he had stayed on in the RAF (he was a navigator, like myself) and eventually gained a senior post in Transport Command.

We didn't do so well on the entertainment front here, as it took some time to convert one hut into a theatre, and so it was some months before it was ready for any real shows.

Jack Murray continued with the choir, and we had a Welsh Society and a Scottish Society, from which we made up a mock eisteddfod festival and then a Burns' night celebration – but we had no haggis or whisky for the latter, sadly!

Collectively, however, our choir continued to rehearse *The Mikado* – hoping to carry on where we had been forced to leave off on exiting Sagan – and at Easter in 1944, we put on *Stainer's Crucifixion*.

By that time, another compound had been built alongside our own, to house American prisoners. Jock persuaded the German authorities to allow us to perform the *Crucifixion* in their compound too, and it went down very well with them. The Americans really showed their appreciation by plying us with cigarettes and other goodies – but even so, and seemingly ungratefully, I came away with a slightly jaundiced view of some of them, an uncharacteristic if not slightly unfair impression that took a long time to leave me.

When we entered their biggest hut (which had hastily been cleared back to provide a mini-theatre just for this performance), we looked closely at their noticeboard in an effort to see what tickled them and the kind of information that they shared – and the joke that struck us most was a notice from their medical officer: 'In future,' it stated, 'the MO will refuse to treat airmen who attend medical parade in their pyjamas'! A silly detail to some, perhaps, but it screamed 'Discipline!' to a few of us.

Further to this, when we stepped out on the makeshift stage, we exchanged glances of dismay between ourselves when we saw the general sloppiness of their attire and dress standards; unshaven faces everywhere, uniforms mostly worn slap-happy and unlaundered here and there – only a tiny handful of officers had made the attempt to smarten up, and so it seemed almost as though they had mostly given up and given in to their bare existence. There was a sea of multicoloured nationals here – something of a rare sight to us Brits at that time – yet for all their apparent scruffiness and languor, they were all to a man highly appreciative of our performance that night, and gave us a thunderous round of genuine applause when we came to the finale – something that made a few of us flush slightly with pride.

Perhaps they weren't such a bad bunch of guys, after all, we thought, if only they'd tidy up their 'act'!

Back in our own compound theatre, we carried on creating shows (albeit much more frugally and hence more inventively than at Sagan) – until, one night, we were to witness its final 'glorious' but incredibly sad exit.

At around two o'clock in the morning we were awakened to very loud, panicked yelling, and as the main chorus seemed to be 'Feuer!', we were all agog and raring to get out of our huts to see what was going on. Somehow, in spite of our hut doors supposedly being securely locked and the windows shuttered externally, most of us managed to get outside, and we immediately saw that it was the theatre that was well ablaze, and it seemed that there was little that we could do but stand and watch its miserable demise. And watch, we did, for – despite the solemnity of the incident – it was well worth witnessing the comedic capers of the Germans in their efforts to extinguish the flames!

The Jerries, of course, had a fire engine – originally designed, it appeared, to be pulled by ponies, or something as small in stature. But they did not have such an animal here; just a bunch of 'trained' goons to pull and manoeuvre it into position. We expected, therefore, to see a fine example of that 'typical Teutonic thoroughness' that they were supposedly famous for – yet it turned out to be far more like a scene from the Keystone Kops!

In line like a team of stagecoach horses, up trotted the Jerries as smartly and as closely as they could to the fire hydrant, whereupon the Feldwebel shouted 'Halte!' Snapping to attention – all for show to us, of course – they dispersed to their individual tasks, connected the hose from hydrant to pump, then ran out their long hoses, coupled the nozzles, and took up their postures and aimed at the flames.

'Stimmt!' cried the leading fireman, and the man at the hydrant smartly wielded his key on the valve … and from the first hose nozzle came a mere, teeny-weeny trickle of water!

Amid roars of laughter from us, these amateur firemen tried every trick that they could to try to coax a decent flow of water pressure out of that hydrant and through their hoses, until, finally, one of the Kriegies tumbled to the solution.

'There's nobody pumping, you clots!' he cried, and as another of our number translated to the bemused crew, in next to no time, a gang of Kriegies had volunteered for pumping duty. Along with them, a couple of chain gangs had been organised and were busily shuttling all manner of bowls, containers and buckets back and forth from fire pond and wash-house to theatre.

Sadly, though, there was just no hope of saving the hut, and in no time at all it was just a smoking heap of charred timbers. The next day, a rumour passed around the camp that among the findings that morning, there was a pile of molten records, the top disc of which was the well-known tune, 'I don't want to set the world on fire'! It eventually transpired that this was a deliberate joke, played by the arsonist who had set the fire, apparently to destroy certain items that the escape committee didn't want found by the Germans in a predicted imminent close search – although those of us who had put so much effort into that makeshift theatre and its productions didn't see the funny side for some time.

Appells continued to be a source of both horseplay and news; those two inimitable jokers, Ken Bowden and Jack Lipton, were always ready for a lark – the only limit was their imagination, it seemed.

Bowden was over 6ft tall, and he had at one time been issued with a Polish cavalry officer's long greatcoat; this was very long indeed, long enough to cover the horse's hindquarters, in fact. He had cut off one of the big pockets from the inside – for what real purpose, nobody knew – and one morning, he and Lipton appeared in the front line of the parade, Bowden standing upright, with Lipton's head tucked under his arm! The latter was bent forward but also standing beneath that voluminous coat, with his head poked through the pocket hole. While Bowden stood there with a deadpan look on his face, Lipton pulled a grotesque caricature expression, with bulging eyes and tongue poking out in imitation of a decapitation, while their room-mates all sang 'With 'er 'ead tucked underneath 'er arm, she walks the bloody tow-er', etc., etc.

This trick caused great hilarity, and even the Kommandant, his adjutant and many of the guards gave in and had a good chuckle – but the two pranksters still earned themselves a day in the cooler for being cheeky.

Not long after that high-spirited episode, however, came that already-mentioned diabolical news of the massacre of the Great Escapers, and the camp was a very gloomy place indeed for some time – made all the more melancholy by the fact that there was absolutely nothing that we could do about it, other than a total mutiny during – say – an engineered riotous appell. But even that desperate, crazy thought was fraught with the risk that several of our number would be killed or wounded if we should attempt such madness – and what then? Even if we did manage to outfight and overrun our captors, what would we do, afterwards? There were some who espoused taking such action, then making for the west-ward-creeping Russian lines to supposed freedom (as we were quite near, it seemed), but in harsh reality, it was an impossible notion – and those who were angry enough to voice such thoughts soon found themselves rapidly smothered by their superiors and fellow inmates.

No one would have blamed the Kriegies in captivity right across Axis territory for taking some kind of revenge action, but it would have led to a wholesale disaster of dire repercussions, one way or another.

Chapter 18

Glen Heydekrug

As might be imagined, a prisoner of war camp was a great place for long stories – some good, some a little tall, but a great many hard luck ones and we all had one of those to tell, for they were the reason that we were all cooped up here together, fallen fliers like so many flightless birds!

Many were simple tales of misfortune leading to quick capture, others were long-winded and punctuated by anticlimax – Alec and I shared that scenario – and some were quite funny. Others were dramatic and often poignant or just plain tragic.

There was Jock Alexander (Grimson's cohort in escape activities); he was a pilot, and when his aircraft was attacked and crippled by a night fighter, he and his crew were forced to bail out. Being the last man out of the stricken aircraft, he became separated from the rest of his crew by wind drift catching his parachute, but he landed safely, and set about determining his next move. Being fairly fluent in German, Jock opted to make his way to Lübeck, a port to the north of his landing zone, and so – hiding in barns by night and travelling by day (much as we had) – he set off, acquiring a long overcoat along the way, and even procured an ancient, rattling old pushbike to help him travel a little quicker.

Upon reaching Lübeck a few days later, he hid down near the docks, to await his chance to get aboard a ship bound for Sweden – and, hopefully, freedom. The docks were swamped with German guards everywhere, and it looked an almost impossible task – but after a night or so in chilly conditions, he finally found an opportunity to sneak past the gangway guards and board a ship flying the Swedish national flag. He stowed away in a lifeboat – his heart in his mouth when he heard the Germans carrying out their standard pre-sailing search – but when they had been at sea for almost a day, he decided that it ought to be safe enough by then to reveal his presence to the crew.

He found the bosun, who took him to meet the captain, who promptly ordered the helmsman to turn the ship around on reverse course back to Lübeck! It transpired that the captain was a German sympathiser, and had Jock locked into a brig-like cubbyhole, to be handed over to the Germans upon reaching the docks. What a sad end to a heroic escape attempt!

In another's experience, the aircraft of Paul Shapiro, a Canadian second pilot, was hit by flak and they were given the order to bail out. Paul grabbed his parachute, clipped it on, but as he stepped over the escape hatch in preparation to jump through, the parachute pack burst open, and he stood there with two armfuls of fluttering silk, yelling, 'Now what do I do?' to the man behind him.

By way of answer, his understandably impatient crew-mate shouted back, 'Hang on, Paul' – then grabbed him around the waist and dropped him through the hatch! Drastic measures, no doubt, but when Paul at last had the sense to let go of his parachute, it flapped and billowed aloft, unfolding and forming a perfect canopy to lower him safely to earth; phew!

Ted Barnett and Doug Redpath were others who had had miraculous escapes. Barnett, a rear gunner in a Hudson, heard an explosion in their aircraft – possibly a direct hit from flak, or something as unwelcome – and suddenly found himself spinning through space, still secured within his turret and unable to get out … until, abruptly, it splashed down into the North Sea, then bobbed afloat just long enough to allow him to escape and inflate his Mae West life jacket. Struggling to tread water with his boots on, he tugged them off and tucked them into the life jacket's strapping, swimming steadily to the shore, which – fortunately – wasn't very far away; very lucky, indeed!

Meanwhile, Redpath had bailed out, but had somehow slipped out of his parachute harness. His foot had fortuitously caught in the ropes, however, and so he floated down to earth, only to crash head-first through a canopy of trees on landing. Miraculously sustaining only minor facial injuries as he dropped through several branches, he was still helplessly suspended upside-down when the Germans rescued him soon after, and he counted his blessings that he only had a few cuts and a twisted spine to show for his perilous descent.

There were hundreds of similar stories, of course, recounted so many times that some were eventually to pass into legend (and some were garnished so much with each retelling that they became almost implausibly fictitious!), but few such tales could be as harrowing as that of Jock McGarvey.

Jock had been a Glasgow policeman before hostilities commenced – a big man, strong as a horse, yet very quiet and calm in demeanour; he was the pilot of a Stirling bomber which, after successfully dropping its load on Hamburg, had succumbed to an electrical storm and icing and was uncontrollable. Too low to bail out, McGarvey successfully ditched the aircraft into the sea just off the Dutch coast – only to find that their inflatable dinghy was riddled with bullet and shell holes, and therefore utterly unusable.

He gathered the crew together, checked that their Mae Wests were all inflated, and they set off slowly toward the not-too-distant shore, following the sight of the anti-aircraft batteries still banging away skywards.

However, there were two very big snags. Firstly, they had come down in the North Sea, which was no place to be immersed in at any time of the year. The temperature in daytime was cold enough, and was lower still at night. Secondly, it was only then that he discovered that his navigator couldn't swim (oh, how I shuddered when I heard this tale when I thought back to what might have happened to me, had I attempted to swim the River Doubs to Switzerland!).

Fortunately, McGarvey was a strong swimmer, having played water polo for Scotland in years gone by, as well as taken a place in their national 'Tug-o'-War' team, and so he took their unfortunate navigator in tow, and launched them all on their way once more. It was later estimated that they were roughly 7 miles from shore, so it was no mean task that they faced.

They kept in touch with each other by shouting, but the bitter cold was always going to be the biggest hazard. McGarvey had the most terrible experience of seeing his crew succumbing to the fierce chill, one by one, as they slowed then stopped swimming, then quietly drifted away beyond any reach. He could do nothing to help, burdened, as he was, with his navigator, who was now unconscious from hypothermia – he could even have been dead, for all that Jock knew at that point – and so it was only his strength and a stubborn survival instinct that kept him going, determined to make it ashore.

And make it, he did, for they had been found almost frozen to death by a German patrol, and hospitalised to thaw out. The navigator was kept in for quite some time – we never did find out where he had been sent after recovery – and Jock eventually joined us at Heydekrug.

Of all the many stories that we had heard of aerial misfortune leading to capture, Jock's account had to be the most harrowing.

When winter came, I had two new experiences. The first, shared with the whole camp, was when the temperature dropped below freezing, and the Swedish Red Cross unexpectedly delivered sets of ice skates, and ice hockey sticks and some very basic kit!

The large numbers of Canadians in our midst were ecstatic, for this was their national sport, and in no time at all we had created a new skating rink in the same fashion that we had at Stalag Luft III – by banking earth on a fairly level section of the appell ground, and forming a chain gang of bucket bearers. We were further north than at Sagan, so the water froze even faster than it had there – practically upon contact with the ground! – and so the Canadians had training and practice sessions organised and under way swiftly, although following some improvised rules in order to avert potential serious injury, bearing in mind the very limited supply of protective padding. But that ice rink lasted exactly two days, when a sudden thaw set in and it melted it into slush! We were all bitterly dismayed (none more so that the Canadians, obviously), for we had all been looking forward to an entertaining display of this fast-played sport – something that few of us had ever seen before. What a let down.

The other notable event – for me, at least – was the New Year. As with Sagan, we were allowed to visit the other blocks on New Year's Eve, to socialise with friends in the other barracks, and to celebrate 'Hogmanay' in traditional fashion wherever we could.

In each hut, special preparations were being made – of the spirited kind! We were all determined to have something to imbibe, and in our hut the man with ideas about this was Neil McGregor, a man from the Highlands of Scotland. He would make a still, he said, to produce some 'whisky', the base ingredient of which would be raisins – a fruit that was in good supply in packets from the Canadian Red Cross parcels that were now trickling through. And so, for the two weeks before Christmas, every man in the hut donated his ration, as issued from the cookhouse (for they had very little use for them anyway) – and for a little while, Alec and I were 'trade kings', as we were the only non-smokers in the hut, and so we bartered our rations of cigarettes with other prisoners for extra supplies of raisins, all to strengthen the contents of the still!

Even the Germans unwittingly contributed to the brew; one of their few usable food issues was a kind of 'jam' that tasted rather like loganberry, and was quite palatable. However, it had a different value to McGregor. If left to stand out in the open for a few days, it fermented like nobody's business – and that fermentation process was just what Mac needed to complete the components for his whisky, nicknamed 'Glen Heydekrug'.

I don't know what other secret ingredients he used, but the really marvellous part of it was the still itself. It consisted of yards of metal tubing, constructed from recycling those ubiquitous 'Klim' tins, all painstakingly de-soldered, cut, re-rolled and re-soldered by a veritable army of deft-fingered technical types, thus creating a contraption that began at a vessel next to Mac's bed, then ran down half the length of the hut before turning across it, and was then draped across several bunk tops before returning to his bed once more where the potent liquid drip-dripped into another container, jealously guarded by Mac and two helpers all eagerly watching the level rise and each anticipating a good wee dram of something special. Only they knew exactly what was going on with this; the guards viewed the whole thing with some suspicion, but did nothing about it. I fancy that Dixie might have had a word in the Kommandant's ear, to allay any distrust that he might have had – perhaps he had told him that we were percolating some form of heating fuel, which wouldn't be far from the truth, except that it would be inside each of us, rather than in the stoves!

New Year's Eve finally arrived, and McGregor himself – rightfully – had the honour of taking the first dram of the amber liquid, and amber it certainly was, although not as clear as we would have hoped.

He sniffed at his cupful, took a sip, then grinned and said, 'No' bad at all, lads!', and to great cheers he downed the dram in one shot – then flushed bright red and coughed sharply as the fiery liquid burned down his gullet, much to everyone's great amusement! He grinned again, though, holding up his thumb and gesturing for all to get stuck in. And so the party began.

Neil had made a surprising amount of the stuff, and everyone in the hut was able to get a good noggin down him. It really was quite tasty indeed, but never much of a drinker, it wasn't long before I became quite squiffy, whereas wee Alec simply became all glowing and giggly.

We had a wander around our friends in the other huts and found that other brews had also been made, but none of them compared with Mac's 'Glen Heydekrug'.

At 'lights out', we staggered back to our own hut – not managing to negotiate those 'red lines' too well now, as one might imagine – and walked into a raucous sing-song. Alec flopped down on his bunk and fell asleep straightaway, so I tucked him in and joined in the sing-along for a time before I, too, began to yawn deeply and decided to turn in. I was doing just fine – until my head hit the pillow and the room immediately began to spin … and within seconds, I was diving for the toilet, where I was to spend much of the night being somewhat sick, finally dropping into an exhausted sleep about four o'clock that morning. Predictably, I awoke with a monumental hangover, and the 'drinker's promise' on my lips – 'Never again!' – and equally, as expected, I was just one casualty among many, but nevertheless, Mac's 'whisky' was voted a great success.

Needless to say, wee Alec was as bright as a button that morning, and wondering what all the sickness and fuss was about!

Chapter 19

Fallingbostel

Our stay at Heydekrug came to an abrupt end in July 1944. We were on the move, yet again!

Ever since the Russians had forced General Paulus to surrender at Stalingrad in January 1943, the Germans had been steadily pushed back until, by the summer, the signs of an inglorious defeat for the great German war machine were beginning to show. Our official German camp paper, 'The Camp', still talked of 'strategic retreats', and then boasted of 'brilliant counter-attacks' – but we, still hanging on to our secret radio (John Bristow's 'Canary'), knew better!

From the BBC came a flow of reports. Firstly, the wonderful news of the Allied invasion via the beaches of Normandy in the previous month (and how we all wanted to celebrate THAT news as soon as we heard it, but had to hold off until the Kommandant officially notified us during the morning's Appell!), and following this, there came a stream of reports from the Western Front. The advance against the Germans was going well, it seemed, with the Americans and British trundling quite rapidly through swathes of France, pushing the Germans back toward their homeland at quite a pace. And so, not unnaturally, our hopes of 'home for Christmas' began to take on some real meaning, at last.

Nevertheless, when we received just one day's notice that we were to leave Heydekrug, it caused quite a panic. With over two years' worth of regular supplies of Red Cross parcels, some others from home and some illicit gains from judicious bribery of the not unwilling 'goons' (and also from some of the very badly-treated Russian prisoners who were seen working outside the camp), many Kriegies had managed to amass a surprising amount of personal kit. Our staff had also managed to save a sizeable stockpile of undistributed Red Cross parcels as a 'rainy day' reserve, but little did we know that we had simply been saving them for the Jerries!

Anyway, one day's notice was all we were given. We were to be allowed just two parcels per man, and as for personal kit it was simply a case of what each man could carry. Most of that day was spent devising all manner of carry-alls and straps so that we could tote as much as possible. Even so, when we set out that fine Summer's day, we left behind a veritable mountain of parcels, clothing, sporting equipment and excess personal belongings, which, the Jerries had 'promised', should eventually catch up with us at our next destination – but never did, naturally!

We were loath to leave even the smallest of our prized personal possessions, and so, by the time we were marched out of the gates and heard them clatter shut behind us, the loads being carried by some men were absolutely colossal! However, as it was a good four miles hike to the railway station, surplus belongings soon began to litter the sides of the road as we marched along, the detritus growing more and more concentrated the further we trudged – most particularly in the last mile or so. Alec and I had very little in the way of extra kit, so we devised a form of webbing to make it easier to carry our four Red Cross parcels and goods between us.

On our way, we had our suspicions of the reason for our move confirmed by casual gossip with the guards – the Russians were getting too close for comfort, and the key phrase was 'Go West, young (Ger)man!' We reached the station, to find the expected cattle trucks awaiting us, '40 Hommes, 8 Cheveaux', and we groaned in anticipation of yet another very uncomfortable and unsanitary journey. We didn't even know how long it would take. Nor, for that matter, were we even sure of our destination, even as we were herded aboard. We could only hope that it would prove to be a short trip, and resigned ourselves to the shift pattern of standing for a few hours, then exchanging places for a very cramped squat, with (hopefully) an exercise break or two along the way.

There had been a rumour floating around that the Russians had cut the last rail link between here and Germany, but this was soon shown to be false as we rattled and jolted on our way. Nevertheless, this was by far the worst journey that we had been forced to make. It was of little consolation to see that the Germans were now finding out what it was like to be on the receiving end of a steam-roller assault, but we drew a little comfort from seeing some serious damage to their war machine, the further we travelled.

After nearly seven days, we finally arrived at our destination – an Army prison camp at Thorn. It was quite a large camp, but in fact, it was to be merely a 'staging post' for us, between Heydekrug and our eventual and final stop at Fallingbostel. From what we saw of Thorn, we were all quite keen to move onwards. One thing about it was certainly memorable. Some of the Army personnel were from a Scottish Highland Regiment. They had two sets of bagpipes, but too many pipers, who made it a point of honour to practise assiduously, all day, every day, taking turns at the pipes. It was always right in front of alternating guard towers, which drove the Germans half-crazy from the constantly skirling din. It didn't do most of us 'Sassenachs' much good, either, it has to be said!

Thankfully, we stayed at Thorn for just six weeks, and then we were off again, this time a much shorter journey to a bare camp at Fallingbostel. We had no Red Cross parcels to give us a good start here. They did begin to arrive much later on, but until then we had to depend solely upon the food ration issued by the Germans, which was very meagre fare indeed. Moreover, as the Allies got more and more on top, and the whole German civilian population began to suffer from the steady destruction of their transport system by way of shortages, the conditions in the camp grew gradually worse.

To begin with, our arrival at Fallingbostel was completely chaotic. We marched into the camp, were allocated barracks blocks, and then found that the bunks had not been prepared in any way for our arrival. As with other camps, the two-tier bunks were quite narrow, and we found them bereft of palliasses, even missing most of the bed boards that would support them. And there were no blankets in sight, either.

The Germans were soon confronted by Dixie and his staff, and were told to get the problem sorted immediately, to which they replied that the palliasses were in a hut in the next compound. The gate guard was 'persuaded' to unlock the gate. We didn't understand what had happened with the usual German efficiency at organising such issues, but the guards made no attempt to stop us, and everybody streamed into the compound to the storehouse within, in orderly fashion. Somebody had been on a quick scouting trip around the new barrack compound and had soon discovered that there was no fuel for any of the hut stoves, so not only were the palliasses all grabbed, but also all of the hundreds of bed boards, and anything else that could be burned!

The end of that chaotic day found us all installed in our huts, with bunks brought up to scratch, and wood of all sorts stowed away beneath the lower bunks. We found that each hut had a large, flat stove, which was useful for heating but utterly useless to cook on. Something had to be improvised, and our intrepid scroungers and inventors set to work, designing all manner of devices that would generate sufficient heat with which to cook (away from the main 'canteen', that is).

They came up with an incredibly efficient gadget nicknamed the 'blower', which produced a fierce heat with remarkably little fuel, something that was to prove very beneficial as our supplies of Red Cross parcels dwindled almost to a stop. This device worked by creating a strong draught of air beneath the fire by means of a fan driven at high speed, this being achieved by a complex gearing system. Some of these 'blowers' were real Heath Robinson contraptions, but they all worked. The wood that we'd acquired during that initial sortie into the compound next door came in very useful for these heaters, but it wouldn't last forever, obviously; that was when we all had to scout around for anything that would burn – within reason, anyway!

A number of the more skilled and mechanically-minded among our number produced and sold these machines to those of us who had neither the dexterity nor the patience required for such intricate manufacturing. As Alec and I fell into that latter category, we had to buy ours, and this is where our reserved stock of cigarettes from Heydekrug came in handy, as they were the main 'currency' here.

Some of the chaps held a contest to see whose design would boil a kettle of water the fastest. Two minutes was about the quickest time. Ours would do it in nearly three minutes if worked vigorously!

Fallingbostel, like Thorn, had originally been designated an Army camp. Therefore, it was run on Army lines, with Regimental Sergeant Majors and Sergeant Majors holding all the key jobs, but it wasn't long before we had a combined Administration of both RAF and Army, headed up once more by our inimitable Dixie Deans.

We gradually settled in there, with conditions far inferior to those we'd 'enjoyed' at Sagan and Heydekrug. But by far the worst aspect here was simply the sheer uncertainty. It wasn't all doom and gloom, however, and we did what little we could to raise our collective spirits. We still managed to play a bit of football now and then, with a tatty football that even a slum urchin would have kicked into a river for good. Our energy levels dictated short matches, however, as those parcels slowed right down to almost nothing.

On the entertainment side of things, Jock Murray formed a choir of sixteen of us, and we gave occasional concerts in the various huts. Books were now in extremely short supply, and primarily individual possessions and thus highly guarded, so the only other activity that we had was the inevitable 'Circuit' out on the Appell ground. So many of us did the rounds so much, there developed a veritable hard-track from the constant shuffle of thousands of boots! This activity wasn't as boring as it might now seem, as we would pair off and chat about all manner of subjects as we paced. We each learned something new most days, often from talking to relative strangers, frequently swapping 'lanes' to start or join in conversations with others, all at the same time as keeping our legs and bodies on the move, rather than slump and stagnate in a hut.

Our one great source of cheer was our radio. The news was mixed, of course. No war ever ran smoothly to plans or expectations, but our newsreaders announced the lot, without censoring or editing the bad stories. Although the Allies' position was steadily improving, there seemed little hope of an imminent end to the conflict in 'the foreseeable future', as the BBC announcers put it. From the Far East, of course, we had heard ever-worsening reports of a war going badly, so things didn't seem so 'rosy' at this time, all of which served to underline the roughening conditions here in our new 'home' as supplies dwindled ever thinner.

The Germans, though steadily losing their dominance in Europe, were still proving to be a tough nut to crack. The second front throughout that year was the source of many rumours and counter-rumours. We had spells of good news, such as Monty's successes in routing the Germans in North Africa, and the Allied landings in Italy, but following these great stories came the dire debacle of the failure to invade and hold Arnhem by thousands of British and Commonwealth paratroopers. It was something the Germans actually crowed about, at the end of one Appell parade, much to the disgust of the gathered Kriegies. We received a small number of prisoners who had been captured during that massed assault, and their stories were not encouraging. It still looked like we had a big fight on our hands with the Jerries, after all.

All too soon after that depressing news came the reports of the Germans' tremendous attempt to break the Allied stranglehold across the Ardennes, and almost immediately, the final set-back to our high hopes of an imminent victory were dashed by stories of the apparent success of the new German 'secret weapons', the V1 'Doodlebug' and the V2 rocket, seemingly causing massive damage to Britain from afar. Could this turn of events bring the Germans back from the brink of loss, and perhaps instead reward them with a diabolical victory, we debated?

Only the complete pessimists could possibly really believe that, but it did seem as though that glorious invasion in Normandy and the subsequent push across France had slowed almost to a halt. The reporting of that seemingly slow progress was developing a mood of depression and a dip in morale, something that needed countering in the camp before any 'rot' set in.

Oddly enough, and apparently, some might say, luckily, we had a spell of foul weather in the run up to Christmas and the New Year. First came torrential rain, turning the 'circuit' track into a churned sludge trap where only the hardy souls would trudge and slither. But someone saw the funny side of that quagmire, thought up a way of boosting morale, and organised a rugby match, right in the middle of the slop!

Once the rain had eased off, out came the brave, the foolhardy and the spectators, all hell-bent on having a good laugh, and that, they did! By the time the teams had 'played' for just ten minutes, they were utterly plastered from head to foot in slimy mud. When a man became too exhausted to play on further, another would willingly take his place while the worn out chap would flounder aside and flop down, creating a huge 'splat' of mud where he lay.

It was an excellent means of raising morale, even for only a little while, but served to lighten many heavy hearts. Almost everyone soon gained extra duties in the ensuing clean-up operation thereafter, such was the state of both players and spectators alike, and it wasn't much better even after a short walk around a slightly less sloppy section of the 'circuit'! At least it lightened the mood for a while, and kept our minds occupied in combating the mess.

With those downpours of rain came the less welcome discovery that every roof on each of the huts leaked like sieves, and the men in the top bunks found it impossible to keep themselves or their bedding even remotely dry. We countered this problem by pushing two bunks together, and all four slept in the lower bunks, cramped together like sardines, very much against King's Regulations!

It was essential, however, not only to keep dry, but also to keep warm in the colder months as temperatures dropped below freezing once more, and fuel for the stoves became quite scarce during that winter. The only problems came along when one man in the middle needed to visit the toilet and had to be careful how to extract himself without too much disturbance to his neighbour. Or if one suddenly needed to roll over to counter an all-too-often bout of vicious cramp, in which case every man would have to be woken and asked to roll over, usually accompanied by a loud 'Thump!' as the man on the outside would be tipped out to land heavily on the floor. At least it gave the other occupants of the huts some-thing to laugh at, even if they were lying there counting sheep with a neighbour's elbow in one nostril.

By this time, leading up to Christmas in 1944, our Red Cross parcels had all but stopped altogether. We were living on what were almost starvation rations provided by our captors – three thin slices of chewy black 'bread', and three or four small (often rotten) potatoes each day, occasionally supplemented by a very watery soup. Alec and I had been put in charge of distributing the rations in our hut, and I remember with some dismay when we went to the sack one day, where we stored our supply of potatoes, only to find that some mice had beaten us to it and relieved us of almost a quarter of that day's rations! A huge mouse hunt was immediately organised, and I'm glad to say that we caught all the villains and evicted them, much to their evident disgust! Even though we were almost starving, none of us would stoop so low as to eat a tiny mouse, so the lads sneaked over to one of the German huts just outside the fence and let the blighters run for cover in that direction.

Just a few weeks before Christmas, on the 7th and 8th of December, I sat my exams for Commercial Mathematics and Economics – courses that I had begun in Heydekrug, working alongside Ted Lacey. Thick snow lay outside, except for the boundary and parade area of our Appell ground. The previously sludgy mud on which those hardy rugby-playing clowns had floundered had frozen solid, and turned rock-hard and razor-rutted, making it very hard on the ankles when walking the circuit. It wasn't much warmer inside the hut being used for those exams! We sat at our tables, wearing every layer that we had available, topped with our great-coats and even blankets, still shivering even with our improvised 'hot-water bottles' (actually stove-heated bricks wrapped in rags!) which only stayed warm for so long. But I persevered and completed the tests with my teeth rattling from the chill. However, I am happy to say that I passed both quite well, although none of us were to hear of our successes until March, 1945. I learned of my own passes through a letter from Evelyn, after she had received my certificates issued by the Institute Of Book-keepers and posted to my home – much to her surprise and evident delight!

I had an odd stroke of 'luck', if one might call it that, on Christmas Eve when I was taken ill with a severe bout of cystitis. I had had this once before the war, and no doubt the wet and miserable conditions had probably contributed towards it, but it seemed much more painful this time around. I was whisked off to the Sick Bay (by wheelbarrow!) and there I stayed for three weeks. The 'lucky' part was, of course, that I was at least warm and dry, and I had a bed all to myself! The rations were just a little more than normal, but while in the Sick Bay I was weighed. My normal weight had usually been around the eleven and a half stones mark, but the scales tipped at barely eight stones! I felt almost as though I was a walking skeleton, but, of course, I was in superb health by comparison to those poor Russian wretches that we had seen on our travels. I counted my blessings for what little I did have.

While in that sick ward, I received a much-delayed letter from home in which Evelyn broke the tragic news that my brother James had, after all, been listed as 'Killed In Action' (I later learned that this particular bombing raid was the last major massed-aircraft effort which took place in March 1944, the target being Nuremberg). I was deeply shocked and very saddened by this news, having hoped that he might one day have simply tapped me on a shoulder and shook hands, grinning in his inimitable way – but it would never be so, now. Naturally, I felt that some small part of me had died with him, and I prayed that Vera and their little boy Alan were coping with their deeper loss.

With James' demise, I simply had to hope that our younger brother William would fare better and see out the war, perhaps in a lesser confrontational role in the RAF, although I knew from our last conversation that he, too, wished to follow our 'flight-path' into aircrew training, one day.

I was discharged from the sick ward in the middle of January, still very sore, and barely able to walk; wee Alec came to my rescue, however, as he saw me struggle down the two steps from the hut. He marched smartly over and shoved his shoulder beneath my armpit, therefore propping me up as we tottered back to our own hut. I thanked him profusely, but he waved away the sentiment and eased me down on the bunk; what would I do without him? Bless his moth-eaten socks.

Chapter 20

The Long March

A month or so later, our numbers were increased by an intake of about 150 American prisoners – and how they were to suffer, for the only accommodation available for them were three large tents.

They told us that they had left their last camp in Poland a month ago, with the ground still snow-covered, and had been marching westward ever since. Despite this trial of their stamina, they were remarkably cheerful, and the main reason for that was that on their travels, they had seen unmistakable signs of the Germans' gradual collapse; the civilian population, they related, were terrified of being overrun by the ever-greater speed of the Russian advance – which confirmed what we had already learned from the radio and, in spite of our miserable conditions, we were all considerably bucked up by the accounts.

The visual evidence of the Allies' superiority in the air, high overhead, further raised our hopes, as Fallingbostel was only about 30 miles from Hanover and roughly the same distance from Bremen, and we were 'entertained' for several nights as we saw tons of target indicators drop over these areas, followed by the deep rumble of heavy aircraft and the subsequent thumps and flashes as the raids lit up the night sky over each region in turn.

The high spot of all this activity came when, one afternoon, a huge formation of probably about 200 or so American Flying Fortress bombers flew almost directly over the camp, with not one German fighter nor a single pop of flak to disturb them; what a sight for sore eyes – and what a cheer that brought!

The arrival of the American prisoners and their reports of events building back home in Britain – added to what we were witnessing above us – boosted our hopes even more. But then, barely ten days after the

Americans had arrived, even as they were just beginning to accept their lot and settle into their damp tented encampment, they were turned out yet again – and this time, we all went with them!

We were informed that the camp was being abandoned, and we were all to be on the march again, but to where? North, toward the Baltic Sea? East, directly into the path of the sweeping Russians? Rumour was rife, but what little information did emerge from the Germans was that we would be leaving the camp in columns of 1,000 men at a time.

Our leaders had forestalled the Jerries to a certain extent, however, for through their now well-established grapevine, they had learned of the plan beforehand, and we were all packed and ready to go when the Germans finally gave the word to do so.

The object of the Germans' plan was – apparently – to serve as a distraction for the many Allied aircraft that seemed to have the freedom of the skies above Germany. But Dixie and his men had somehow managed to notify the Allies too, for once we were on the move away from the camp, every Allied aircraft that came near our column would swoop down, waggle their wings, and fly off, with us waving very energetically and enthusiastically in their wake.

This act gave us a great feeling of confidence, and though we had little to carry but the clothes we stood in and a few personal belongings, and hastily snatched supplies, we strode on with much lighter hearts. Yet the Long March (as it was to be called after the war) was not without incident or tragedy.

We were far from fit enough for this trek to who-knew-where, but our guards (very understanding, now!) allowed us frequent rests. Half starved as we were, we would try anything that seemed edible. At night, we were usually planted in some farm outbuildings, and it was no surprise what things we found to eat within such sheds and barns. On one occasion, four Australians had caught and dispatched a sheep, and had it sliced and diced and prepared for consumption as quickly as you might say, 'Bob's your uncle'!

At other times, we found apples, potatoes, corn and even some turnips – all was grist to our dietary mill – but as a result of eating such frequently 'past-its-prime' fare, about half of us ended up suffering from various

levels of dysentery. I had a very embarrassing incident because of this;
I, too, had succumbed to that awful condition, and as we were walking
mainly through a country area without anything that might serve as a
public convenience, when a Kriegie was 'caught short' he simply shuffled
to the side of the road and performed, to the usual accompaniment of
jeers and ribald comments.

My own bad moment occurred when we were just outside the gate of
a large field that contained only two scrawny-looking rams. I hastily
dropped my trousers to half-mast and squatted down and was just settling reasonably comfortably, when a strange thing happened – one of
the rams pushed open the gate and came to investigate 'this strange
phenomenon'! He walked right up behind me, and although I tried to shoo
him away (all the time, fighting to hold my balance), the ram just blinked
at me and stood his ground. He moved forward and nudged me off balance, and kept doing so enough to put me right off what I was trying to
do! I ended up having to hastily hitch up my trousers and move off, while
he stood there as if to say, 'This is my patch, mate – get lost!' I had to find
another, quieter spot in a ditch further along the road, much to Alec's
amusement.

On a more successful occasion – during a foraging 'expedition' – someone uncovered a potato clump, and we were all hobbling across the field
towards it when I spotted another row of green plants. On investigating
closer, I saw that they were in fact leeks, but apparently nobody else knew
what they were; my northern upbringing had proved its usefulness, and
the leeks were all lifted for our 'pot'.

Our guards were simply walking beside us now, apparently resigned
to the fact that effectively, for them, the war was over. If anyone of our
number thought that they could do better by going off on their own,
the guards made no attempt to stop them; they simply didn't have their
hearts and minds on their job any more. A few of our chaps did wander
off, intent upon finding the battle lines in order to cross to the Allies,
but we were advised (by the 'canary' no less, as the radio was still being
set up and used in barns on night stops!) to stay together as a column as
it was safer that way; there were, it was said, 'pockets' of German soldiers
lurking around who were bitter with defeat, and were liable to shoot first
and dispense with any questions.

The radio news indicated that the war was all but over; all we had to do was keep going together, and to listen out for instructions when they came via the BBC.

We had been on the march for about two weeks by now, and thanks to some successful scrounging at the places where we stopped, and the daily, continuous exercise of the walking, we were a little fitter and stronger and could move a good deal more fluidly – which proved to be just as well for many of us, one morning.

We were striding along at a regular pace in bright sunshine when we were 'visited' by three Hawker Typhoons – easily identified by our recognition experts. The fighters zoomed overhead, one after the other, as we smiled up at them and waved in friendly greeting. They swung away to our right, did a full turn – then swooped down on us, all guns and rockets blazing away!

Shocked out of our skins, we dived and jumped in all directions to get away from that deadly strafing; Alec threw himself head-first into a ditch to our left; I followed his example and rolled over him, and although I kept my head down I could see others leaping behind trees, through hedges, into the ditch on the other side of the road, while others fell dead, dying or wounded as the bullets and cannon shells ripped up the road in tragic, destructive fashion.

The shock, the noise and the ferocity were terrifying – even more so, knowing that these pilots were our own – and we all stayed down, clinging to the reeds, grass and debris where we lay, waiting for a second run and possible death … but the Typhoons' engine noise dwindled as they flew off, and slowly, fearfully, we gradually emerged from our hiding places to a scene of utter carnage. We simply could not believe what we had just experienced, and were now seeing in its tragic outcome.

There were bodies and body parts strewn all over; I saw one poor bloke – a New Zealander I knew who had been a prisoner of war almost from the start of this conflict – cut in half at the waist. Another had tried to get behind a tree, but had been decapitated before he could reach safety. Many were wounded but mercifully for themselves, unconscious; others were wide awake and either too shocked to utter any sounds, or just subdued and quietly pleading for help.

One chap I noticed was sitting propped against a tree with a rocket through his thigh – evidently a dud projectile, fortunately for him and for those near him when it had hit – and he was calmly sitting there, puffing away on a cigarette as he waited for medical attention.

As airmen all, we had had almost no previous opportunity to witness this kind of carnage so horrifically close at hand – perhaps with the exception of seeing and aiding crew-mates who had suffered battle injuries when airborne – but it shocked us to the core. When the full count was completed, we had forty-two POWs and twelve German guards dead, and over seventy wounded, many quite seriously. I heard, some months later, that another six had perished from their wounds, so the toll eventually stood at sixty needless deaths.

All these years of struggling in captivity, all this way on a forced march – only to be cut down by our own. Then, Dixie Deans arrived upon the tragic scene.

From the moment we had left Fallingbostel, he had commandeered a couple of old bicycles (one for himself, and another for his accompanying elderly German guard), and he had been cycling back and forth along the column, keeping each 'block' of marching men in touch with one another. When the Typhoons had struck, he had been right at the extreme rear of the column, and had put a spurt on as the fighters had zoomed off, but when he arrived, we could see the shock and the rage in his eyes, the same as every one of us.

Normally a calm man, even in the most provocative situations in prison camps, he gave quiet vent to a few choice expletives before taking a serious decision – and that was to seek out the Kommandant and demand to be allowed to cross through the German and British lines, with guaranteed safe conduct passes for himself and his guard (on a promise that he would return), in order to put a stop to any further disasters such as this. The Kommandant readily agreed (for he was understandably angry too, having lost twelve of his own men so unnecessarily), and Dixie was issued with a letter of safe conduct. Both German and British forces honoured the letter, and soon Dixie and his guard reached the nearest Allied brigade HQ, whereupon his message was immediately passed on to Air Command. Further to this request, Dixie described the injuries sustained, and necessary medical supplies were issued for transfer. Dixie and his guard were returned to the column in a Jeep under a Red Cross flag, and our medics were finally able to treat the wounded with decent supplies.

Thankfully we had no further trouble from aircraft. The seriously wounded were taken into a cottage hospital somewhere nearby (it was felt that they would be safe there anyway, as they were likely to be overrun and back in Allied hands very soon), while the dead were placed in the tender care of the local pastor, who organised their non-denominational burials.

Finally, after much reorganisation, the rest of us marched on in sombre mood with only a few German soldiers escorting us, being completely ignored even though they still carried rifles. I later heard a story that some of the elderly guards were so worn out by now that some of our chaps even carried their guns for them!

Five days later, a platoon of British soldiers under the command of two officers finally caught up with us, and that was that – we were 'liberated', at last!

They disarmed our guards and marched them off, and we were officially free from that moment on, every one of us wanting to shake hands with the platoon members in very grateful thanks. Actually, it was something of an anticlimax, but nevertheless a great moment, long awaited by many.

The officer issued instructions for us to try to make our way to Lübeck, 'as we've got bugger all by way of transport available for all you chaps! Sorry and all that, but you'll just have to beg, borrow and steal whatever you can find to carry you. The roads are quite clogged, but you'll get there.'

From somewhere, we managed to procure all manner of vehicles – motorbikes, pushbikes and even a horse and cart for one bunch of lads – and he was right, it was incredibly slow, and not without hold-ups by our own 'officialdom' from time to time – but the majority got organised and chugged along.

Alec and I had the excellent fortune to scrounge a ride with about twenty others in an army van, just one vehicle in a huge convoy that stretched away into the distance. Although we were all very happy now, our weariness was taking its toll.

My immediate neighbour in this van was a lanky American – a thin, talkative man from West Virginia – who began a one-sided 'conversation' aimed at me, rather than with me, and he drawled away for quite some time while my head nodded and lolled as I tried hard not to fall asleep out of politeness. Twice, I tried to raise my hand to interrupt him, simply to ask if he would please refrain from talking so that I could sleep as I was just exhausted, but both times he ignored my attempted gesture and blared on (even the others were giving him weary looks, now), until, unexpectedly, he went very quiet and I jerked awake because of the verbal 'ceasefire'; I suddenly realised that he had asked me a question, and even though I was really fuzzy-headed from fatigue, I decided to answer him in French in the hope that it might put him off and shut him up.

'Je ne sais pas, Monsieur?' I said, adding a convincingly Gallic shrug to punctuate my answer – and his face became a picture of frustration.

'Goddamn!' he grumbled. 'Been talking to maself, all this tahm!'

With that, he shook his head and turned away. Perhaps I should have been a little more forthright and just told him to 'Shut up, please, and let me sleep,' rather than be rude in that way, but he had simply worn out my already spent patience. The ruse worked, however – and as I turned to face Alec, who was sitting directly opposite me, I caught him trying very hard not to laugh and that set me struggling to suppress my own grow-ing mirth! I managed to quell the urge – for now – but when we stopped within a minute or so at a level crossing, the West Virginian spotted one of his friends in the back of a canvas-covered truck and yelled across to him, then jumped out of our van, ran across the road and leaped in with his pal.

All this time I was struggling to hold a neutral, innocent expression on my face, really fighting the urge to let fly with a guffaw – but as soon as the other truck rolled away out of sight, Alec burst out laughing, and I just couldn't stop myself from joining in. It felt so good to laugh uproar-iously after all that we had been through together over those few years, and we just kept laughing until our ribs ached and we wept with sheer fatigue. Our other colleagues in the van were grinning and some were creasing up with us, but most of them didn't know what we were laughing about, until finally I stopped chuckling just long enough to explain the joke – and then they roared with laughter too!

Eventually, I gave a mighty yawn and felt myself drifting off into sleep, a smile on my face (so Alec told me, later). I dreamed pleasant dreams of home, for the first time in years – and awoke with a gentle jump as we finally bumped off the road and stopped in a spotlessly presented tented encampment.

Alec was the first to alight from the van, then myself, and Doug Redpath, then Sam Swinton (another Scotsman), who was followed by the other fellows. We stood in an untidy gaggle, each of us stretching our arms and legs and rolling our necks to ease our cramps and numbnesses, all as scruffy as can be, while around us strode the most immaculate specimens that the British Army had ever turned out. Without exception, they were bronzed, well-built and cheerful – and by comparison, we all felt like utter tramps.

We made an effort to shuffle into two straight lines, and did our best to march along to join the others all clambering from the other vehicles in the convoy – but hardly anyone spared us much of a glance. We had 'arrived', but without the kind of welcome that we might have hoped for; very much a let down after all we had suffered – but what else had we expected, really? There was a war still to fight, after all!

We rose the next morning to a breakfast of the loveliest porridge I'd ever tasted, followed of course by the traditional bacon and eggs; 'God's in his heaven – all's right with the world', I found myself thinking, for this was certainly heavenly fare – it was superb! It wasn't long, however, before our tummies all ached from eating 'so much', after the very meagre rations that we had existed upon … but what a lovely ache to endure!

Two or three days passed by, and the only fly in the ointment was the fact that there was no word or sign of any further move. We had naively expected that we would be off home as soon as we'd joined forces with the army, but obviously there was a tremendous amount of organisation required before that could be implemented with such great numbers. So out of boredom, we did a little bit of exploring. The camp was just outside a small village, strangely untouched by the war, but looking quite attractive. After a brief wander around, we sauntered back to the encampment, enjoying the beautiful warm weather and almost at peace with the world. There was always a bustle of activity in the camp – always the way with headquarters of any armed force, it seemed – but we were still being largely ignored as we strolled back to our tent; it almost felt like we were invisible.

After tea, Doug disappeared to try to find some of his New Zealand mates, while we just sat comfortably and gossiped. Just before dark, Doug reappeared with a large parcel under his arm, looking very smug.

''Ello, 'ello, 'ello,' I said, in my best impersonation of a British bobby. 'What 'ave we 'ere, then?'

'Come into the tent and see,' he invited, tipping a wink as he bent beneath the canvas flap.

Intrigued, we followed him within, whereupon he unravelled his parcel – to reveal a huge full side of luscious-looking ham; we were astonished!

'Where the heck did you get that?' we gasped, almost drooling in anticipation of a real feast.

'I'm not telling you,' he replied, churlishly, 'so that if anyone asks you, you can plead innocence with a clear conscience!'

So we questioned him no further, but instead began to make plans for a feast the next day. Alec was already rubbing his hands in gleeful anticipation, for he had been a grocery shop manager before joining the RAF and therefore knew the best way to cut such a huge slab of ham. We retired to our beds, looking forward to the next day, which turned out far better than our modest expectations, so used to frugality were we now.

After breakfast, a special roll call was announced, and we lined up smartly, both the army personnel and all of us RAF ex-POWs, all agog. 'Gentlemen,' announced the camp CO, 'I have a very special announcement to make. Today, General Eisenhower has accepted the unconditional surrender of the German Army!'

A massive, thunderous cheer burst from over a thousand happy throats, and everywhere around there were men shaking hands and hugging one another; finally, it was all over!

The ecstatic cheering continued for quite some time, and the grinning CO had long stepped down from the bonnet of his Jeep and disappeared into his HQ tent before the merriment finally died down and the men began to disperse; it was definitely the best day for at least the three years that Alec and I had spent in captivity; all we needed now was that flight home, and we'd be happier still. That was the only discordant note, here. We had been liberated and released on 2 May , but here we were on VE Day, 8 May, and still in what was effectively a 'collecting camp' as more POWs were brought in, with no apparent hint of any decision to send us home as yet.

But Doug broke the morose mood with a brighter idea: 'Come on, lads,' he urged us, 'how about a celebration with that ham, eh?'

'Damned good idea!' we chorused, and made our way back to the tent to collect it.

'Hey,' prompted Sam, 'why don't we try someone down in the village? I'm sure they'd be happy to cook it and share it with us? I should think they'd be as pleased as we are that it's over.'

We all agreed and set off for the village, carefully hiding our prized ham as we looked for signs of local life, and hoped that they would indeed be willing to join our celebration.

At the far end of the main road, we came upon a fairly large house with net curtains at the windows, and a sizeable well-kept garden before it.

'This looks promising,' I said, and walked up the path to the front door, then rang the bell.

The door was opened very cautiously by a pleasant-looking, neatly dressed woman, with a girl of about eight or nine years old peeking around her waist. Understandably, they both looked very nervous, even scared, for although we had all cleaned up our 'act' since arriving at the collection camp and were barbered and shaved, our old uniforms were somewhat tattered and dishevelled; we must have appeared a desperate mob indeed!

Always the spokesman, and in somewhat halting German, I did my best to assure them that we meant them no harm. She hadn't yet heard the news that the war had been officially declared over, so we told them of the surrender, and with tears of relief and evident joy, she shook hands with us all. Then she and her daughter had an excited conversation in their native language, and the mother said, 'Kommen sie', and led us into the house.

Her natural trepidation had gone – evaporated along with the hostilities of the nations – and, carefully, I explained that we were look-ing for someone to share a joint celebration of the end of the conflict, and then Doug produced his pièce de résistance, that juicy great side of ham, and she opened her eyes in astonishment.

'This is for the feast,' we managed to explain, and she smiled and happily set about making preparations for the meal. While she was busy, her little girl – Anna, she told us – was quickly losing her shyness and tried her best to talk to us, and with the help of some simple sign language, we were managing quite well in a very short time, 'chatting' away cheerfully – very reminiscent of those French farms that Alec and I had visited on our way to Switzerland all those years ago (how it seemed like another world away, even then!).

Anna's mother, Frau Erikson, soon joined in and conveyed to us that her husband was still in the army, but they didn't know where.

'But now,' she managed in clear English, 'he will soon be home!'

Altogether, we passed a very happy afternoon with them, our German language improving by the hour until, finally, it was time to eat. She had cooked the ham to perfection – it literally fell apart to the touch of our knives and tasted absolutely delicious, as did the baked potatoes and cabbage that she had added to supplement the meal. Anna had decorated the table with lilacs from the garden and, all in all, it really was a very pleasant celebration indeed. The war was over, and we were all glad to be able to look forward again.

We left the still substantial remains of the ham with the Eriksons, then made our way back to the camp for what we hoped might be our last day in Germany – and so it turned out!

The next day, they flew us to a 'staging base' in Belgium, in a couple of Douglas C47s that were run ragged with many shuttle flights back and forth on that day and the next. We stayed in Brussels overnight, and many of the lads went down into the town from the barracks where we were quartered. They returned with some weird and wonderful tales, for the people of Brussels were still going strong with their second full day of liberation partying, grabbing and dancing with every single Allied uniform that they could get their hands on – something that the young, single lads greatly enjoyed, obviously!

Finally, on 10 May we were herded into a collection of RAF bombers and flown home in the late afternoon. Alec and I boarded an Avro Lancaster, and as I sat down beneath the mid-upper turret, I couldn't help but look up and think mournfully about my younger brother James, for that might well have been his crewing post; I had no idea which turret he would have manned, or what squadron or type of aircraft he would have been in on his last night in action, but the details didn't matter as I felt my previously joyous mood plummet. Alec – true to his ever-sensitive form – picked up on my upward glance and deepening mood.

'Och, Jack – you never know,' he said, 'your brother might still be alive out there – just not out, yet.'

I felt a twinge of hope, of course, that he had been caught and incarcerated in another POW camp somewhere and we would soon meet again. I managed a smile in return for Alec's good intentions and nodded agreement, and we settled down on the floor between the wing spar and turret.

The Lancaster, being a military aircraft, wasn't fitted with large windows for passengers' sight-seeing enjoyment – just tiny spotters' portholes here and there – so we had no easy way of viewing the English coastline drifting by below us as we crossed it (and any movements were frowned upon in flight anyway, for fear of shifting masses if everyone jumped up at the same time), but the pilot – evidently an appreciative and decent sort – sent a crewman back from the cockpit to tell us of the moment, and we gave a little cheer of thanks and relief as we exchanged broad grins, then we droned onward for another hour or so.

Inevitably, Alec and I debated what was really a moot point about how we might have fared on that fateful night when we crashed in D-Donald, had we instead been equipped with a Lancaster (ironically, we had learned from fellow 101 prisoners captured later that 101 Squadron had converted to these heavy bombers soon after our mishap!), and we came to the conclusion that, yes, we would almost certainly have made it home on three engines … but would we have safely completed the tour? Even if we had made it back to base in D-Donald that night, might we have fallen victim to a more fatal destiny, later? We would never know –– but we were both very happy that we had survived the war and our sometimes-harsh imprisonment, and were able to sit, now, in this marvellous aircraft and talk so casually about such issues as we flew home.

As we came in to land at Cosford amid dozens of similar flights of repatriated RAF personnel, I have to admit that when we touched down gently on the runway and rumbled to a halt, I (and several others around me) became somewhat emotional; we were back on home ground once more – something that I had sometimes wondered might never happen.

The engines stopped, and as we all began to rise from our places, the pilot appeared in the cockpit gangway and clapped his hands for attention.

'Gentlemen,' he said, 'welcome back to Blighty!' With that, he wriggled down between us all until he reached the side door (already being opened from the outside by ground crew), then he grinned and shook hands with every man as he saw us all off; his gesture was very welcome and heart-warming indeed, appreciated by us all.

After the initial documentation procedures, etc., we continued on to the sergeants' mess and sat down to the biggest mixed grill we'd ever seen, served by what must have been the most glamorous WAAFs the RAF could muster for the occasion; they were certainly doing their best to welcome us home!

After a few essential speeches we were packed off to bed, to be ready for the next day when we were scheduled to have medical examinations, followed by kitting out with new uniforms (we really looked a right scruffy bunch, by now!), and we would then be given our leave passes – for a glorious six full weeks! This evening, though, we were issued with special express posting forms to let our families know when they could expect us on the biggest day of all – when we went home.

On that momentous day, it all went off exactly as planned. As Alec and I left Cosford and went our separate ways (he to Glasgow, I to Newcastle, initially), we shook hands with firm double-clasps and great affection, for we had endured and survived, and had vowed to stay in touch as firm friends always promise.

After a couple of route changes along the way, the last train in my journey home – the final link from Newcastle to Ashington – was miraculously right on time as it chuffed into the station, and as I moved through the scrum of passengers toward the end of the platform, my wife Evelyn and son John were right there to greet me.

There were great hugs and tears flowing plentifully as we embraced right there in front of everyone, but we noticed no one else but ourselves in this understandably emotional blur of happy reunion, and it took some time before we untangled ourselves enough to walk hand in hand the last mile to our home in Tweed Street.

So, it was all finally over. Two years of action and three years of captivity, in the latter of which Alec and I had had some good moments, and other times of dire depression and grim despair, but we had never faltered in our certainty that we would win through and get home safely.

I often look back on those years – the excitement of the training and operational flying, our crash-landing and attempt to evade, then the anticlimax of capture and imprisonment – but rather than curse my luck at the captivity, I remember those three years as something of a different kind of adventure, not all bad and almost all of it an education in living with one's fellow man in sometimes diabolical conditions. And I thank God that I managed to live through it all.

It sometimes seems, though, that we survived the war almost by accident through that crash and the hardship of incarceration – and in truth and by statistics, that survival might well have been very doubtful indeed had we succeeded in getting home that night and then carried on flying in action. Ironically, we had that misfortune to thank for our continued longevity!

I have to admit to have largely enjoyed the thrill of it all and the experience of acute danger on occasion – especially on those flights through hellish flak and searchlights, and during our march by moonlight to the Swiss border. But most of all, I really wished that I had learned to swim!

Epilogue *by Barry Love*

True to his spirit and keeping his word as a close friend, Jack maintained contact with rear gunner Alec Crighton over the years following the war, occasionally meeting when passing by each other's homes, but he had no idea what had become of the pilot, John Beecroft, Brad, and front gunner, Henry Hanwell. Had they got home? Had they survived the war? Might they even still be alive, perhaps? When we began to research some of the technical details, some very good news came to light, albeit also accompanied by a tragic postscript.

My grandfather and I had headed to the RAF Museum at Hendon with a long list of questions needing in-depth answers, there also to meet with the gentlemen running the Bomber Command Association. We were stunned to discover that Beecroft and Hanwell had in fact successfully made their 'home run' from Switzerland! Beecroft had returned to active service as a pilot in a night-fighter squadron in de Havilland Mosquitoes, while Hanwell had become a master instructor at an Air Gunnery Unit, training fresh aircrew in the arts of aerial defence.

Jack was a very happy man upon this discovery, but the joy was immediately dampened by the sad discovery that poor Brad had drowned, after all, attempting to cross the River Doubs, and I left him alone for a few minutes to come to terms with the shock; it had obviously affected him very deeply.

When he had recovered his composure, we returned to the BC Association office to delve further into the 101 Squadron ORBs (Operational Record Books) to see what else we might discover.

Sure enough, other information confirmed that Beecroft and Hanwell had survived the war, although this information did not necessarily mean that his ex-comrades were still alive then – in 1989 – but he perked up almost immediately when I promised him that I would search for Beecroft and Hanwell, to try to find out if they were still 'with us', and if so where they might now be living. We left Hendon with a wealth of material and references – and Beecroft and Hanwell's old addresses, as listed on their 'demob' papers.

Back then, such personnel searches were rather more difficult than they are today (in 2015); for a start, the Internet didn't exist except as a dream in the boffins' minds, so my first port of call, therefore, was the local town library and what promised to be a daunting trawl through the shelves of telephone directories – hoping, of course, that neither of the gentlemen were ex-directory and subsequently unlisted.

By nothing short of good fortune, I quickly found John Beecroft's number, registered at his old address, and set up a call to him that evening while Jack sat beside me, understandably nervous yet as excited as a schoolboy. Once connected, and when I explained who I was and what the call was about, Mr Beecroft merely exclaimed 'Good God, man!', and after a brief chat with him, I passed the receiver to Jack and left them to their telephone reunion (but taking notes from aside when I could!). For Grandad, it was a very blissful and emotional hour or so, and a happy outcome for all of us.

It was a scenario that was repeated just two days later when I returned to the town library to look up Henry Hanwell. He took a little more work to find as he had moved from his old address, but after a couple of false starts with namesakes, I spoke to Henry, and he was ecstatic at my news that Jack was still very much alive and very active … as was John Beecroft, did he know? It transpired that Henry didn't know, and so, after Jack had returned home a little later that day – and following another joyous 'reunion' via a conversational phone call, in which contact details were exchanged – a physical reunion was mooted and agreed, to be organised for the next year.

This took place in one of the hotels that they had frequented in Cambridge when they were based in Bourn, their RAF base only a few miles west along the old A45 from the city – and it proved to be quite an event, with Anglia News filming the occasion for their evening news show.

Out of this reunion, happily, came old comrades' pledges to stay in touch with each other – along with a promise from both Beecroft and Hanwell to write a résumé of their intriguing departure from Switzerland, then their subsequent evasion though France via the Pat O'Leary escape line, and back to England via a trawler to Gibraltar.

This episode is quite an epic journey in itself and, rightfully, I have added their experiences to this book to complete the entire picture, adapted from their own hand-written letters and corroborated from the official MI9 intelligence reports and other sources.

The following 'travelogue' is their story.

Home Run from Switzerland

'After Henry, Brad and I had shaken hands with Jack and Alec and bade them good luck,' wrote Beecroft, 'we felt saddened at having to split up with them; we fervently hoped that we would meet up on the other side of this raging torrent, somehow, but for now we needed to make haste, lest we be discovered by the German border guards.

We began to strip off our outer clothing, stuffing the items into small sacks that we had acquired in preparation for crossing the river, and just at that moment – as luck would have it after our efforts to find a method of crossing by trying to use that rolling log barrier – we discovered another smaller log close by, floating freely. We glanced at one another, and just as I considered calling out to Jack and Alec to come back, to take their chances with us by holding on to the log while Henry, Brad and I attempted to push and tow it, we suddenly heard shouting from upstream and a dog barking, sounding much too close for comfort; had Jack and Alec been seen, we wondered? We exchanged fearful glances, and then quickly slipped gently into the shockingly cold water – we could dally no longer!

Packing our sacks on to the log, we wedged them tight against stubs of branches and waded in as quietly as possible, pushing the log ahead of us – and almost lost control of it as the current snatched at it and pulled us away from the bank. I held on to the log, with Henry taking strong strokes alongside and Brad struggling to stay with us on my other side. The current took us swirling back toward the French bank only a few yards downstream. We all kicked, pushed and thrashed out like madmen, burning far too much energy too soon as we fought that powerful current – and soon we were all caught in the torrent and powered toward the middle of the river, where we travelled on downstream at quite a pace.

This, I knew, could be even more dangerous if we were spotted, and so I urged the lads on once more. We pushed ourselves again, swimming as hard as we could. The water was very much colder than I had thought it might be – surprisingly so, for the month of June – and we were all becoming quite short of breath from the shocking chill and the tremendous effort of having to manhandle and force the log forward.

By the time we eventually found a calmer spot in which to attempt to reach the far bank, we had travelled quite a way with the current and I was almost depleted. I saw that Henry was struggling hard too, and Brad had slipped away from the log, dropping back a little and flailing about a bit. However, there was no chance here of trying to tread water or perhaps even shout encouragement to him, for I was almost breathless myself – we just had to keep going and push through that last barrier of exhaustion.

Within a few moments, my hands touched the gravelled bottom of the bank on the Swiss side and I splashed wildly as I tried to stand and rise out of the water, and as Henry crashed into me, I grabbed him and the log with both hands to stop myself from going under. Between us, we pulled the log into a grounded position, then floundered on to the bank and collapsed heavily, utterly spent.

Seconds later, we heard Brad's gasping shouts for help – and, tragically, we were just so utterly and physically burned out that we could do nothing as we saw him slip beneath the surface almost mid-stream, to be swept away by the current. It was some minutes before either Henry or I could even attempt to sit up – let alone think about trying to stand – and we were absolutely mortified and distraught at what we had just witnessed. It was such a damned disastrous end to a brave endeavour, and after such a long and hazardous trek.

We were utterly devastated at losing Brad; Henry was visibly moved to tears, and I felt that heavy emotion. Although I fervently hoped that Brad might have held his breath and strength long enough to have survived the 'ducking' and perhaps reached the bank further along, my heart was leaden with the higher probability that he had most likely drowned before our very eyes.'

It seemed beyond doubt that this was indeed a tragic end to their epic journey.

Beecroft and Hanwell were utterly exhausted and lay sprawled on the bank, their lower legs still in the water as they gasped and panted for breath, peering into the gloomy darkness in the hope that Brad had found enough strength to surface and flounder back to them. After a few more minutes, however, there was still no sign of him, and they wearily extricated themselves from the log's stumpy branches and retrieved their clothes sacks.

Having dressed once more, they recovered Brad's sack of clothing from the log, and then trudged a few feet into the trees away from the riverbank. Still shivering from the chill and shock they followed the river, all the while straining their eyes into the darkness as they plodded on, searching and hoping to find Brad, but to no avail. Eventually they came across a small riverside café, although this arrival at what they hoped would be a sanctuary was not such a joyous moment, having lost three good friends so quickly, by different means.

The sky was greying toward dawn by then and, naturally, there was no sign of life within the building at that hour, but they were so chilled to the bone and in need of help and sustenance that they felt compelled to try to wake the inhabitants and trust in safe assistance.

Beecroft nodded at Hanwell to reassure him, then braced back his shoulders and rapped hard with the brass doorknocker, and in a few moments the proprietor parted the window blinds and scrutinised them carefully before unlocking the door. He looked very confused and seemed about to give them a telling off for disturbing him, but Beecroft shortcircuited his anticipated challenge by opening his coat to show him his RAF uniform.

'Je suis aviateur Anglais,' Beecroft told him, borrowing their navigator's oft-used phrase (well-remembered for this occasion, he hoped!).

The café proprietor beamed them both a wide smile and bade them enter, and his wife – who had been standing hidden behind him – made quite a fuss of welcoming them within before she set about boiling the kettle to make hot drinks for everyone. Her husband asked some fairly basic questions to try to establish their story and credentials, but even though they were still in the habit of giving only vague answers their replies evidently satisfied him, and they soon settled down to drink coffee as the proprietor telephoned the authorities.

Quite soon, there came a gentle rattling of the door and a smiling frontier guard joined them to share a hot drink and ply each of them in turn with more questions.

They carefully repeated their story (still just a little imprecisely) and he beamed again, happily accepting their tale. He congratulated them both on their success in escaping – but they were all then disheartened to hear from him, the confirmation that the Germans had indeed captured 'two airmen' on their side of the river and had shown them off to the Swiss bridge guards – a point that explained, to Beecroft, his immediate acceptance of their story.

'At least Jack and Alec should be OK, even though they're obviously "in the bag",' Beecroft commented to Hanwell. With that miserable news out of the way, they discussed Brad's probable tragic fate; the guard asked if they could remember exactly where this had happened and, once confirmed, they agreed that they should guide him back to the spot where they had last seen him.

They thanked the café owners profusely as they left with the frontier guard, and soon returned to the place where they had floundered on to the riverbank. They paced slowly back along the bank in the downstream direction, searching intently as they moved, but even with strengthening daylight they could find no trace of poor Brad, and so they were forced to abandon their sad quest. The Swiss guard promised them that a full search would be carried out along the river and then took Beecroft and Hanwell to his home, whereupon his wife cooked a delicious breakfast of bacon and eggs, which they devoured ravenously.

Soon after, the guard escorted them the short distance to the nearest town, La Chaux-de-Fonds, of which they saw very little except the inside of the prison! They were treated very kindly, however, and given the opportunity of a long, hot bath and shave each, followed by a medical examination and a good evening meal – but even so, after all this kindness, they were locked up in separate cells for the night.

The next morning – following an excellent breakfast – they were taken by train to Berne, where they were interrogated by senior officers of the Swiss Army Air Force. Beecroft and Hanwell told them simply that they were escaped prisoners of war because, under the terms of the Geneva Convention, this gave them the right of repatriation. Had they merely declared the truth that they had crashed, then walked across France and crossed the River Doubs (and were therefore evaders, rather than escapers), they feared that the Swiss might suspect them of being German 'planted' agents, and so might well have interned them instead – still effectively prisoners of war, and very much forced to sit out the conflict in the same captive manner.

Fortunately, the Swiss accepted the story without further ado or challenge, and so – later that day – two thoroughly disreputable-looking 'tramps' presented themselves at the British Legation.

Luckily, the Legation staff were not at all dismayed by their shoddy appearances; they were all very patient and exceptionally well qualified to attend to any matters, and were – it seemed – well used to dealing with escape and evasion issues.

Beecroft was enthralled to discover that the military attaché was Colonel Henry Cartwright, who had been a famous escaper of the First World War, and whose own book, *Within Four Walls*, was a classic tale of escape that Beecroft had already read with tremendous interest – and, he admitted, had drawn upon his memory of its pages for inspiration throughout their own escapade – hence, Beecroft paid rapt attention to Colonel Cartwright's words as they discussed the trek to his very office. The air attaché was no less a man than Air Commodore Ferdinand 'Freddie' West, VC, awarded thus for his 'rare courage and determination' on a flying sortie in August 1918, when he was unfortunate enough to lose his left leg under fire from at least seven enemy fighters, but managed to fight them off and return to base; two of Beecroft's boyhood heroes, met in real life! He felt duly humbled in their presence.

The staff set about caring for their needs; foremost of those was fresh clothing. They were taken down to a room in the basement where clothes were stacked, looking very much like a rummage sale – but with Beecroft being 6ft 4in tall, none of the suits would fit him! However, one was borrowed from somebody almost as tall, and a few days later he and Hanwell were sent to an outfitter, where they chose suits and other necessities.

They had been lodged in the Hotel Metropole and each given the equivalent of about £3 spending money – an amount that they dispensed with quite quickly that day, when presented with all manner of temptations upon which to spend it! They were to return to the Legation almost daily thereafter for 'top-ups' of pocket money, such was the good life that they led while ensconced at Berne.

The next couple of weeks proved to be the most relaxed and pleasant antidote to their recent exertions and stresses, and also from the black-out of war-torn Britain and France, and so they enjoyed the bright lights as they spent most evenings savouring the delights of many of the café verandahs and courtyards; the war did indeed seem hundreds of miles away, just then.

While Beecroft and Hanwell were enjoying these leisure pursuits, wheels had been set in motion to organise their return home. Sadly, too, came the confirmation that Brad had indeed drowned in his very brave attempt to swim that raging River Doubs; his body had been recovered from the river the next day, and he had been buried with full military honours in the cemetery in Vevey St Martin; the news naturally dampened their spirits for a time.

Their planned return home actually involved not a simple flight or two back to Blighty, but would require them to 'escape' from Switzerland into adjoining unoccupied (Vichy) France, and thence travel back under escort through an organised escape route either by using a mountain pass to Spain, or (more likely) a coastal destination to meet a boat.

Quite soon, they were photographed and equipped with forged identity cards – they were now Czech students, of which, apparently, there were plenty in unoccupied France, for some reason – and were also given genuine Basque berets for use in a later stage of their proposed journey.

Soon after these were issued, the pair were moved to a small hotel (pension) in Geneva, to await further instructions – all very cloak and dagger, as Hanwell joked. However, once there, they still had a few days to wait, and so spent much of the time swimming in the huge lake and generally relaxing.

Here, they were joined by Anthony Deane-Drummond, a commando who had escaped from an Italian prison camp, crossing the border by burrowing under the frontier wire fence and then allowing himself to be accosted by a Swiss guard – much like Beecroft and Hanwell, at the latter stage of their escape. Together, Beecroft, Hanwell and Deane-Drummond sampled many of the restaurants and cafés along the shores of Lake Geneva. But as pleasant as the rich-sounding lifestyle was, they were becoming bored and restless and wanted to get home to their families, and perhaps even back into action.

At last the message came, and they were sent to receive their movement instructions in true clandestine fashion! The three fugitives were told to go, at the appointed hour, to a certain place where there would be a man wearing a light grey suit and trilby hat, and he would be reading a particular newspaper.

They duly arrived, doing their very best to contain their excitement – and there stood the contact! Beecroft approached him in as casual a manner as he could muster and identified himself, and – almost farcically – the agent's stage-whispered message was that the three were to be ready to move before dawn the next day, when the agent would collect them from their pension and take them to a designated crossing point at the Swiss/French border; they were on their way, at last.

Sleep that night was nigh impossible as the tension rose while the clock ticked slowly toward the dawn, but, finally, there came a sharp signalling rap on their room door and they almost jumped out of their skins. Deane-Drummond leaped to one side of the door, ready to pounce as the lock turned and the door creaked sharply open – but fortunately it was the guide and they exhaled in sharp relief.

The agent handed them ration cards and French money, and they set off in his car to a cemetery on the outskirts of Geneva. They were then instructed to pass through the graveyard to a point in the far boundary wall, whereupon, the agent told them, they were to climb over the wall (dry-stone, as it proved to be, and therefore quite easy to negotiate), then to cross a shallow stream and go through two large coils of barbed wire!

After thanking their guide for his efforts they moved off through the early mist, stepping their way through the headstones, then clambering over the wall. They managed to wade quietly through the gentle stream, and then picked their way carefully through the barbed wire; it was a very slow and occasionally painful task, with all three collecting a few cuts in the process; Beecroft also managed to tear a small hole in his trousers, much to Hanwell's barely concealed amusement.

Finally, they were through, and slowly scaled a grass bank on the French side to find a road stretching away before them into Vichy France. Their instructions from that point were to continue walking along this road, and sometime soon would be met by a man who would be pushing a bicycle.

In the event, it seemed to be taking such an interminable time that Beecroft stopped and challenged Deane-Drummond about their direction, thinking that he might have possibly misheard their guide's whispered instructions; Deane-Drummond was about to argue and refute Beecroft's doubts when the bicycle-riding guide came clattering along the road toward them at breakneck speed before skidding to a halt and apologising between deep breaths for being late.

With Deane-Drummond's honour restored and acknowledged by Beecroft and Hanwell, they followed their new guide to his home, and very soon enjoyed a healthy breakfast set before them by his very plump wife.

They were shortly joined by their next guide, whose name (real or supposed, they weren't told for security reasons) was Henri; he took the three fugitives to his own home in a very roundabout route, occasionally telling them to wait while he approached guards or police officers, and after brief conversations with them he bade them to carry on ahead of him. He would then catch up, walking briskly, smiling and chatting amiably as he steered the trio along street after alley, until they finally reached his house.

They stayed with him for most of that day, and a most enlightening time it proved to be, too. They learned of the risks, dangers and arrests that took place among the helpers and agents along this escape line, and how the Gestapo were quite active and too successful with discovering 'safe houses'. ('But do not worry, mon amis! You are safe with me!' Henri declared, trying to put them at ease as soon as he'd recounted this information.) His stories were intended, it was believed, simply to put the men on their strongest guard for the rest of the journey, and was – in all fairness – a reasonable tactic. German Gestapo men in plain clothes were abundant here, he said, and so they needed to be extra careful with their movements around the streets.

Their next move was to be by night train to Marseilles, and another guide would keep an eye on them while they travelled thus.

Henri left them in his house while he walked to the railway station to buy the necessary tickets, and soon after his return they prepared to leave, checking that they had left nothing by which he might be incriminated, should he be visited by those secret police.

Somewhat tensely, they tried to amble as nonchalantly as possible the few hundred yards to the station where they boarded the train and settled in a compartment, seated apart, and as soon as the train pulled out of the station they pretended to sleep.

At some time during the night, a nasty incident occurred right outside their compartment, attracting the unwanted attention of the railway guard and a couple of police officers, when a woman passenger lit up a cigarette; an innocent, everyday act to Englishmen, but not to the 'native' gentlemen in the compartment, who became quite irate and called up the guard to report her. The three evaders didn't understand what all the fuss was about, but the lady was forced to extinguish her cigarette, and the guard and two police officers searched her, confiscating her cigarettes and an elegant-looking gold lighter.

Eventually the blazing row died down, and they settled back into their faked sleep, wondering what it had all been about. (It wasn't until they told their next host about the incident that they learned of a quaint prohibition law regarding cigarette smoking in Vichy France; apparently, tobacco was in such short supply in the region that all stocks had been declared an exclusively male-only reserve! They were astonished to hear that women were forbidden to smoke – most certainly in public, at any rate – hence, the reason for the co-travellers' angst over the unfortunate woman.)

At about seven o'clock the next morning, the train steamed and clanked into Marseilles station, and they alighted a discreet few paces behind their guide, but as Beecroft, Hanwell and Deane-Drummond left the station and were 'transferred' fluidly into the guidance of another chap, they became acutely aware of being scrutinised by a couple of sinister-looking persons.

These nefarious characters squinted after the trio as they made their way down the main street, and as they entered another small café for a welcome breakfast, Beecroft hazarded a glance back, to see the two suspicious-looking characters quite blatantly taking up observation points on opposite sides of the café. Naturally, he was somewhat worried and mentioned them to their unnamed guide, but he merely smiled and shrugged, waving them to sit down and be served coffee. Evidently, being spied upon was commonplace, and the guide was simply indicating that they should all simply ignore the 'agents' (if, indeed, that was who they were).

The scenario gave Beecroft and Hanwell something of a chilled feeling as they ate, but Deane-Drummond acted unperturbed and, soon, they vacated the establishment and followed the guide through some very narrow, winding streets. As they left the café – keeping distance from the guide once more – Beecroft had noticed that those two particular 'spies' seemed to have disappeared – perhaps content that the group were just innocent visitors, after all – but he was very nervously alert and continued to subtly scan the faces of every person that they passed as they wound their way through the poor quarter of this grubby part of the city. Likewise, Hanwell and Deane-Drummond did their best to avoid eye contact with anyone – just looking long enough to try to determine whether they were being scrutinised through sidelong glances and other such subterfuge – and eventually, they all managed to assure themselves that they weren't actually being followed by anyone.

It was a highly stressful and worrying walk, but finally they arrived at a very grimy apartment block, there to meet a young woman who was to escort them on the next stage of their journey through the dusty streets. They were introduced to her, but she acknowledged simply by nodding to each in turn; they were then told to merely follow her discreetly, and not to try to converse or otherwise make contact with her – and so they shuffled out of the building, using the rear exit for discretion and to try to confound any potential watchers.

After winding their way through numerous grubby alleys and streets, they reached a fairly modern, clean apartment block overlooking the old harbour, only to find a gendarme standing guard at the doorway. Unperturbed, their guide strutted right past the gendarme as if he was of no consequence at all, and the trio followed suit as casually as they could manage, but still inwardly nervous of being stopped and engaged by him. They needn't have worried. The gendarme averted his gaze as they passed, and they breathed deep sighs of relief; quite probably, they realised, the gendarme might well have been a member of this clandestine organisation.

They rode in the lift to a fifth-floor apartment, where they were introduced to Louis and Reneé Nouveau, who were to be their hosts in luxurious surroundings for the coming days. Louis spoke perfectly clear English, and he explained the strict house rules. These were essential for keeping the neighbours at bay, for he couldn't be sure of where their allegiances lay; they could be Vichy sympathisers, and as there were usually only two people living and moving around in the Nouveaus' apartment regularly, they had to be as quiet as possible.

It was made clear that the fugitives were not to appear by the window all together, nor were they to wear shoes; Beecroft enjoyed the use of a pair of slippers loaned to him by Monsieur Nouveau, but Hanwell and Deane-Drummond had to make do with small rectangles of carpet tied to their feet as they shuffled around!

They took it in turns to sit by the window and soak up the magnificent view, but they had to be very vigilant against making any noise, and even had to chatter no louder than in stage whispers. Toilet visits were to prove awkward, too, in that they had to curb the automatic habit of trying to flush the toilet by pulling the chain – something that Louis forestalled by shortening the chain to make them think twice when reaching for it.

They enjoyed the Nouveaus' hospitality for ten days in all, during which time other evaders and escapers joined them, causing some cramping within the apartment – something that must have been very nerve-racking for everyone, as each person sought to move around without interfering with or bumping into a fellow occupier, and all the time, trying to be as quiet as mice, to avert neighbourly interest.

One of the new arrivals was Squadron Leader Whitney Straight, an American serving in the RAF, whose escape from internment in a French port had been engineered by O'Leary; the British Air Ministry was very keen to get him back, they were told.

In mid-July, they all embarked upon the next stage of their journey – and 'embark' was the operative word. They had been led to believe that they were to be taken over the Pyrenees into Spain, but there had been a change of plan due to various hitches with Spanish authorities interning anyone they caught travelling that way, and so they were to be picked up by boat in the dead of the night instead, from a quite beach somewhere west of Marseilles – something that had been set up by Pat O'Leary in a visit to Gibraltar, in anticipation of those Spanish problems.

When they left the Nouveaus' apartment, their number had increased to seven fugitives; they had been joined by another three evaders, Sergeant Stefan Miniakowski, Private Charles Knight, and Sergeant Johnson, and the 'crowd' now leaving the building had to be very discreet indeed, the first one leaving with their next guide, and the others following in pairs, to reunite at the railway station, there to board another train.

This time, they were bound for Canet-Plage, near Perpignan. They arrived without incident and were escorted to a small cottage just inland of the beach, there to await the appointed hour.

At about eleven o'clock that night, they were led out along separate paths toward the beach, then winding their way parallel to the sand in the darkness between large boulders. Finally they scrambled down a rock incline on to the beach itself, where the surf showed vividly white in the weak moonlight.

They were urged to keep absolutely silent at this stage, as there were residential and holiday villas dotted along the rear edge of the beach along that stretch; their English-speaking guide told them that they were aiming for a point along the beach, roughly midway between the visible lighthouse beams, and that was their agreed rendezvous.

Off they trudged and, at around midnight, their guide judged them to be in the right spot and ushered them to squat down between the rocks as he pulled a torch from his coat pocket. This was fitted with a special blue filter, and his radio-signalled instructions had been to point its reflector out to sea, then to wait until he saw two long dashes, which he should then answer with three short flashes from his torch.

The appointed time of 1am drew closer, and the band of men became increasingly nervous that the weather might worsen and cancel the pickup. By now it had started to rain and the group were getting wetter by the minute, worrying as each second passed by without a signal. And then, at 1am precisely, two faint blue flashes pin-pricked the darkness out at sea, and were answered by our guide. There were smiles of relief, and they waited, expecting the boat to take roughly twenty minutes to reach them ... but half an hour passed, without any view of a craft nearing the beach. Their guide set off a few more Morse code flashes from his torch, but didn't elicit any answering flashes from offshore.

Time ticked by very slowly, with still no sign of a boat, and the tension rose within the group. Their guide was beginning to consider abandoning the rendezvous – to return to the cottage where they'd set off and to arrange another collection time – when they saw a single blue flash from close by in the surf; then came a strange noise, which proved to be the sound of muffled rowlocks, and at 2.45am, a ship's lifeboat beached before them.

Relief flowed though the group as two burly British Navy able-bodied seamen shipped their oars, and an immaculately uniformed midshipman stood up from the boat's stern and grinned a welcome as the escapers trudged down the beach to greet them.

They piled aboard the boat and were soon under way back to the ship, with two of the evaders lending a hand with a second pair of oars, and as they rocked and rolled along as quickly as the rowers could power them, the midshipman told them that the delay had been caused by an unexpectedly brisk offshore wind, coupled with a strong tidal current; after one effort to row ashore with just a single oarsman, they had had to return to the ship for a second oarsman, to counter the swell.

Quite soon, they sighted the outline of a small ship. A few moments later they bumped against the hull and, after clambering up a draped scaling net to be hauled aboard by many willing hands, they were taken to the fo'c'sle for much appreciated enormous mugs of Navy cocoa, each laced with a generous tot of whisky (rum was apparently in short supply!), and overwhelmed with bread, jam and cheese.

They were elated to be back in the company of British countrymen, absorbing all their enthusiastic cheer and hospitality as crewmen paid excited visits to see them, simply to bid them welcome and reassure them that they should be safe from that point onward – even though they all knew that they still had to run the gauntlet of German Navy U-boats and warships on their voyage home.

Once the ship had got under way, the captain of the vessel joined them. 'Gentlemen, welcome aboard the HMS *Tarana* – glad to see you looking so well!'

They returned the greeting and chatted for some time, then one of the fugitives asked how the ship could sail and operate so close to the enemy shore without interference, and the captain merely grinned and winked.

'You'll see in the morning,' he said. 'We're decked out just like a small fishing trawler – wouldn't hurt a fly, us lot, eh, lads?' A couple of crew-men chuckled at their captain's comment, adding their grins to enliven their new charges, and then their leader turned serious. 'Rule number one for you chaps,' he began. 'If any of you are on deck in daylight, and should we be visited by any aircraft, you are to drop below decks immediately and stay there until told otherwise. You don't look in the least bit like trawler crew, and we don't want to arouse any suspicions, do we?' The fugitives concurred, and he continued. 'Right, time for you to get some shut-eye – you need it, by the look of you! You won't be required to do anything for a day or so, so just keep your heads down and try to stay out of the crew's way as best you can. Other than that, enjoy your taxi-ride!' With that, he left the cabin, and the rescued men sorted themselves into bunks and dropped into exhausted sleep.

Come the daylight – which proved to be a bright sunny day – they soon discovered the captain's meaning; the crew were shambling around in grubby reefer coats and shabby trousers and caps, and the ship did indeed look exactly like a dirty brown trawler, with coils of rope and heaps of nets shoved into every nook and cranny on deck. But beneath those untidy-looking heaps lay a few secrets, in the shape of several swing-up machine-gun posts! The big steam winch in the fore-deck was in fact a 5.7in naval gun, and mounted just beneath the machine-room hatch was another sizeable weapon (possibly a Bofors anti-aircraft unit), so HMS *Tarana* was, in fact, a genuine Q-ship of old tradition, and looked more than capable of defending itself against most aggressors!

Their course was due to take them to Gibraltar, but they ran into a huge storm on their first night at sea, so rough that the trawler dived, lifted and rocked sideways so violently that it seemed to the fugitives that they might even capsize; obviously a worrying prospect, given all that they had endured up until that point in their bids to return home. Some of them were quite seasick – as indeed were some of the hardened crew – in what the captain later confirmed as one of the worst summer storms that he could remember.

Eventually the tempest subsided, and they continued on their way. There was another rendezvous to keep before making Gibraltar – this time at sea – to take on fifty Poles who had also managed to flee across Europe and had collected in Vichy France by way of another escape organisation dedicated to their own cause. They, too, had had to ride out the same storm – but they had really suffered, having been cramped below decks in a tiny ship little more than a quarter of the size of the *Tarana*, and were in a very pitiful state when helped aboard and down into the trawler's capacious hold. The Poles were treated for injuries and given medication where needed, and made comfortable for the rest of their voyage.

The *Tarana* got under way once more, but stopped again soon after to take another couple on board from a small boat – this time a Greek man named Leoni Savinos and his German wife, who were apparently key 'players' in the Pat O'Leary escape line who had been compromised, and were therefore being evacuated for their own safety.

The trawler continued on her journey and things quietened down – but when they were about a day and a half from reaching Gibraltar, the captain announced that that evening would be 'painting night', drawing mystified looks from his passengers as his crew grinned.

As soon as it had grown dark, everyone aboard (who was physically capable, at least) was issued with a pot of grey paint and a large brush, and were set to work along the decks and structures, painting the entire trawler a universal shade of Royal Navy battleship grey! By four o'clock in the morning, the job was done and the stench of sticky paint burned every nostril aboard (not the first time that this disguising operation had been carried out, Beecroft judged from the layers of paint) – and when the sun rose the next morning, its rays fell upon a glittering ship complete with its British white ensign flapping in the breeze, and a crew now resplendent in crisp, clean uniforms. It was a moment of true pride.

Beecroft and Hanwell were very impressed; their hearts swelled with joy at the transformation, and they finally began to feel like they were really going home. But first, the *Tarana* had to traverse a good stretch of the Mediterranean Sea and then wait outside the harbour until dark, which was the only time the port authorities would allow them in past the protective harbour boom; the threat of unseen U-boats was still casting fear in their minds.

Once safely docked that night, Whitney Straight and the Savinoses were whisked away in the darkness – to be flown home in an express fashion – and Beecroft, Hanwell and the others were transferred to a troop ship, the SS *Llanstephan Castle*, due to leave Gibraltar the next day. Under escort from two destroyers, they enjoyed what seemed like a leisurely cruise as they ploughed their way up the Atlantic. Their escort handed the troop ship over to another pair of destroyers roughly at the halfway point, and finally sailed into the River Clyde on 30 July.

All of the remaining fugitives were overjoyed to see the green and very welcoming shores of Britain drifting slowly by as they reached port. Once the ship had docked and they had passed through the 'immigration' procedure (this existed still, even in wartime!), they were taken to London by train – under armed escort, no less – to the headquarters of MI9 (which was the Escape and Evasion Section of Military Intelligence) for full debriefing. Then, at last, they were sent home on indefinite leave – much to the delight of their unsuspecting families!

And so ended the fantastically brave wartime escape story of Nos 30 and 31 – Beecroft and Hanwell – through the famous Pat O'Leary line.

After a spell on leave, Beecroft returned to operational service by joining 256 Squadron, a night-fighter force, later being based in Malta when the invasion of Sicily got under way.

Hanwell was rested from active service, becoming a master gunnery instructor, passing on his experience and skills in aerial defence techniques to newly enlisted air gunners.

Index

C

D